Money & Happiness

Money &
Happiness

A GUIDE
TO LIVING
THE GOOD LIFE

LAURA ROWLEY

WILEY

JOHN WILEY & SONS, INC.

Published by John Wiley & Sons, Inc., Hoboken, New Jersey.
Published simultaneously in Canada.

For general information on our other products and services, or technical support, please contact our Customer Care Department within the United States at 800-762-2974, outside the United States at 317-572-3993 or fax 317-572-4002.

Wiley also publishes its books in a variety of electronic formats. Some content that appears in print may not be available in electronic books. For more information about Wiley products, visit our web site at www.wiley.com.

Library of Congress Cataloging-in-Publication Data:

Rowley, Laura.
  Money and happiness : a guide to living the good life / Laura Rowley.
     p.   cm.
  Includes bibliographical references and index.
  ISBN 0-471-71404-6 (cloth)
  1. Finance, Personal.   I. Title.
  HG179.R693   2005
  332.024—dc22
                                                    2004027092

Printed in the United States of America.
10   9   8   7   6   5   4   3   2   1

To my parents, Eugene and Jane Rowley

CONTENTS

ACKNOWLEDGMENTS

Thanks to Lisa Queen of IMG for believing in this project and being a first-class agent and person. Thanks to a talented group of professionals at John Wiley & Sons, Debra Wishik Englander, Greg Friedman, and Kim Craven. Thank you, Deb, for your infinite patience and voice of reason and calm.

I am privileged to work with an amazing brain trust at *Self* magazine: Lucy Danziger, Paula Derrow, Holly Pevzner, Kate Lewis, and Dana Points. Thanks for your creative insight and continuing support.

I am indebted to Dr. Richard Easterlin, Dr. Tim Kasser, and Dr. Sonja Lyubomirsky for help in reviewing the research on subjective well-being; certified financial planners Doug Flynn and Kevin McKinley, and CPA Richard Berse for your excellent feedback on the technical aspects of investing. Thanks to Seton Hall intern Brian Matthew for assistance in crunching the survey numbers.

Thanks to my sisters, Barbara Scherer, Therese Rowley, Mary Moye-Rowley and Ann Gilbert for your feedback and encouragement; my brothers Gene, Ed, John, Tom, Paul and Dan (webmaster extraordinaire) Rowley for your friendship and advice. To Cynthia Rowley, a swell cousin and a swell muse—you rock!

To writers and kindred spirits Lynne Pagano, Amy McCall and Judy McLaughlin—your enthusiasm for the craft means more to me than I can say. To the many women who agreed to long interviews for this book: It is a privilege to tell your stories. I am awed by your honesty and generosity in sharing your money lessons—instructive, amusing and heartbreaking—that will no doubt help other women to better manage their financial lives.

Thanks to the two people who inspired this book—my mom, Jane Rowley, for your remarkable wisdom and faith; and my dad, Eugene Rowley, who taught me everything I know about money and values.

Finally, thanks to Jim, Anne, Charlotte, and Holly Hilker, for your steadfast love and support throughout the course of this project, and for reminding me every day where true wealth lies.

INTRODUCTION

I was once asked to give advice to a reader of *Self* magazine who I will call Mia. Mia is in her mid-20s, working for a social service agency in a major city, earning $42,000 a year. Her ultimate financial goal is to be a millionaire. "I want to live the way I want to live and never worry about making ends meet," she says. Mia isn't thrilled with her job; she hopes to quit and start a public relations firm. She has a busy social life, dining out three to four times a week at $75 a pop. She attends parties and premieres that demand a designer wardrobe at a cost of about $500 a month. Asked to name her most important investment, Mia describes a $540 Louis Vuitton handbag. She is maxed out on 13 credit cards, on which she carries an $8,000 balance. She owes another $28,000 in student loans, but hasn't started paying them back. She has no savings and doesn't contribute to her firm's retirement savings plan. "I always feel a little panicky that I'm not going to be able to pay my bills and have money to live," she says.

Obviously, Mia needed an extreme financial makeover. There was a gigantic disconnect between her goals—becoming a millionaire, starting her own business—and the decisions she made about money. But ironically, I have met other women through the *Self* column who didn't struggle with debt, had some savings, education, and good jobs—and felt every bit as anxious as Mia. For some women, money is a like a guy who can't commit—it shows up with flowers, wine, and dinner reservations, but disappears at the mere mention of long-term goals. For others, money is like commuting to work; it must be confronted on a daily basis, but brings minimal pleasure. For still others, money is like a computer that arrives in a million pieces—it's exactly what they need, but they have no idea how to make it work for them. Money can be a source of fear, dread, envy, guilt, regret. It can also be a tool that brings confidence, peace, and happiness. It all depends on what money means to us, how much we know about it, how much control we exert over it—and most importantly, how closely money is aligned with our larger values and goals.

When I was a journalism undergrad at the University of Illinois, I had a brilliant professor named Ted Peterson, an author and expert in media theory. He stood barely five feet tall with a shock of white hair, thick-framed black glasses, an unlit pipe clenched between his teeth. I recall one morning stumbling in late to his seminar, guilty of not reading the assignments due for the day. He paused while I slid noisily into my seat, leaned back in his chair, gazed at me intently, and said, "So, Ms. Rowley, what's the meaning of life?" Caught off guard, I answered his question with a question: "To be happy?"

What I didn't know at the time was that nearly 2,500 years of philosophy supported my off-the-cuff response. In 400 B.C., Aristotle suggested that we are all born with a purpose in life, and by cultivating our reason and working toward our highest calling, we can achieve happiness. While my journalism degree led to a career covering personal finance and business for CNN and other media, Professor Peterson's question inspired a side trip to divinity school. I now write the money column for *Self* and teach a university course called "Contemporary Moral Values." Those experiences culminated in what is hopefully a very different kind of personal finance book. Most money guides operate under the assumption that if you have enough information and take action, you can build wealth and be happy. But that leap from wealth to happiness is neither easy nor obvious. I believe that you first have to define what "the rich life" means to you, what ideas, activities, and relationships you value, and what you're striving for personally—then use money to build that life. Too often it works the other way around: Someone chooses a particular career to get money, and then lets money define what she does, what she values, who she is, and what her life looks like. Or, like Mia, someone creates a life that's unsustainable and results in massive debt, because there is no rational connection between the goals and the money. That connection is essential. I occasionally get e-mails from readers that say, "I have $1,000 to invest. What should I do with it?" My response is always: What is the money for? What do you value? As my wise old instructor Ted Peterson would ask, "What's the meaning of life?"

This book offers a road map to wealth with practical financial tools and positive strategies for creating "the good life" in a personally meaningful way. It looks at how to identify our authentic values and overcome unconscious beliefs and personality traits that frustrate our efforts to manage money in a healthy manner. It also explores decades of research into behavioral economics—uncovering how to be happy with whatever you have, while you move toward your larger financial goals. It offers the stories of real women who talk about their money triumphs, failures, and lessons. Because so many of those lessons are so personal, the women I interviewed for this book did not want their full names disclosed; some allowed me to use their real names and last initials; others asked that a pseudonym be used. But they are all real people and real money situations—there are no composites here.

Why is this personal finance book for women in particular? Because our money situation is unique: We live longer than men; earn less on average; often bear the financial brunt of divorce; and are more likely to drop out of the workforce to care for family members (the average is 10 years). In addition:

- Women are more than twice as likely as men to live their retirement years in poverty, and twice as likely to live in a nursing home, according to the Administration on Aging.
- More than half of the elderly widows now living in poverty were not living in poverty before their husbands died, the Administration found.
- Among women 35 to 55 years old, between one-third and two-thirds will be impoverished by age 70, according to research by the National Endowment for Financial Education and the AARP.
- The average woman born between 1946 and 1964 will likely be in the workforce until she is 74 years old because of inadequate financial savings and pension coverage.

- While women contribute a higher percentage of their earnings to retirement plans than men, they tend to invest more conservatively, so their investments don't grow as quickly. They are three times more likely than men not to know what kinds of investments offer the best returns, according to a study by Dreyfus and the National Center for Women and Retirement Research.
- Three out of four working women earn less than $30,000 a year, according to the Women's Institute for a Secure Retirement; nine in ten earn less than $40,000.
- A woman is more likely to work a minimum wage job than a man, and three times more likely to work a part-time job, according to the U.S. Department of Labor.

This book will give you both the knowledge and power to change your relationship with money and grab hold of your financial destiny. Personal finance is both a science and an art. It's about numbers, but more importantly, it's about how those numbers fit into your real life, how they help you achieve a fulfilled life. I hope this book inspires you to seek genuine happiness, with money as your partner.

1

WEALTH AND VALUES

Julie D., 29, calls herself "a hippie at heart." The Florida teacher just bought her first house: a 1960s cement bungalow painted periwinkle blue, a shade inspired by the nearby Gulf of Mexico.

The charming three-bedroom home boasts a nicely landscaped yard, tiled patio, and a small pond with a fountain. New homebuyers like Julie typically spend $6,500 on furnishings and improvements in the first year of ownership, statistics say.

But Julie isn't the typical new homebuyer. Instead of shopping, she "dumpster dives."

"Every Thursday night, the town lets you put anything at the end of your street," Julie says with enthusiasm. "People throw away good stuff and it's free! We got wrought iron chairs and tables for the patio, little plant stands, and stuff for outside the house."

Julie earns $34,000 a year teaching preschoolers with special needs, a passion she stumbled upon in a high school child care course. "Being with children made me feel good," she says. "I wanted to do something that made a difference in the world." Julie has money automatically deducted from her paycheck for retirement and sets aside a little cash every month to splurge on travel. Last year, she was laid off after the state cut funding for the pre-K program where she taught. She took $2,000 out of her savings and went to the Caribbean for a month. "My boyfriend had a friend who was house-sitting a gorgeous villa," she says. "We stayed for free, we went to the grocery store, I brought a yoga tape and did yoga, and there was a boat for us to use. We pretended we were movie stars. That's why I save up money and why I have a nest egg—because if I get sick of it all, I'll be able to quit and go to the Caribbean and still pay my mortgage."

Marilyn N., 31, is also a saver, but in a town where it's tough to save—New York City. "I was always the kid counting my money in my piggybank instead of spending it," she says. Her parents divorced when she was young, and she lived with her mom and sister in modest circumstances. Married with one child, Marilyn now enjoys a household income of around $300,000 a year. But old habits die hard: "As one of my friends says, we're the cheapest rich people she knows," she jokes. "We just don't want crazy things. That's part of my upbringing. I could never in a million years bring myself to pay $500 for any item of clothing—which a lot of people in New York do. When we buy extravagant things, like a car, we labor over the decision forever."

Like Julie D., Marilyn N. has found her calling, as a documentary film producer. When asked about her best money-related experience, she answers quickly: "Winning scholarship money in college. I have peers with a lot of student loans. If I had loans, there's no way I could have taken the jobs that led me to where I am now. I started in film as a researcher, at $10 an hour with no benefits."

While their incomes are miles apart, Marilyn N. and Julie D. have much in common. They have discovered the secret to financial happiness: aligning their money and values. What does this mean? They are clear on what is most meaningful to them, and focus their money around it. The way they earn, save, and spend is in sync with what's most important in their lives. Managing their money makes them feel "good," "smart," and "empowered." They consciously prioritize their money goals: They know what they want their money to do, and more importantly, understand how to manage it so it maximizes their happiness. They have defined "the good life" in a way that's authentic to them, and use money to realize a personal vision.

Back in the 1990s, I worked as a producer at CNN business news, and went to seminary at night. Few of my business journalist friends understood why I was studying theology. Few of my peers in the master's program (most of them ministers in training) understood why I was interested in Wall Street. I lived in a dualistic world, covering the financial markets by day and biblical Greek by night. I was fascinated by both, and still am: Today, I write a money column for *Self* magazine and teach a university course called "Contemporary Moral Values."

Here's what I have learned about money and meaning: You can't separate them. Think about the definition of cash itself: It's an entity that stores value. Understanding what value it holds for you can be life altering because we structure our lives around money; it defines the choices we make; it shapes the person we become. To be successful at achieving wealth, you first have to discern what *wealth* means for you.

Most personal finance books make this difficult to do. They define wealth as a numeric formula: The difference between your assets and your liabilities—between what you have and what you owe. They focus on financial instruments—those three-letter, three-number combos like IRA, Dow, 529, SEP, and 401k—and discuss investment concepts—diversity, liquidity, tax efficiency. You're smart enough to understand all this information—but what does it mean to your real life?

Theology poses the same problem: "Where theology becomes overly abstract, conceptual, systematic, it separates thought and life, belief and practice, words and their embodiment, making it more difficult, if not impossible, for us to believe in our hearts what we confess with our lips," says theologian and author Sallie McFague.[1] The same is true for money: If you don't start with what you believe in your heart, all your money management is just lip service. You'll join your company's retirement plan because it seems like a good idea, then run up your credit cards because what you really value is a canvas lounger on a Caribbean beach in February. It's okay to value these things—but pursuing them simultaneously doesn't work. Your net result is a paltry 401k and a lot of debt. Both make you unhappy and anxious.

This book gives you the financial tools you need to succeed. But *first,* it shows you how to bring together your thoughts and your life, your beliefs and your practices, your words and their embodiment—so that you mean what you say and take action that achieves what you desire. You'll be able to fully engage your finances because you'll know how to put your money where your heart is. Your money will reflect your energy, imagination, and passion. This book also explains the findings of three decades of research into money and happiness, and helps you figure out how to be more satisfied with whatever you have, while you move toward your long-term goals.

The aim of this book is to help you create your own definition of wealth based on what you truly value. The first few chapters offer tools to uncover the source of your values—family, community, and personality—and explain how experiences and character come together to create a larger belief system about money. Once you identify unconscious beliefs that control how you view and use money, you have the power to change them and better align your finances and values. Later chapters tackle the nitty-gritty of getting out of debt, spending, saving, and investing, with a special look at money and relationships and what to do when you achieve certain financial milestones. The goal is to connect these financial concepts to real life, so the book is built on the experiences of women like you—stories about their money choices, how money has shaped their lives, and how they have used money to facilitate their genuine happiness.

How Wealthy Are You?

Let's start with an assessment of your wealth. Do you consider yourself rich, poor, or somewhere in between? Use the following wealth assessment to get some perspective on where you stand:

	Yes	No
1. I have easy access to food and clean water.	____	____
2. I live in a home that has heat and running water.	____	____
3. I feel safe in my home and in my neighborhood.	____	____
4. I can comfortably spend more than $2 a day.	____	____
5. I am employed or supported by someone who is.	____	____
6. I exercise regularly.	____	____
7. I get at least eight hours of sleep a night.	____	____
8. I have health insurance.	____	____
9. My children have access to affordable medical care.	____	____
10. I fully expect to live until I'm 70 years old.	____	____
11. My children are enrolled in a good school.	____	____
12. I graduated from high school.	____	____
13. I earned an associate's degree.	____	____
14. I earned a bachelor's degree.	____	____
15. I earned a master's degree.	____	____
16. I earned a PhD.	____	____
17. I earned a professional degree (law or medicine).	____	____
18. My household income is at least $43,300.	____	____
19. My household income is at least $50,000.	____	____
20. My household income is above $75,000.	____	____
21. My household income is above $100,000.	____	____
22. My household income is above $150,000.	____	____
23. I have a checking account.	____	____
24. I put money away into savings last year.	____	____
25. I own stocks directly or through mutual funds.	____	____
26. I pay off my credit cards in full every month (or don't use credit cards at all).	____	____
27. The credit card debt I carry is less than $1,000.	____	____
28. I own a car.	____	____
29. I save money for retirement.	____	____
30. I own my home (with or without a mortgage).	____	____
31. My home is worth more than $169,900.	____	____
32. I have no student loans.	____	____
33. I have meaningful relationships.	____	____

	Yes	No
34. I have opportunities to express and develop my skills and talents.	___	___
35. I have the ability to strive for my goals.	___	___
36. I like my work.	___	___
37. My day is filled with meaningful activity.	___	___
38. I have enough time to enjoy my life outside of work.	___	___
39. I notice and appreciate small daily pleasures.	___	___
40. I feel in control of my life.	___	___
41. I have a strong sense of self-respect.	___	___
42. I participate in the life of my community.	___	___
43. My life has a spiritual dimension.	___	___

Scoring the Wealth Assessment

The assessment is based on a broad definition of wealth, including material needs and comforts (questions 1 through 5), health (questions 6 through 10), education (11 through 16), and assets and liabilities (questions 17 through 32). Finally, questions 33 through 43 list intangible values that create a rich life—from the quality of relationships to the ability to control your destiny and develop as a human being. We'll get to that section in a moment. First, let's look at how your wealth compares to others. On questions 1 through 32, give yourself one point for every time you answered "yes."

Part 1: Basic Needs

1. *I have easy access to food and clean water.* Some 840 million people in the world are chronically undernourished, meaning they consume too little food to maintain normal levels of activity; 1.2 billion people lack access to a reliable water source that is easonably protected from contamination.[2] In the United States, about 11 percent of families—or 35 million people—were "food insecure" in 2002, meaning they lack the means to ensure themselves of healthy meals and are vulnerable to at least a mild form of chronic malnutrition.[3]

2. *I live in a home that has heat and running water.* About 924 million people, or roughly 15 percent of the world's population, lived in slums in 2003.[4]

3. *I feel safe in my home and in my neighborhood.* The most recent government survey found 29 percent of Americans say there is an area near their home where they would be afraid to walk at night.[5] Worldwide, more than 9.7 million people were refugees from their home countries in 2003 because of persecution related to race, religion, nationality, political opinion, or membership in a particular social group.[6]

4. *I can comfortably spend more than $2 a day.* In 2003, more than 2.7 billion people lived on less than $2 day, about 43 percent of the world's population.[7]

5. *I am employed, or supported by someone who is.* About 6 percent of Americans were unemployed in 2004.[8]

Part 2: Health

6. *I exercise regularly.* Just 40 percent of Americans do the regular physical activity recommended by the U.S. Surgeon General (30 minutes of brisk walking a day). One-quarter of all U.S. adults are not active at all.[9]

7. *I get at least 8 hours of sleep a night.* Only 37 percent of Americans get the recommended eight hours of sleep needed for good health, safety, and optimum performance.[10]

8. *I have health insurance.* Almost 45 million people—about 15 percent of U.S. population—were uninsured in 2003.[11]

9. *My children have access to basic medical care if they need it.* More than 10 million children die each year in the developing world, the vast majority from causes that could be prevented by good care, nutrition, and medical treatment.[12]

10. *I fully expect to live until I'm 75 years old.* In 2003, life expectancy worldwide is just over 65 years; in sub-Saharan Africa, 46 years.[13]

Part 3: Education

11. *My children are enrolled in a decent school.* Worldwide, 115 million school-age children are not enrolled in school at all.[14]

12. *I graduated from high school.* 84 percent of Americans ages 25 and older have completed high school. The average annual salary for

a high school graduate was $25,900, compared to $18,900 for nongraduates.

13. *I have an associate degree.* People with an associate degree earned an average of $33,000 in 2000.

14. *I have a bachelor's degree.* About one in four Americans ages 25 and older has attained a bachelor's degree. Average earnings were $45,400. Over an adult's working life, people with bachelor's degrees earn an average of $2.1 million, compared with $1.2 million for high school graduates.

15. *I have a master's degree.* For someone with a master's degree, average earnings were $55,641 in 2000. Over a lifetime, those with a master's degree earn an average of $2.5 million.

16. *I have a PhD.* Average earnings were $86,833 in 2000 for people with a doctorate, and lifetime earnings averaged $3.4 million.

17. *I have a professional degree (law or medicine).* Average earnings for this level of education were $99,300 in 2000. Professional degree holders average lifetime earnings of $4.4 million.[15]

Part 4: Assets and Liabilities

18. *My household income is at least $43,300.* This is the median income in the United States. Half of incomes are above this mark, half are below. Nearly 36 million people—about 12.5 percent of the population—lived in poverty in 2003. The poverty level is defined as annual income of $18,810 for a family of four; $14,680 for a family of three; $12,015 for a family of two; and $9,393 for individuals.[16]

19. *My household income is at least $50,000.* 57 percent of Americans earn $50,000 or more. A survey by researchers at the Centers for Disease Control and Prevention found Americans with incomes of more than $50,000 reported fewer days of feeling "sad, blue, or depressed" than those who earned less.[17]

20. *My household income is above $75,000.* Some 28 percent of Americans earn more than $75,000.

21. *My household income is above $100,000.* 15 percent of Americans earn $100,000 or more.

22. *My household income is above $150,000.* Just 4.6 percent of U.S. households earn more than $150,000.

23. *I have a checking account.* About 87 percent of U.S. families have a checking account.[18]

24. *I put money into savings in 2003.* About 59 percent of Americans saved money in 2003.[19]

25. *I own stocks directly or through mutual funds.* About 52 percent of Americans had one of these investments in 2001.[20]

26. *I pay off my credit cards in full every month (or don't use them at all).* About 55 percent of American families pay off their credit cards in full every month.[21]

27. *My credit card debt is less than $1,000.* About 48 percent of credit card holders owed less than $1,000; about 10 percent had balances of more than $10,000.[22]

28. *I own a car.* 85 percent of all Americans own some kind of vehicle. The average car costs $3,000 to $6,000 a year to operate.

29. *I save money for retirement.* About 6 in 10 Americans save for retirement.[23]

30. *I own my own home.* Nearly 68 percent of Americans own their homes.[24]

31. *My home is worth more than $169,900.* This was the median home price in the United States in 2003—half of homes cost more, half cost less.[25]

32. *I have no student loan debt.* College students who borrow to finance their educations graduate with an average debt of $18,900. The average debt for all graduate students is $45,900. Law and medical student borrowers report an average accumulated debt from all years of $91,700.[26]

Scoring

Parts 1 through 4 of the wealth assessment cover food, shelter, work, health, education, and assets/debt. Based on your answers to questions 1 through 32, here is where your scores ranks:

30+ points	Tremendous wealth
20–29 points	High wealth
10–19 points	Moderate wealth
5–9 points	Living paycheck to paycheck
0–4	Living in material poverty

But wait—we're not finished yet! Part 5 of the assessment focuses on variables that are highly individual—that can't be compared with others. Review your answers to questions 33 through 43. Give yourself one point for each time you answered "yes." Add that to your previous score. This is your total score. Now consider again: Are you wealthy, poor, or somewhere in between?

The purpose of this quiz is to assess your wealth in a holistic way. The first four sections acknowledge the fact that when it comes to money, we cannot help comparing ourselves with other people. We like to know how we're doing relative to our peers. For instance, I'm a regular reader of the *Wall Street Journal* online, and one day I stumbled across an interactive feature called "Keeping Score." It allows you to click on your income bracket and find out how much other people in your age group have in stocks, bonds, retirement accounts, checking accounts, and so on. You can see if they drive fancier cars or live in homes worth more than yours. The first time I saw this feature I found it riveting. In some parts of my financial life I was above average: I had more put away for retirement than other people in my age and income group. In other categories, I was inferior: my beater minivan was worth about a quarter of the value of vehicles my peers owned. Then it dawned on me that while the exercise is fascinating, it is utterly meaningless. Should I be concerned about what my neighbor has in her retirement plan, or focused on whether I can afford the kind of retirement I desire? If my home serves my family's needs for safety, comfort, and style, what difference does it make if someone else's mansion is featured in *Architectural Digest*?

Scientific research supports the link between happiness and avoiding comparisons. In a series of studies, Professor Sonja Lyubomirsky of the University of California-Riverside had her subjects perform a word-game task. She then planted false indicators of success or failure, such as allowing participants to see that other people completed the test more quickly. Lyubomirsky found that happy people are better at disregarding information about others' success. They concentrate on their own abilities instead. When happy people do consider how others are doing, it's typically to learn something to improve their own performance. Meanwhile, unhappy people tend to dwell on negative feelings about themselves and others. Such negative comparisons, studies found, actually inhibited a person's ability to perform the task.[27]

My point is this: It's a waste of energy to look around and measure our wealth based on what other people have. I have met people who are rich in monetary and material assets and genuinely miserable; and people who live paycheck to paycheck who lead truly joyful lives. The only way to benchmark your wealth is to create your own definition and judge how you're doing against your personal standards; to identify and visualize what wealth means to you, and then see if your life jibes with your definition. So questions 33 through 43 are based on academic research into other essential "wealth factors" that bring lasting happiness: meaningful relationships, work that allows us to express our talents, community involvement, spirituality, and a sense of autonomy—the idea that our activities and our paths in life are self-chosen. (The research on happiness is explored in Chapter 4.)

What about My Stuff?

By now you may have noticed something missing from the wealth assessment: It doesn't include any of the things typically associated with "the good life." There are no questions about designer clothing, exotic travel, mansions, vacation homes, sports cars, four-star restaurants, spa treatments—the consumer indulgences that bombard us in every form of media. Truthfully, I would be the last person on earth to deny the pleasure of a new pair of shoes, a night on the town, or a great massage. So why leave them out of the assessment?

Here's why: Your values come from who you are, not from the things or services you can buy. Your values are integral to your character, to your life's purpose, to the way you create your future. Your lifestyle, attitudes, choices, and habits; the way you see the world; your goals for the sort of person you want to be—all come from your core values. Defining your values empowers you to make meaningful choices and gives momentum to your actions. When you know what you value and make money decisions that are value-driven, you can be true to yourself. You can shape the course of your life with freedom and self-determination and find genuine happiness with money as your partner.

The alternative is never identifying what you value and flying blind—spending your money on what others say will make you better, cooler, smarter, more important, more attractive, more successful, more comfortable, more loved—instead of spending your money on what is meaningful to you, on what creates lasting happiness. Paying too much attention to our stuff—and the stuff that other people have—can knock us off course, derail us from living in a truly satisfying way. That's because desires for material goods are often driven by emotions, rather than values. (Chapter 5 looks at the feelings that drive certain spending behaviors.)

Moreover, using your values as a screen for your money choices can simplify your life and provide more peace of mind. In *The Paradox of Choice: Why More Is Less*,[28] Swarthmore Professor Barry Schwartz explains how life has become more complex because of the overwhelming number of everyday choices—from picking a doctor to setting up a retirement plan. (Just think about how many decisions you had to make the first time you ordered coffee at Starbucks.) Being forced to sort through hundreds of options a day requires people to "invest time, energy, and no small amount of self-doubt, and dread," writes Schwartz, an expert in psychology and economics and author of six books. Excessive choice can lead to perpetual stress, even depression, he argues, while eliminating choices can streamline our lives and reduce anxiety. Knowing what you value provides the discipline to focus on what's really important and ignore other choices.

We have to start our path to wealth with the knowledge of what we really value in life—which comes from who we are, not what we have. We need to judge the richness of our lives by an absolute standard—a personal values standard that has no relationship to what people around us are doing or consuming. Knowing what we value, we can also determine what we don't need, things we can eliminate, because our decisions will be internally driven, rather than motivated by someone else's approval. Before we get into the luxuries you want, use this book to help you figure out the values and qualities on which you want to base your life, and how money can become a tool to facilitate that reality.

A Look at Some Values-Based Decisions

Stacy E. is a 26-year-old college counselor in Iowa, earning $31,000. She grew up in a farm town of 3,000 people, where her dad was a land surveyor, a part-time police officer, a dry wall contractor, and a city council member. "He calls himself a jack of all trades and a master of none," Stacy laughs. Her mom, who is retired, worked in a supermarket and a factory over the years. "My parents taught me the importance of hard work," she says. "Growing up in a loving environment was far more important than anything material my parents could have provided."

Stacy has a master's degree in education and is considering getting a PhD. She calls her education her most important investment. So far, she has accumulated $48,000 in college loans. Her payments are $250 a month for the next 35 years. To some people, that debt might feel crushing. But Stacy takes it in stride: "If I work hard, everything will work out," she says. "I don't let money affect too much of my life. I kind of go with the flow, so it doesn't overwhelm me. I pay the bills when they come and everything seems to work out."

Jill B., 38, earned a substantial salary as a financial planner in Ohio. When she was pregnant with her first child, Jill asked to go part-time after the baby was born. The company agreed, but when the time came, she was told the offer was no longer on the table. Faced with the option of working 60 to 70 hours a week or not working at all, she quit. She cut her household income in half and lost her family's health benefits. They now purchase private health insurance for $600 a month. Because her husband works on commission, some months are tighter than others.

"We used to stress about money so much," Jill says. Then she discovered a "Christian Money Management" philosophy through her Catholic Church. "We provide food, housing, medical care, and education for our family, and once those basic needs are taken care of, we begin to provide for the needs of others," she explains. "It's not always money—sometimes we'll volunteer our time. We started to bring God more into our life, and started feeling more peace about everything. Whenever we're in a stressful time, I pray to God to help us—and it just seems to work out."

Why do things "seem to work out" for Stacy and Jill? When money is in harmony with values—for Stacy, education; for Jill, family and faith—things really do work out. The energy of their lives is aligned with their priorities. But make no mistake—that's not a simple thing to do. It requires focus, discipline, commitment, and action. Living by their values is a daily struggle. Jill admits she would love to be working again in the world of adults. Instead, she channels her ambition into nurturing her two young daughters and slashing household expenses: She swaps babysitting time with neighbors, clips coupons, and buys food in bulk—making several dishes at once and trading with her sister. She's learned to make things last—soaking t-shirts in vinegar to take out stains, rather than throwing them out; cutting off the bottom of the toothpaste tube to get the last drop. Although she knows raising her kids is priceless work, it's the kind of job where the fruits of her labor won't be seen for years, and it's a world away from the financial rewards and prestige she used to enjoy.

Stacy, like her parents before her, took a second job, working part-time in a retail store to shore up her finances. "I only work one night a week, but during the Christmas season I work an extra 25 hours a week," she says. For entertainment, she and her fiancé take walks, watch television, or attend college basketball and football games. They rarely travel. "It's not a high priority," Stacy says. Both Stacy and Jill made significant trade-offs to live in harmony with their highest values.

Sometimes following your values means making even more difficult sacrifices. Jennifer L., 29, is the oldest of four children. She's had a passion for investing ever since she opened a passbook savings account at age 6, with a little help from the tooth fairy. "I'm one of those people who's excited to read the *Financial Times*," she says with a laugh. When she was 14, her parents started a restaurant, and she began waitressing at night. Her father encouraged her to save up for substantial needs, like a car, rather than frittering money away on day-to-day distractions. "That really hit home with me," she says.

In 2000, fate demanded Jennifer act on her values. She was four years out of college, working for a financial planner in a booming economy, moving up quickly in her career. Then her mother was diagnosed with breast cancer. "At first I was taking care of her, running my family's restaurant business, and managing my job," she recalls. "But I couldn't go on doing that. So when I was faced with a decision between my career and my mom, I chose my mom."

Jennifer moved home to help care for her mother and teenage siblings. Her career in finance fizzled. She toiled in the family restaurant, watching college acquaintances pass her by. "A lot of my friends, people I'd gone to school with, said I should be more concerned for me. How would I get back into the financial world?" she recalls. "I said I would worry about that when the time comes, but right now I'm worried about how my mom is doing. I know for a fact some people looked down on me, but to be honest I don't care. The people who looked down on me aren't really my friends."

Two years later, with her mother in remission, Jennifer set about rebuilding her career. She landed a marketing job in financial services, where she earns about $45,000 a year. She is studying for her broker's license. "It's not a time I'd want to relive, but not one I regret at all either," Jennifer says. "I definitely thought money was much more synonymous with happiness before—I thought success was measured in money. Now I know success is being happy with yourself."

Jennifer's happiness is a direct consequence of living according to her values despite the cost. Her decision was especially difficult because she had to choose between two of her highest values—family and work she loved. When she left her job, she had no idea what the future would hold. She chose to be guided by her own integrity, rather than the opinions around her. She had the courage to leap into the unknown because she had a grip on her values. Acting on her values made that leap possible—it didn't make it easy.

Meanwhile, despite the detour in her career plans, Jennifer's values helped her stay in charge of her money. Keeping in mind her father's advice about saving for big needs, she socked away 20 percent of her income every year, hoping to buy her own place before age 30. She closed on a 1,500-sq.-ft. condominium in spring 2004—six months before her 30th birthday.

How Do You Identify Your Values?

Like Jennifer, sometimes we don't become aware of what we value most deeply until we are faced with a crisis. Values are often invisible—a product of our family life, social training, education, personality, friendships, and our larger beliefs about the world.

Values can be tricky to identify and easily confused with wants or needs: "I really value air conditioning on a day like this." Or: "I really value this vintage Gucci handbag." But values run deeper than comforts or pleasures. Jennifer's story points up a crucial truth about values: They are life giving. They are often rooted in love. Following them can lead us down a rocky path—but it's a journey to our truest selves. There is a deep sense of fulfillment when we act according to our values—and a deep sense of revulsion when someone or something violates our values. As part of the research for this book, I sent a survey to hundreds of women. Respondents were asked to name their top three values (no choices were given). They overwhelmingly valued the people in their lives: 81 percent said family, 49 percent said friends. The next highest value was health, at 42 percent; happiness, at 17 percent; and faith, at 10 percent. Four percent said they valued travel; 3 percent, education. The other values named were more abstract—6 percent listed freedom, for example.

Values are qualities that foster growth. They help us, and those around us, become the people we were meant to be. You don't have to believe in a particular God to recognize you were born with specific gifts and talents, you cherish certain beliefs and are more satisfied and fulfilled when you have the opportunity to express them. Values are inescapable—the choices we make every day about how we live and what we do reflect a value system. One way to start clarifying your values is to examine the motives behind your daily activities. Simply questioning why you do something can reveal your underlying values. I know this sounds rather obvious, but when was the last time you honestly asked yourself why you do what you do, or why you chose what you chose?

For example, I choose to live in New Jersey. Stop laughing. I know my state gets a bad rap, which it truly doesn't deserve. Maybe it's because New Jersey is the most densely populated and the most developed place in America. Maybe it's the stunning view of the gas refineries from the Turnpike as you drive from New York City. Maybe it's our unusual politics. (The state's married governor resigned in 2004 after his gay lover accused him of sexual harassment on the job—imagine how it feels to have a leader the tabloids call "The Love Gov.") Living in New Jersey requires certain financial sacrifices. My sister's house in Iowa has twice as much space and cost half as much. I pay about three times what she pays in real estate taxes. Even my utilities cost more—which boggles my mind, since it snows in Iowa for, what, eight months of the year? Most of my family is in the Midwest. So why would I live in New Jersey?

New Jersey actually has many wonderful qualities (the subject of another book), but the main reason for me is location: I'm just 40 minutes by train to Manhattan. I visited a friend in New York City when I was 21 and was so enthralled I spent the next six days of my vacation at the library and on the phone (no Internet in those days) trying to land a job. I moved four months later and stayed for 15 years. I love the electric charge I get the moment I step off the train. I love hearing four different languages on the subway. I love that the Korean woman in the store below my first apartment would shout "Hello, Pretty!" every time I walked in (no matter what I actually looked like). I love that a stroll down any street is a visual circus. I even love the fact most of the dogs on the Upper East Side wear more fashionable sweaters than I do.

Obviously, I value an exciting, challenging, diverse environment. So why did I move to New Jersey? Because some serious competition showed up to rival my love for the city: my kids. The suburbs afforded a better quality of life for them—more space (indoors and out), less noise and pollution, the ability to set up a lemonade stand on the sidewalk and not have a cop ask you for a permit. I value the quality of my environment, but I value the quality of my kids' environment even more. So I found a relatively diverse suburb that was a train ride away from the city. And that's where I put my money.

This example brings up another important aspect of values: While some of the qualities we value—honesty, justice, joy—may remain constant throughout our lives, other values tend to shift with major life changes. Maybe in college you greatly valued independence and self-reliance; when you find a life partner, you may put a higher priority on compromise and cooperation. You'll find greater happiness by shifting your money habits to reflect that change in values—whether it means an equitable method of sharing bills or a discussion of how to spend your cash. When I became a parent, my values began to conflict (kid-friendly environment versus exciting city environment), I had to prioritize, and then realign my money. (If my income drops drastically someday, I may have to realign again, because I value living within my means more than living close to New York City. Look out, Iowa!)

Start to identify your values by looking at how you spend your day. On a sheet of paper, make two columns: On the left, list all of your activities today, on the right, the reasons you did these things. Here's an example:

Activity	Reason for Activity
Got up at 7, showered and dressed, drove to work.	*I have to go to work.*
Ate a bagel and coffee at my desk.	*Hungry, no time to eat at home.*
Went out to lunch with work friends.	*Enjoy socializing.*
Went to the gym after work.	*Like to stay in shape.*
Went out for drinks and dinner with friends.	*Enjoy socializing.*
Watched TV.	*Needed to relax.*
Went to bed at 12 midnight.	*Wanted to get 7 hours of sleep.*

Now interrogate each of your reasons. Let's look at the example:

Why did you get up, shower, dress, and drive to work?	*Because I have to go to work.*
Why do you go to work?	*Because I enjoy my work.*
Why do you enjoy your work?	*Because it offers a chance to do things I'm good at in a fun environment.*

We've just identified some values: the opportunity to use your skills in a fun environment. We could ask further questions to explore what's particularly fun about the environment, and we would discover more values. When you are thinking about how you spend your time, pay close attention to your physical response, to what your gut tells you. Do you feel a rise in energy, a sense of satisfaction when you meditate on your daily activities, or a feeling of dread, a sudden weight on your chest? Your emotions are just as critical as your thoughts in guiding you toward what you value.

Now let's suppose the responses were different:

Why do you go to work?	*Because I have to make money.*
Why do you have to make money?	*To pay my bills.*
Why do you have to pay your bills?	*Because I need to be responsible for myself.*

You've just identified a value: responsibility. But in this case, you may want to question if working at this particular job is the best way to serve that value. Maybe you can make other choices. Maybe you can reduce your spending, so your bills are lower. Then you would have the opportunity to take a job that pays less but is more satisfying—and still pay your bills and be responsible. A different vocation might accommodate some of your other values, along with responsibility.

Try this exercise with activities you do monthly or even annually—hobbies, trips, interactions with other people—and see what they say about your values. Here is a list of some of the values cited by women surveyed for the book. Do any of them resonate with you? How do you incorporate them into your life? How does money relate to them?

Children

Community

Connection with Spirit

Creating Memories

Creative/Artistic Expression

Cultural Arts

Education

Environment/Surroundings

Excitement

Exploring New Things, Places, Ideas

Faith

Family

Freedom

Friends/Friendship

Fun

God

Happiness

Health

Home

Independence

Job/Career

Joy	Peace of Mind
Kindness	Safety/Security
Laughter	Sanity
Leisure Time	Self-Respect
Love	Stability
Marriage/Partner	Travel
Opportunity	Variety

The road to money and happiness begins when we identify our values—those deeply held principles and ideals that promise us a rich life, if only we have the courage to follow them, and to align our money with them. We can uncover values by asking direct questions about the choices we make. But that leads us to other questions: Why do I value that? What's the source of that value? We examine those questions more closely in the next chapter.

IDENTIFYING YOUR VALUES: FAMILY, COMMUNITY, PERSONALITY

When Chicago marketing director Wanda H. was growing up, her parents told colorful tales of their struggles during the Depression in the 1930s. "I would hear about how my dad started his first job delivering newspapers at 4 A.M. when it was 30 degrees below zero, and how my mother lived with 11 people in her house because they were all too poor to have their own homes," she recounts. "They were both frugal but not stingy."

In this chapter, we explore some of the key influences on our values, including family, community, and personality. By far, family has the greatest impact on what we hold dear. We listen to stories, observe what relatives do and internalize beliefs, attitudes, and practices related to money. When asked who had the biggest effect on their spending habits, close to 100 percent of the women surveyed for this book mentioned one or both parents. As for savings, 84 percent said a parent was the greatest influence. (Spouses came in second; for more on money and relationships, see Chapter 9.) Think about your childhood experience with money: What role did it play in your household? What emotions were attached to financial experiences? How was money discussed?

Wanda's parents consistently preached the virtues of saving for the future and explained the nuts and bolts of investing. One of five children, Wanda opened a passbook savings account at age 5, started babysitting in fifth grade and by seventh grade accumulated $1,000—which she invested in a real estate partnership with her dad. At 16, she started working in retail and waitressing after school. Today, Wanda jokingly calls herself "a no-debt kind of girl." And indeed, at age 40, her assets are substantial: She earns $120,000 a year. She maxes out her 401k contributions and has significant retirement assets. She saves something from every paycheck to pay for big-ticket items like traveling and skiing trips with girlfriends. Wanda says managing her money makes her feel "responsible and in control."

Anyone in our immediate family can inspire the way we handle money as adults. Lisa T., a 38-year-old journalist based in Tokyo, makes saving and investing a top priority. When she thinks about her childhood experience with money, she recalls her grandmother's thrift—and generosity. "She lived with our family—she taught me that every little bit counts," Lisa says. "She worked nights as a waitress at a Howard Johnson's, and every day she'd empty her tips—pennies, nickels, dimes, and quarters—into a small tin can in her bedroom, and write the total in a notebook. At the end of the week, she'd take all the change to the bank. She was very careful with her money. And yet she, not my parents, bought me my first 10-speed bike. They bought one for my younger brother for his birthday and didn't understand that I, the older kid, felt bad still riding a little kid's bike. My grandmother understood this. I remember thinking about the price and trying to add up how many pennies and dimes it cost her. This made me appreciate even more what she had done for me."

Some parents, like Wanda's, have forceful opinions about what money means and how it should be handled. In other cases, they say nothing at all—and we make assumptions based on our observations and experiences. Janet M., a nonprofit executive in her early 40s, says it took her years to get a handle on her money. "Savings in our family was never discussed or emphasized," she recalls. "I know nothing about my parents' savings or how they will finance their retirement." Raised with four siblings in an upper middle-class Pennsylvania suburb, Janet's formative experiences with money revolved around the pleasures of spending: "My mother took us each shopping before the school year. Those days were among the few times I would have my mother's undivided attention."

The excursions were paid for with credit cards, with no further explanation of how the bills got paid. When Janet graduated from college, she says, "I measured my level of success and independence by how many credit cards I could apply for and get." That led to wild spending for a number of years. "I didn't know how to handle money or live within my means. I had no financial goals. I was in such agony over credit card debts—I'd pay them off with consolidated loans and ring them up again," she recalls. She joined Debtor's Anonymous and worked with a therapist on her money issues. Today, she pays the bills before she considers the rest of her income discretionary, and saves something every month, even if it's what she calls a "symbolic" amount, like $20.

Janet's success at changing her approach to money gave her the opportunity to make key decisions in harmony with her values. When she was laid off, she had a savings cushion. "It gave me peace of mind and freedom—not the 'do I go to Monaco or Hawaii?' kind of freedom—but the 'do I need to go back to work when it's snowing every day or take this month off with my children?'" she explains. Ultimately, controlling expenses and saving allowed her to switch from a corporate job to the nonprofit sector, giving her more time with her children. But the shift to living within her means and spending on what she most valued took several years of soul searching and financial education.

We absorb ideas and attitudes from our families almost by osmosis, by living in a specific time and place, with particular people. Our money attitudes become actions, our actions become habits, and habits become a financial way of life. By examining where that way of life came from, you can uncover the beliefs that drive your behavior, and ask, "Are these life giving? Are they helping me flourish in all ways as a person? Are they helping or hurting the people around me? Are they genuine values on which I want to base my life?" If the answer is no, you can learn to adjust those money behaviors, as Janet did. (The specifics are covered in later chapters.)

Changing a Lifetime of Habits

What happens when parents disagree on their attitudes toward money? Children may gravitate sharply to one style or the other, or end up with deeply conflicted feelings about money. Sometimes the discord is resolved only by "hitting bottom." Deb W., an East Coast publishing executive in her early 40s, is the product of a "mixed money" household. Deb's parents divorced when she was young. Her father made a fortune in advertising. He owned several luxurious homes, a collection of antiques, and a boat. By contrast, her mother was conservative to a fault, spending minimally and squirreling away nickels and dimes from her mid-level civil service job, where she worked for 30 years. "My mother had the last laugh," Deb says. "She has had a fabulous retirement, she and her boyfriend ride around [Florida's] intercoastal waterway on their yacht. My father had health setbacks and made some bad business decisions and lost all of his money. He died penniless in a small apartment."

Starting out after college, Deb adopted her father's attitude: "Go for the gusto and live for today." She earned and spent significant amounts of money before she had children. Then everything changed. Shortly after the birth of her first child, her marriage fell apart. "My ex-husband was not at all responsible about money and neither was I, but I was the one with the credit cards," she says ruefully. "I ended up filing for bankruptcy. I was a single parent with no money and no job—analogous to where my father had gone, but I was only in my early 30s."

Deb knew she didn't want to end up like her father. She got a finan-cial coach and "started unlearning a lot of the behaviors I had seen growing up," she says. She met her second husband just before the tech-nology boom hit in the late 1990s. He worked as a consultant and she got a job at an Internet start-up. "Everyone was raking it in hand over fist," she recalls. "We bought a house that really required that income, and we did $80,000 in renovations immediately. Then my company folded and my husband was out of work for eight months." The debt began piling up again.

Work was sporadic for both Deb and her husband over the next two years. Then Deb managed to land a wonderful job, earning more than six figures. She decided to reorganize their finances so that her income covered almost all of their expenses. That meant selling the landmark arts-and-crafts-style home she treasured. "I drew a line in the sand and said, 'We're in debt and we're not going to get into any more debt.' It was a tense time. My husband wasn't happy about it, and the children were not initially happy about it because we loved the house and neigh-borhood," she explains. "I looked for almost a year. I found a house I was able to get outrageously cheap—there were 10 people and a ferocious pit bull living there." They were able to keep their children in the same schools, clean up most of their debt, and begin earmarking her hus-band's income for retirement and college savings.

The new house is architecturally mundane, with a seriously outdated kitchen (complete with faux wood-grain formica countertops). But Deb is willing to tackle the upgrades a little at a time. "The first mortgage payment I made without any problem was such a huge relief," she says. "I used to come home and think, 'it's going to take another $2,000 in credit card debt to pay for this.' The thing about downsizing is it has the connotation of giving something up. But for us, downsizing was about giving up anxiety."

"For me the happiness is not in having the money, because I have been in a place where my household income was more than twice what it is now," Deb explains. "But the happiness is knowing the money is sufficient for us to live on, and be comfortable, and not be worried about money all the time. The big question is, what makes me feel prosperous? In the final analysis, the thing that was going to make me feel prosperous after all these years of being on the roller coaster was not being on the roller coaster anymore. I feel lucky—we worked really hard and were willing to make choices and abide by them, and change the habits of a lifetime."

Visualizing Prosperity

Deb's experience raises a critical question: What makes you feel prosperous? What does prosperity mean for you? Webster's dictionary defines prosperity as "the condition of being successful or thriving; especially economic well-being." Think of the times you have felt you were truly thriving in your entire life, not just your economic life. What activities and people were involved? How did you allocate your time? What were the common threads in those experiences? If nothing comes to mind, then consider the following questions and visualize a prosperous life:

1. What kind of work would you do if money were no object? Think about what you love doing; what comes naturally to you; what's meaningful and pleasurable; what skills or abilities have others recognized in you? Mihaly Csikszentmihalyi (*MEE-high CHICK-sent-me-high-eee*), former chairman of the Department of Psychology at the University of Chicago, is a leading researcher on both creativity and happiness. Growing up in Europe during World War II, he saw some adults who were destroyed by the tragedies of war and others who maintained courage, reached out to help others, and found a sense of purpose and meaning to their lives. That inspired him to study psychology, specifically how one could create a more fulfilling life. Csikszentmihalyi developed a concept he calls "flow," a state of being that is reached when we are deeply engaged in a challenging activity that matches our skills and abilities—so much so that we forget the passage of time. "How we choose what we do, and how we approach it, will determine whether the sum of our days adds up to a formless blur, or to something resembling a work of art," he writes.[1]

2. Consider the kind of work environment you most enjoy. Do you like being part of a team, working in a noisy, social office, or alone in lab, pursuing your own research? What larger values do

you want to express through your work? Imagine a colleague is introducing you at an award ceremony after 25 years on the job. What would you like her to say about you?

3. Where would you live? How would you spend your time off? What kinds of relationships would you have, and how would you spend your time with those people?

Picture your prosperous life in detail. Doubts may crop up immediately: "How can I pursue a career as an artist and pay the bills?" "I can't live on a boat, how would I earn money?" Don't think about dollars and cents right away, or whether others would approve of your choices. Talk to the voice of doubt: Who is speaking—you or someone else? Family can influence our money values for better or worse—not only how we save or spend it, but also how we earn it. They may discourage us from chasing certain dreams out of love—they don't want to see us make a mistake, get hurt, or fail. But disappointment and failure are indispensable stepping-stones on an authentic path. Would you rather be safe and secure in a routine job that pays the bills, or walk through your fears and take a shot at achieving your happiest life? Even if the outcome is not what you expected, the experience of setting goals that reflect who you are (rather than how you earn money), working toward them, and facing adversity will leave you stronger and wiser. Happiness may lie in the lessons you learn, the people you meet, and the person you become because you were willing to embark on that journey.

The Influence of Community

While family is the strongest influence on our values, community is a close second. The communities we belong to—whether by circumstance or by choice—are critical in forming our values. Communities can be informal—a circle of old friends, workplace colleagues, a book club, your neighbors—and formal, such as religious, social, or political institutions you ascribe to, and where you may pay dues to belong. Informal communities can be just as influential as formal ones, particularly when it comes to spending decisions.

Consider Shari R., 40, who calls herself an "activist at heart." She works at a public radio station, although she could earn much more at a for-profit one. She has served on committees in her town, was vice president of the Parent Teacher Association at her sons' school and is involved in her synagogue. "I'm concerned about politics and what goes on in the rest of the world," she explains. "That's just how I was raised."

Shari grew up in Brooklyn, New York. Her parents divorced when she was four, and her mother, a teacher, was forced to move back in with her parents. "We had to choose which bills to pay—you'd pick a bill to pay, and that's what you'd pay," Shari recalls. "There were literally times we wanted to order a pizza on Friday night, and if it was before my mother got paid, we'd look for change in the couch. I didn't realize we didn't have money until much later. Nobody had a lot in the neighborhood; most of my friends' parents were divorced. But I grew up in a house filled with love. My house never had a lot of heat, but it was the house everybody hung out in."

Shari says that her community's focus on the simple pleasures of family and friendship gave her a great deal of confidence when she faced a financial crisis. "When I was pregnant with my first son, my husband got laid off, and we got a notice that we had to vacate our apartment because we were subletting and the owner hadn't paid the rent," she recounts. "We went from living on $150,000 to $30,000 and we were pregnant with no place to live. I kept telling him, 'It's going to be fine.' And sure enough, we found an apartment, he got a job, we had the baby—it makes for a good story. I don't have a lot of fear. As much as I love shopping, if I couldn't do it, okay. I've got a great family, we're all healthy and we all love each other. The money is just the icing, it's not the cake."

Today, much of Shari's happiness comes from consciously surrounding herself with communities of people that reflect and support her values, which helps her maintain a healthy perspective on money. "It's not a goal to be rich—that's the end result of something. You have to focus on doing something that matters to you," she explains. "It's not about driving a Porsche. I always tell my kids that the person who wants everything never gets what he wants."

In their book, *Character, Choices and Community: The Three Faces of Christian Ethics,* authors Russell Connors Jr. and Patrick McCormick talk about the way formal communities influence us. They begin as informal groups of people who take action and make choices, which crystallize into institutions. The institutions develop structures and systems that, over time, become internalized by people, shaping their ways of thinking, communicating, and behaving.[2]

Consider the American Revolution: A group of people in Philadelphia decided they could no longer live under the tyranny of a king. They took action that led to the formation of a new nation—with new laws, customs, and practices. Over time, the systems and structures gave the government shape, and it took on a life of its own. Because of that, Americans sometimes forget that the institution is the result of the people who form and sustain it—an institution of, by, and for the people. In the same way, we belong to communities that were originally formed by groups of people. We are socialized through membership in these circles, we internalize their messages, and we accept their values—sometimes without questioning them. Think of several communities to which you belong—your workplace, the city where you live, the social clubs you have joined, or the educational institution you attend. What duties does the group have to its members? What rights and responsibilities do the members have? What are the specific values espoused by this group? Are they meaningful to you? How do you manifest them in your daily life?

Communities include our circle of friends, and they can have a significant influence on how we value and use money. Friends can be what I call "money boosters" or "money busters"—talking us into, or out of, healthy money habits. For instance, Jane L., an administrative assistant in the Midwest, stumbled into debt with a friend. "When I was in my early 20s, I got really carried away with my credit cards. Some of it was because my girlfriend and I started shopping a lot together," she recalls. "We'd talk on the phone and plan out the weekend, with lunch and dinner. We both went hog wild, shopping all day on a Saturday, going to malls and outlet centers. It was horrible—I bought anything and everything—clothes, shoes, gadgets for this and gadgets for that. She would see something I had to have, and I would see something she had to have." Jane shopped to distract herself from other issues: "I was unhappy in my life. I didn't really care for my job at the time. I was having lot of difficulties getting along with my parents. I felt that they were trying to run my life. What better way to run my own life than to shop for things? When I look back, I see they were probably just trying to guide me. It took eight months to pay off the debt and I never let it get out of control again."

Money busters may have the best intentions. During the midst of a difficult divorce, Rhonda J., a Wall Street executive, recalls a friend inviting her out to cheer her up. "We went to Saks before dinner to get a makeover at the Bobbie Brown counter. The woman doing the makeup started selling me: 'Oh, this is great color!' Before I realized it, I had bought $325 in makeup. My friend said, 'So what? It's $325 in makeup. This is a once in lifetime experience. Stop being ridiculous.' I went home and I didn't feel good about it. So that weekend I went to Saks locally and told them that I was in New York, had bought all this makeup, came home, and my husband had a fit. They took it all back. That's so me—there was no way I could have lived with that."

On the other end of the spectrum, Yvonne B., a mom of two in Hawaii, relies on her best friend to help her keep her spending in check. "We'll talk each other down from a purchase," she explains. "I was traveling on business and in this store looking at bedding that cost over $2,000. I thought, 'I'm calling her, she's going talk me out of this.' She said, 'Put down the pillows! Walk away from the bed! Walk out the door, get in your car, and drive away!' The last thing I talked her out of was probably a purse. She has a ton of purses."

Similarly, Kay S., an executive at a Fortune 500 company in the Midwest, is careful not to become a negative money influence on her close friends. "There are certain friends we enjoy hanging out with—if I had my way, we'd go on vacation with them every year," she explains. "But if we pick a more elaborate location, I don't push it, because I understand the cost implications and wouldn't put them in that position."

Meanwhile, Wanda H. has made it a mission to get her friends to join their company retirement plans. "I guess I started preaching what my dad used to preach to me, so my friends took the initiative to be proactive with their investments and savings," she says. "Now they say, 'Thank you for telling me to do that, because I never would have thought of it.'" How does your community of friends affect the way you handle money? What's your role: Are you a money booster or a money buster? Being intentional about the communities we join can make a remarkable difference in our financial happiness.

Connors and McCormick suggest another exercise to help identify the values that derive from community: Imagine you are organizing a youth group for a child you love—your own or a relative's or friend's. What kinds of values and beliefs do you want this group to instill in this child? What practices would you want the group to engage in to teach these values?

Identifying Your Money Personality

While our families and communities play a large role in shaping our money values, personality also comes strongly into play. Obviously, we are all unique individuals. But in interviewing women for this book, I discovered there are certain characteristics, tendencies, motivations, and areas of interest shared by people that can be roughly grouped into five different "money personalities." Take the quiz that begins on the bottom of this page and continues on pages 32–33 to assess your money personality. Each statement reflects a belief or tendency toward behavior that you must decide is either "like me" or "unlike me." The scoring follows.

Money Personality Quiz		
	Like Me	Unlike Me
1. The main purpose of money is to provide security for the future.	_____	_____
2. The main purpose of money is to provide freedom and options in life.	_____	_____
3. The main purpose of money is to help other people.	_____	_____
4. Money is a way to keep score, to measure success.	_____	_____
5. If I want it, I buy it. I'm into immediate gratification.	_____	_____
6. I am generally frugal: I clip coupons, brown bag my lunch, etc.	_____	_____
7. Creativity in a job is more important than money.	_____	_____
8. I frequently lend money to friends.	_____	_____
9. Money increases your personal power.	_____	_____
10. I enjoy buying extravagant gifts for loved ones.	_____	_____
11. I do a lot of research before I buy an expensive item.	_____	_____
12. I don't mind having credit card debt—sometimes it's a necessary evil.	_____	_____

(continued)

Money Personality Quiz *(Continued)*

	Like Me	Unlike Me
13. It's very important to give money and time to causes you believe in.	_____	_____
14. Getting laid off from my job would make me feel like a loser.	_____	_____
15. I tend to shop when I'm depressed, bored or lonely.	_____	_____
16. I know my monthly expenses, and never spend more than I earn.	_____	_____
17. I spend a lot of money on vacations and travel—it's a high priority in life.	_____	_____
18. I don't really understand money and wish people didn't place so much importance on it.	_____	_____
19. I chose my current home because it was in the "right" neighborhood, economically and socially.	_____	_____
20. I often feel guilty about spending.	_____	_____
21. I hate debt. The idea of carrying a balance on my credit card freaks me out.	_____	_____
22. When I shop, I tend to buy things that express my unique personality.	_____	_____
23. Money often causes problems between people.	_____	_____
24. When I shop I buy the best, high-end luxury brands—I like fashion and making an impression on others.	_____	_____
25. I would put my money in an investment without much research if a close friend recommended it.	_____	_____
26. I do my own investing, and check my investments online frequently.	_____	_____
27. I occasionally pick up the tab in social situations just for fun.	_____	_____
28. I rarely shop, and have little interest in fashion.	_____	_____
29. I frequently live above my means.	_____	_____
30. When I see someone who has more money or material goods than me, I often feel deeply envious.	_____	_____
31. I read the business section, subscribe to personal finance magazines or surf websites on money.	_____	_____
32. I have met or would like to meet with a financial planner because I think investing is important, but don't have much interest in it.	_____	_____
33. Having money would solve a lot of my problems, but I'm not sure how to get it.	_____	_____
34. When I think of powerful people, I think of wealthy people.	_____	_____

(continued)

Money Personality Quiz *(Continued)*

	Like Me	Unlike Me
35. I often spend money I don't have because I don't want to miss out on a dinner, trip or other activity my social circle has planned.	___	___
36. I have an extremely strong work ethic.	___	___
37. The main purpose of money is to create lasting memories.	___	___
38. I have dreams for my life, but don't know how money relates to them.	___	___
39. It's important to pick up the tab in most social or business situations.	___	___
40. When I shop I tend to buy clothing, cosmetics, jewelry or other items that make me feel good and look more attractive.	___	___
41. When I shop I look for high-quality classics on sale.	___	___
42. Rich people have more opportunity to lead better lives.	___	___
43. I think of money in terms of energy.	___	___
44. I don't love my job, but I am highly competitive and the financial rewards are fabulous.	___	___
45. More money would definitely bring me more happiness.	___	___

Scoring: If you answered "like me" to the question, circle the letters below. Add up the total number of times you scored PL, A, M, P, and I.

1. PL	8. M	15. I	22. A	29. P	36. PL	43. M
2. A	9. P	16. PL	23. M	30. I	37. A	44. P
3. M	10. I	17. A	24. P	31. PL	38. M	45. I
4. P	11. PL	18. M	25. I	32. A	39. P	
5. I	12. A	19. P	26. PL	33. M	40. I	
6. PL	13. M	20. I	27. A	34. P	41. PL	
7. A	14. P	21. PL	28. M	35. I	42. A	

TOTALS: PL ____ A ____ M ____ P ____ I ____

If Your Highest Score Was PL, You Are a Planner

Attributes: You tend to be a careful budgeter, cautious spender, and conservative investor. You like having a steady paycheck, live within your means, and save on a regular basis. You may use financial software, pay bills online, or thumb through the money magazines at the grocery checkout. You equate money with security or safety for yourself or your family. You eagerly monitor your monthly investment statements and can ballpark your "number"—the amount it would take to retire. You bring your lunch to work and stock up on energy-efficient gadgets. You adore *Consumer Reports,* avidly research big purchases, and seek the best value. You don't necessarily enjoy shopping but love to get a deal, particularly on high-quality classics (Ferragamo at the Nordstrom shoe sale, Anne Taylor at the end of the season, jewelry at Costco, Michael Graves at Target). You are a goal setter, list maker, spreadsheet builder. You take pleasure in watching your savings grow.

How Your Personality Works in Your Favor: Knowledge gives you confidence around money. You're savvy about investment concepts and that gives you the power to achieve what you plan, which increases your self-esteem. You have an internal barometer for success; you have zero interest in keeping up with the Joneses.

How Your Personality Works against You: You may be a workaholic, or hang on to a bad job longer than you should out of a sense of financial duty. You may hoard cash or tend to be a cheapskate—heavy into self-denial ("I'll walk and save the $2 bus fare") or stingy (you invite a friend for coffee and then divide the tab down to the penny, noting that her cappuccino cost 75 cents more than your latte.) You can also be a judgmental smarty-pants: Observing the seasonal wardrobe changes and dazzling social schedule of the woman down the hall, you smirk, "She's eating cat food when she retires!" You may be so afraid of losing your money you don't take the appropriate risks to make it grow. If you do take risks, you may brood over financial injuries ("Why didn't I sell Lucent at $60?").

Your Money Motto: Live within your means. Pay yourself first. Never pay retail.

If Your Highest Score Was A, You Are an Adventurer

Attributes: You tend to be a high-energy optimist, an extrovert who relishes life's challenges. You equate money with freedom, choices, and options—whether it's hiking the remote highlands of Irian Jaya or starting your own real estate firm. You are independent and achievement-oriented, but not necessarily interested in power. You spend your money on vacations, electronics, sports gear—things that express your unique spirit (first gal on your block to use a Blackberry, send a photo from your cell phone, drive a Mini, own an Ipod). You keep up with fashion, but are just as delighted with a quirky garage sale find as one from a high-end boutique.

How Your Personality Works in Your Favor: You think life is a big band orchestra, you're Duke Ellington, and money is the instrument that helps you hit the high notes. Because you know yourself well, your spending is focused on what brings you delight and creates memories. You tend to choose jobs strongly correlated with your skills, and insist on life balance (or you're one of those people who sleeps four hours a night and does triathlons, writes novels and builds houses for Habitat for Humanity in your spare time).

How Your Personality Works against You: You can be pathologically optimistic and not realize how far you've overshot your income. Saving is something you think is valuable, but boring; you don't do it automatically, so it can easily fall by the wayside. You find budgets a tiresome distraction from your globetrotting exploits, and that can get you into trouble with debt.

Your Money Motto: Life don't mean a thing if it ain't got that swing!

If Your Highest Score Was "I," You Are an Indulger

Attributes: For you, money is a source of comfort, love, happiness. You crave luxury goods for the sensual pleasure of them. You are extremely focused on the present, impulsive and spontaneous in your spending. You want immediate gratification, whether it's for you or someone you love. Your shopping bag is full of cosmetics, trinkets, shoes, and clothing (often something you already have two of, but probably on sale). You lease cars you could never afford to buy. You're a social butterfly—you love fine dining, good wine, entertainment, spa weekends—anything involving friends.

How Your Personality Works for You: You are generous to a fault. Your thoughtfulness attracts a circle of loyal friends—you're the one who remembers the birthdays of everyone in the office and collects for the cake, throwing in the extra five bucks to personalize it. You're dramatic in the best possible way—the first to shout for joy at a friend's promotion, and the first to suggest a champagne celebration. You're good to yourself and you never deny yourself the pleasures money can buy.

How Your Personality Works against You: All that indulgence comes at a high price—you probably carry credit card debt and feel some guilt or shame about it. When you're blue or want to treat yourself, you head for the mall. You like to feel a sense of belonging, so you make friends with salespeople who persuade you to buy things you don't need. If you're in a relationship, you may hide some of this spending from your partner, which compromises your trust. You tend to believe a little extra money will solve all your problems. You envy people who are more affluent, assuming they must be happier. At the end of the month, you have no idea where the money went. You might sign up for the company 401k to please the friend who suggests it, but the idea of following a budget is thoroughly depressing. (It makes you want to go to the mall.)

Money Motto: When the going gets tough, the tough go shopping.

If Your Highest Score Was P, You Are a Power Tripper

Attributes: For you, money means success, status, prestige, self-esteem. You spend your day focused on amassing money so you can prove your worth, keep score, expand your power. You look for jobs that have unlimited earning potential. You have a list of the Forbes 100 Wealthiest Americans pinned up on the wall. You think life balance is for wimps. Your purchases showcase your status—luxury cars, designer clothing, country clubs, and real estate (although in truth you may be mortgaged up to your eyeballs). You pick up the tab to show how powerful you are. You pay retail just to prove you can. You wouldn't be caught dead in a Costco.

How Your Personality Works for You: You're an alpha babe who takes no prisoners: You crush competitors in your field, you're a brilliant negotiator, you get what you ask for. You're probably highly educated and dressed to the nines (because you're always trying to impress everyone). You live better than most people on the planet. Neiman Marcus has a dressing room with your name on it.

How Your Personality Works against You: You will never have enough money to satisfy your desires because you constantly compare yourself to others and compete with those who have more. Because you think money is power, you tend to use it to control other people. You rarely budget ("What's the point—the next big deal is right around the corner!") You've probably had amazing experiences in travel, dining, and luxury living that most people would give their eyeteeth for, but you barely appreciate them. You *are* the Joneses.

Money Motto: She who dies with the most toys wins.

If Your Highest Score Was M, You Are a Mystic

Attributes: You are a dreamer, an intuitive, a romantic—you don't just see the big picture, you are one with it. To you, money is simply an energy force that ebbs and flows—not something that can be captured or stored up. You likely work in a helping profession. You align your money with your kind spirit—you're the person who gets a thrill out of paying the toll for the driver behind you.

How Your Personality Works for You: You would never let money take over your life—a possibility for all the other money personalities. You know how to be happy with or without it. You are completely genuine, uninterested in materialistic goods. You give time and money to causes and charities. You remind the rest of the world that peace and compassion are more important than cold hard cash.

How Your Personality Works against You: You have a hard time taking money for your work. You feel it may somehow taint you and are quick to lend it or give it away to anyone who needs help. You don't have a checking account—maybe don't even own a wallet—you just keep a couple dollars in your yoga mat bag. You are naïve—you'll invest in a friend's business without even thinking to check out the financials of the company. (You have no idea what "financials" means.) You're imaginative—you dream big dreams, build castles in the air—but because you believe the universe is in charge of your destiny, you don't know how to use money to lay the foundation for them. Deep down you hope to be rescued from your money dilemmas.

Money Motto: It is better to give than receive.

How to Make Your Money Personality Work for You

All of these personalities have strength and weaknesses. All of them can learn something from one another. The idea is to take the best of your personality's attributes and then balance them with traits from an opposing personality, so you use money with both wisdom and passion to create a truly rich life. Some suggestions follow.

The Planner

If you're a planner who tends to be a workaholic, stingy, or judgmental, start by borrowing some of the strengths of the indulger. While you tend to live in your head and map things out in detail, the indulger lives in her heart and spontaneously embraces pleasure. Since spontaneity is not your strong suit, try to schedule moments of joy in your month. The truth is, you secretly envy the woman who lives for the moment and spends without fear—so stop judging and plan some fearless spending yourself.

Make a list of five things you would really like to do for yourself this month—not to achieve a goal but just for pure enjoyment. At least two of them should cost money, even a nominal amount, say $20. Then make a list of five things you can do to bring joy to someone else. Again, budget at least $20 for this list. To counter your ardent work ethic, schedule at least two of these events so that you must leave your desk at 5:30 P.M. (The office conference room is not a suitable location for fun.)

Borrow a page from the adventurer and put your planning talents to work saving up for a truly blockbuster vacation. Lean out of your comfort zone—instead of the usual bus tour of nine European cities in eight days, consider a vacation that allows you to volunteer for a cause and meet new people (groups like the Sierra Club and the American Hiking Society offer these trips, or check out globalvolunteers.org).

The Indulger

Learn from the planner: Confront the details of your spending so you don't continue to bleed money from an emotional place. Since you tend to work from the heart, make a list of how you would like to feel about your money: Knowledgeable, confident, savvy, in control, calm, responsible—whatever it may be. Then, for each adjective, write down one step you can take this week, to achieve that feeling. Next to "knowledgeable" you might write: "I will locate all my credit card statements and write down the amount I owe and the interest rate for each card. Then I'll decide which card to pay off first." For "in control," you might write: "For two days, I'll brown bag it and control my spending on lunch." Next to "savvy," you might write: "By the end of the week, I will visit the web site bankrate.com and find a savings account that pays the highest interest on my money. I'll download and print the enrollment forms, or stop at the bank to get them, and open the account by the end of next week." Be sure to put a specific time frame on each action. Since so many people fall into the indulger personality type, Chapter 5 is devoted to controlling your spending.

Finally, take a page from the mystic, and separate money and happiness. Make a list of five pleasurable activities to do this month that cost nothing—check out a book from the library, watch an old movie, play poker with girlfriends, volunteer for Meals on Wheels and bring dinner to an elderly shut-in, offer to babysit for a new mom. You'll begin to recognize that fun and generosity don't always involve money.

The Adventurer

When you think about money, you think of great experiences—so you don't understand why people get a charge out of piling it up in the bank. Since you love a challenge, try to turn money management into a game. For instance, one adventurer put all of her accounts on a simple Excel spreadsheet in her computer. When she feels so inclined, she pulls out her last statement and enters the new balance in the column—and gets a more visceral thrill from seeing the numbers grow. Make savings automatic so you don't have to think about it (see Chapter 6). If you've got assets, think about hiring someone who actually likes investing to take care of them for you (see Chapter 9). Finally, if your wanderlust is putting you in the red, consider ways to cut your expenses—fly for free as a courier or drive someone else's car cross country. (For details and more ways to save on travel see Chapter 6.)

The Power Tripper

Borrow a page from the mystic, go on a retreat and do a little soul searching: What kind of person do you really want to be? What relationship is most important to you? (Ideally, this should be a living person. And not you.) Try writing your epitaph: How do you want to be remembered by others? *She had the chutzpah of Martha Stewart and the heart of Mother Teresa. . . .* Reduce the materialism in your life before you turn to white-collar crime to support your conspicuous consumption. If your unsecured debt surpasses five figures, get yourself to a credit counselor immediately (see Chapter 5 for details). Rent the video *Baby Boom* with Diane Keaton. Okay, you can buy the DVD.

The Mystic

Get a grip, my ethereal friend. Even His Holiness the Dalai Lama approves of a little legal tender on the path to enlightenment. "Money is good. It is important. Without money, daily survival—not to mention further development—is impossible," he told author Thomas Kostigen in *What Money Really Means.*[3] "At the same time, it is wrong to consider money a god or a substance endowed with some power of its own. To think that money is everything, and that just by having lots of it all our problems will be solved is a serious mistake." Accept the rewards of your labors: Imagine the universe has chosen you to receive money because you know how to do good works with it. (When the Dalai Lama won the Nobel Prize in 1989, he didn't refuse the scratch—he established the

Foundation for Universal Responsibility, to promote peace, interfaith dialogue, and ethical education.) Remember the universe demands both meditation and action. When you cross the path of a spiritually minded financial planner, offer to barter your services—acupuncture, massage therapy, meditation training—for a solid analysis of your cash flow. Create your own reality—get started building some savings for your future foundation. (See Chapter 6.)

By now you should have a good handle on the most important sources of your values—family, community, and personality. In the next chapter, we look at how all of these influences come together in a comprehensive framework of beliefs through which we analyze and interpret money. We look at how to adjust beliefs and debunk money illusions that can block your progress toward prosperity.

3

WHAT DO YOU BELIEVE ABOUT MONEY?

Maria B. is shepherding her energetic sons, 3 and 4, through a busy day in the suburb of a large southwestern city. She and her husband are careful budgeters and savers, regularly investing for retirement and college. Her family's income is about $180,000. "I don't worry about necessities, but I'm very cautious about luxuries," she says.

Not everyone would share her definition of "luxuries." Shoes, for instance: "I'll wear the same pair of shoes until there are holes in them," she says lightheartedly. "My husband will look at me and say, 'Please go buy a new pair of shoes!' I'll usually say, 'Honey, it's the middle of winter, they're going to get ruined anyway, I might as well wear these until the end of the season.'" Or take family outings: When her husband

wants to visit the local aquarium, she balks at the entrance fee. "I'll always say, 'Why don't we just go to the park today and have a picnic?
That doesn't cost anything,'" she laughs.

Amy P., 34, a married mom of twin girls, has a different philosophy:
"I am very free about spending money, if it either makes my life easier
or creates a memory or experience," she explains. While she and her
husband were living overseas for his job, she paid $1,500 to fly back for
the weekend for her mother's 60th birthday. "I most likely won't remember the money I spent five years from now, but I will have the
memory. I would hate to think I hoarded money that could have afforded me or someone I love an experience or a memory." Her approach
to spending makes it tough to plan ahead. "We don't have a whole lot
saved for the future," she admits.

In Chapter 1, we emphasized the importance of aligning money and
values to achieve happiness. In Chapter 2, we looked at some of the
sources of our values. In this chapter, we look at how values, family,
culture, community loyalties, personality, and experience all combine
to create a complex framework through which we analyze and interpret the world. That framework, or worldview, determines our larger
belief systems about money. For example, we might say Maria is frugal, Amy more carefree—and leave it at that. But this doesn't identify
the larger worldview at work. Both women could be making more
satisfying money decisions if they recognize the belief systems that
govern their actions. Our money styles emanate from internal pre-
sumptions that are often unconscious and hard to separate from our
identities. Sometimes our deeply embedded worldviews act like an invisible hand—guiding us smoothly through life, or clutching us by
one ankle, sabotaging our progress.

For instance, money was scarce when Maria was growing up. Her father was a European immigrant who came from a poor village, where
his family owned the clothes on their backs and not much else. He
worked as a college professor. "Throughout my childhood, I always had
the feeling there was never enough," she recalls. "He would make me
feel really guilty if I wanted a new pair of shoes—he'd sigh like it was
really burdensome. Through almost all of my life there was never a
dime spent without thinking about it."

Money—or the dearth of it—also aroused feelings of shame. "My mother used to drink a bit, so we always had those paper wine bags from the liquor store, and that's what we brought our lunch in to school," Maria recalls. "Everyone else had trendy lunch boxes and here I am with the bag from the liquor store. I don't think the children knew but the teachers obviously looked at that and thought, 'hmmm . . . ' At school, it was important to dress well and look nice. I didn't dress well or look nice, so I was always feeling the lack—the world telling you you're not okay because you don't have money."

Now that she has money, Maria spends it on her family. She doesn't hesitate to enroll her sons in activities or buy them clothes: "You better bet when their shoes are the least bit scuffed, they're going to get new shoes!" she declares. At the same time, her worldview is so tied up in childhood experience, she is reluctant to spend money on herself. Even her financial frame of reference seems frozen in time: "I have such a problem buying clothes for myself, because when I was growing up, a pair of pants was $10," she explains. "So when I see pants for $80, I cannot justify it." Maria's worldview seems to say: *I can't afford to spend money on myself, because I don't deserve it.*

Meanwhile, Amy says the purpose of money is to make life easier and more pleasurable, and she has no qualms about treating herself. "I didn't flinch at a $100 massage when I was pregnant because I deserved it!" she laughs. "If I want something I generally buy it, as long as it's within reason. It's $20 for a shirt at the Gap, not a Mercedes." Amy says she doesn't know where her money style comes from—she approaches money differently than anyone else in her family. In fact, she's the exact opposite of her mother. While her mother is a tenacious bargain hunter, Amy places a premium on convenience over price. "My mother will drive an extra five miles to get something cheaper at the grocery store," she explains. "She won't buy a steak if it's more than $4.99 a pound. I'll walk around the corner and pay through the nose because it's easy."

Amy says her worldview comes from the upper middle-class environment in which she was raised, although her mother's experience with extreme childhood poverty must have made an impression. Amy's mother spent several years of her childhood living in a displaced persons camp in Europe after World War II. Amy's worldview seems to say: *Who knows what tomorrow may bring? Live for today.*

At the same time, Amy acknowledges, "I should be a little more careful with money. I treat it as though it's readily available—because I think more in the here and now than in the future. I'd have a lot more money if I didn't run out to Starbucks and buy $4 Frappuccinos. I waste a lot of money simply by not thinking about it. But I'm not going to change, so why have any guilt about it?"

The goal in identifying your worldview is not to feel guilty, but to decide if it's working in your favor, and if not, adjust it so it does. Once you are in touch with your worldview, you have more power. You can acknowledge, "these beliefs caused that money behavior"—and then choose to change your actions. Amy is an adventurer personality, with childhood and community experiences that nurtured that style. Her money mind-set reflects the importance of living joyfully in the moment—a wonderful value. But it doesn't acknowledge that someday her children may need financial help to attend college, or that she and her spouse will reach an age when they can no longer work. On the other side, Maria is a planner, with childhood and community experiences that strongly influence her style. Her tendency to restrain her spending is beneficial to her goal of planning for the future—also an admirable value. But her approach doesn't seem to leave room for a spontaneous treat for herself every now and then, something everyone deserves.

Recognizing their worldviews, Maria and Amy can make different choices and change their relationship with money. If Amy is worried that curbing her spending will make her feel deprived, she can tell herself, "I have enough money to buy this shirt, but I'm going to spend it differently today. I'm going to put it away for my children's education." Maria can create room for spontaneous buys by putting a "slush fund" in her budget—even if it's only $20 a week—that is strictly reserved for self-indulgence. That way she can adhere to her long-term goals and still experience the pleasure of spending without thinking about it—and realize she deserves it.

How Your Worldview Affects Your Work Life

Our worldview determines not just how we spend and save, but how we think about work and opportunity. Nancy G., 33, says that managing her money makes her feel "ill, dizzy, and confused." She earns $58,000 a year as a communications manager for a nonprofit agency in New York, and runs a holistic health counseling practice in her spare time. "Initially, money makes me feel overwhelmed because I'm not a numbers person," she explains. "On top of that, there are emotions that come along with money—the anxiety of not knowing what I have, or what to do with it, or not having enough, or confusion over 'Did I spend too much for this or am I getting ripped off on that?' Remember the cartoon *Mister Magoo*? He crosses the street and the cars are coming but he doesn't get hit. That's how I feel around money—trying to make it through the fog."

Nancy strongly values helping other people and has often thought of starting her own nutrition counseling practice. Her interest in the field started a few years ago, when she developed an allergic reaction to certain foods. She made the rounds to multiple doctors who couldn't identify the source. Then she enrolled in an institute that teaches alternative therapies. "After two weeks of going to the school, I healed myself," Nancy remarks. "My weight is different and my energy so much clearer. I want to help other people feel that way. There's a lot of confusing, conflicting information about nutrition. People need a little guidance and coaching. It can make a huge difference if you make a few changes." She visualizes her life as an entrepreneur and strategizes her business plan, including the number of clients she would have to attract to pay her bills. But she is reluctant to take the risk of starting her own venture.

In Nancy's childhood, money was never candidly discussed. "My dad had his own business," she recalls. "He would win a case, and we would have a lot of money, and he would come home with a boat. One time he picked us up from school in a pink Cadillac." In between cases, her father would voice anxieties about not having enough money and regret some of his spending. "I would see that we were living well and then hear his concerns, so my experience didn't match what was being said," she says. "Then money would show up again. It was a big mystery."

Nancy's parents were generous, paying for college and setting up investment accounts for her future. But she didn't know precisely what she had in those accounts and didn't think of them as anything she could touch. Ironically, having additional resources only reinforced her sense that money was something that's difficult to get a handle on.

She internalized that experience of mixed messages and developed a belief on some level that said: *Money is elusive.* As a result, Nancy's money behavior was somewhat contradictory: She would set aside money for retirement, but then use credit cards without considering the interest rate. She would pay bills late and get hit with late fees, or stop using a service to save money, only to find it was still being charged to her credit card every month. "The idea that I'm not on top of my money creates fear," she says. "There are concepts about money I don't understand and it's not interesting to me. It makes me anxious and tired."

Even though she had enough resources to quit her job and start her own counseling practice, her anxiety around money undermined the confidence she needed to make the leap. "To create my own situation, where I'm completely depending on myself to make it happen, is different than having the structure of a job where I know a paycheck is coming in," she explains. "It's scary for me to have to drum up my own business."

Fortunately, Nancy realized the dynamics at work in her worldview. She started paying her bills online to eliminate late charges and set up a savings account that automatically withdraws money from her checking account every month. She worked with her fiancé to organize all of their accounts on a spreadsheet. By taking action, she was able to change her worldview and focus on the positive lessons she took from her childhood experience. Now she has a new paradigm: Work at what you love, and money will show up.

A short time after our initial conversation, Nancy got married and quit her full-time job to launch her holistic health practice. "As I know more about money, I feel more empowered and more in control of my life," she says. "I really think to do what you want takes confidence—not money. If you have the confidence and drive to do it, you can do it. It doesn't matter how much money you have."

Dere N., president of a midwestern paint and cleaning accessories company, agrees heartily. She grew up in a close-knit family with five siblings, and her parents constantly encouraged them to take risks. Failure was never condemned, and "when you succeeded, there was a considerable amount of applause that went with it," Dere laughs. As a result, her worldview about work has always been: *Taking a chance is an adventure, and failure is an opportunity to learn.* Dere says her best money-related experience came when she worked for a small software development firm. "The company had a difficult time, it was up against the wall financially," she recalls. "The president of this seven-member company said, 'Here's the deal: We need more money. I'll offer you a proposition: If you want to give up all or some of your paycheck, we'll give you stock. You might get more money back, or you might not get any of it back.'" Dere sacrificed a significant portion of her paycheck for several months. Within a year, the employees who took stock rather than pay received 12 times the amount they invested. "Obviously, that's most unusual," Dere admits. "It was a question of taking a risk—can you afford to do it, what's the upside of it? It was such a terrific group of people and such a great experience, we kept one another motivated through the course of those times. It's really and truly easy to say in hindsight, if it had not worked out, it still would have been worth the money."

How would you have responded to the president of the software firm? Would you take the risk or prefer the steady salary? Your worldview greatly determines what you do for a living, and often, how much you earn. If you believe the job market is a dog-eat-dog world of hypercompetition, or people with your skills are a dime a dozen, you'll be afraid to ask for a raise or look for a better job. Your lack of confidence will create your reality. If you believe you offer unique gifts and valuable experience, odds are that an employer will agree, and you'll have the self-assurance required to negotiate the salary you desire.

In 2001, my company laid off 400 people after a merger. I loved my job, and the layoff was a huge disappointment. But I have a peculiar worldview: I am the tenth of 11 children. In most families, I would never have been born at all. As a result, I tend to think anything is possible. Growing up in that lively environment, I saw my parents overcome many challenges by staying committed to their values and taking a longer term view rather than sweating the details. My mother's classic line was: "This too shall pass"—a philosophy that carries no small amount of hope. When I experienced a setback, such as losing a scholarship competition, she would insist there was something more worthwhile waiting for me. Because of this I have spent my life trying to figure out the hidden opportunity in the crisis. (It beats weeping in public.) I looked at my layoff as a challenge to restructure my work life around my kids, and it turned out to be a wonderful gift: I published my first book about a year later. Did I mourn the loss of my job? Sure. Was the transition terrifying at times? Absolutely. Did I despair? Never. My worldview made the difference.[1]

Challenging Your Belief System

Consider this: How much money would you like to earn next year? Let's say it's $75,000. Now say to yourself: *I'm going to receive $75,000 next year.* Is there a part of you that's laughing? Is there a voice telling you that's ridiculous? One way to discover the unseen forces that block our money progress is to have a conversation with that voice of doubt. To recognize our money mind-set and start to change it, we need to listen carefully to the inner voice of protest and question it. We need to understand the assumptions that are operating behind that voice and where they came from; and to challenge those assumptions on a deep emotional level.

Several years ago, one of my sisters was working as a business consultant. She has a master's degree, an MBA from a top-ranked business school, and a PhD. At the time she worked 60-plus hours a week, not including coast-to-coast travel required to see clients. She made a solid salary, but realized some of her peers doing similar work were earning more. One year, while laying out her goals, she declared: "I want to make X this year." Immediately she heard a discouraging voice from within, telling her it wasn't going to happen for her. She said she felt a block in the pit of her stomach. She sat with the internal response in silence and questioned it: *What is this block I feel and why can't I get past it? Why can't I make more than I am making now?* The response: *Because you're already working to capacity. You can't earn more unless you work harder. How can you possibly work any harder than you are now?*

The voice revealed one of her deepest fears and a critical part of her belief system: *You can't earn more unless you work harder.* She says she looked critically at her worldview: First, was it true? No, in fact, it wasn't: She knew some people who worked fewer hours but made more money. Second: Where and when had she started to believe that? Who or what experience was the model for that paradigm?

Immediately, she thought of our dad, who worked long hours to support the family. "He worked so hard and spent all his money on his children because he loved us. What right do I have to earn more than he did, no matter what I do in life? How could I work fewer hours and feel okay about earning more than he did?" she told me. "My belief system told me that I wasn't worthy of earning more than my father." She meditated on her childhood, reviving memories and emotions, experiencing her dad's love again. "I thanked him for all he sacrificed, and all he did for us, and all he gave up for our sake, and I honored his life," she explained. "Then I realized that dad gave us everything so we could have our own lives. He would want me to follow my own path and to be abundant in every way. He would want me to move forward in ways he couldn't even imagine."

That year she went into business for herself and broke through her internal salary barrier, doubling her income. Ever since, she has worked fewer hours and earned more money. "I learned to work passionately, not hard," she says. The shift occurred only after she confronted a belief system to which she had a strong emotional attachment.

Money Myths

By identifying our worldview, we can overcome the money myths that paralyze us. Do you cling to certain myths about money? Here are some common money illusions, and examples of inspiring women who have proven them wrong:

The Myth: I hate my job, but I can't make a change because I need the money.

The Truth: What kind of money could you earn if you pursued your passion? J. K. Rowling, author of the *Harry Potter* series, was a single mother living on public assistance with her baby daughter the year she finished her first book. "I didn't need money to exercise the talent I had—all I needed was a Biro and some paper," she told an interviewer in 1999. By 2004, she had sold 250 million books, and *Forbes* estimated her net worth at $1 billion.[2]

The Myth: You have to have money to make money.

The Truth: Madam C. J. Walker, the first Black female millionaire, was born in 1867 on a Louisiana cotton plantation. At age seven, she was orphaned and later she was widowed with a two-year-old daughter. Working as a laundress, she managed to send her child to college. In 1906, with less than two dollars in savings, she launched her own line of hair care products and set up a mail-order business. A decade later, her company employed 20,000 people. "Don't sit down and wait for the opportunities to come," she once said. "Get up and make them!"[3]

The Myth: The only way to get wealthy is to be an entrepreneur.

The Truth: There are many roads to wealth. Meg Whitman, the low-key CEO of online auction company eBay, has been a "company woman" her entire career—including positions at Hasbro, Stride Rite shoes, Walt Disney, and Procter & Gamble. Her net worth is estimated at more than $1 billion.[4]

The Myth: To be wealthy, you need to study business.

The Truth: The path to wealth has many stepping stones. Carly Fiorina majored in medieval history and philosophy at Stanford University, then dropped out of law school to take a job as a salesperson at AT&T. Today she is chairman and CEO of Hewlett Packard. *Forbes* named her one of the world's 10 most powerful women in 2004. "Love what you do, or don't do it," she said in a speech in 2000. "Make the choice to do something because it engages your heart as well as your mind."[5]

The Myth: I don't have enough education to become wealthy.

The Truth: Persistence is paramount. Lucille Ball was a high school dropout who enrolled in acting school in New York City, only to be told she lacked the ability to sing, dance, speak, or move with grace. She struggled for years—moving back home several times—before her comic genius was recognized. She also became one of the first women to head a major studio, Desilu Productions.[6]

The Myth: If I had more money I'd be more powerful.

The Truth: Personal power has nothing to do with money. Rosa Parks, the mother of the Civil Rights Movement, was a tailor's assistant at a department store in Montgomery, Alabama. (She lost her job after her arrest for refusing to give up her seat on a bus to a white passenger.) She had no economic, social, or political power, but she had the extraordinary personal power that came from living according to her values.[7]

The Myth: I can't become wealthy because I have no connections.

The Truth: You can make your own connections. Oprah Winfrey was born to unwed parents in Mississippi. Her mother was a housemaid, her father an enlisted man in the armed forces. Her grandmother raised her in a house with no electricity or running water. She turned a talk show into a media empire. In 2004, *Forbes* estimated her net worth at more than $1 billion.[8]

The Myth: Wealth will turn me into a greedy, materialistic person.

The Truth: Wealth is a tool that can be used for good or ill. Joan Kroc was a teenage mother and cocktail bar pianist before she married Ray Kroc, the founder of McDonald's, in 1969. By the time of her death in 2003, she had given all of her fortune away—to university programs for the study of peace and nuclear disarmament, hospice programs, AIDS research, homeless shelters, the Special Olympics, relief organizations, and National Public Radio. She bequeathed $1.5 billion to the Salvation Army to build 25 to 30 centers for recreation and the arts for the poor.[9]

The Myth: I'm not meant for financial success—I've tried before and failed.

The Truth: You can try again. In the late 1930s, Katharine Hepburn was dubbed "box office poison" after a string of five movie failures. In 1939, she created the role of Tracy Lord, the spoiled socialite, in *The Philadelphia Story* on Broadway. On the advice of a friend, billionaire Howard Hughes, Hepburn bought the film rights and headed back to Hollywood, where she sold them to Louis B. Mayer for a reported $250,000 (and approval of the director and leading men). Instead of taking a salary, she negotiated a percentage of the profits. The film broke box office records. "If you're given a choice between money and sex appeal, take the money," Hepburn once said. "As you get older, the money will become your sex appeal."[10]

Analyzing Your Approach to Money

In interviewing women for this book, I asked them a range of questions designed to uncover their broader worldviews about money. Write your responses to the following questions. Don't dwell too much on each one, just write the first response that comes to mind:

1. If I could describe my approach to spending in a sentence, it would be _____ .
2. My most important investment is _____ .
3. Most of my money goes to _____ .
4. My biggest indulgence is _____ .
5. What I owe _____ .
6. Managing my money makes me feel _____ .
7. My ultimate financial goal is _____ .
8. The thing that is missing in my life due to lack of money is _____ .
9. If I won the lottery I would _____ .
10. For me, the purpose of money is to _____ .

Now review your answers and ask yourself the following questions. (Some of your answers may relate to specific saving and investing techniques, which are covered in later chapters.)

1. Why is that my approach to money? Where did that come from? What beliefs does it imply?
2. Do my most important investments reflect my highest values? If not, what beliefs and values do they reflect?
3. Does most of my current spending reflect my highest values? If not, what does my spending say about my beliefs?

4. Why do I choose the indulgences I do? What are my beliefs around entitlement or pleasure? Can I indulge in the present and still invest some of my money for the future? If not, why not?

5. Who do I owe money to, and why? What does that say, if anything, about the way I believe money should be used? Are these debts for necessities of life, such as education or a car, or for investments, such as a home? If not, what do I buy now on credit instead of saving up to buy? Why do I believe I must have it immediately?

6. Why does managing my money make me feel this way? If I feel negatively about it, what would I have to change to feel positively about the way I manage money? Think of times in your life when you felt you were successfully managing your money: What things did those situations have in common?

7. How did I choose my ultimate financial goal? Is it aligned with my highest values?

8. Are the things that are missing in my life because of money really things I value? If so, how can I change my approach to money to achieve them? If they are desires rather than values, what is fueling those desires?

9. Is there a reasonable way to do right now any of the things I would do if I won the lottery?

10. Why did I answer as I did about the purpose of money? What larger belief is operating here?

What illusions about money are blocking you from grabbing hold of your financial life? Whether your money issue is related to earning, spending, or saving, here are eight steps to changing your worldview:

1. Make a radical proposal to yourself around wealth:
   I want to earn/have/do _____ .
2. Listen to the inner voice of protest:
   You can't because _____ .
3. Challenge your doubts:
   That objection is false because _____ .

4. Identify the beliefs behind them:
   I thought that way because I believed _____ .
5. Examine the origin of the beliefs:
   I learned that when _____ .
6. Revisit the experiences and emotions that gave birth to the beliefs:
   That lesson took hold when I experienced _____ .
7. Challenge the belief system:
   The belief is untrue because _____ .
8. Shift to a new paradigm:
   The truth is, I can earn/have/do _____ because _____
   _____ .

The Power of Choice

We are not victims of our worldview. The way we manage money, our attitude toward it, is ultimately a choice. No matter what money mindset we have developed over time, through life experience, we have the power to change it. We can work around our money personalities; we can choose different communities; we can reject our parents' approach and choose a healthier set of values.

Just ask Jeanne H., a 30-something manager of a nonprofit group. In her childhood, her family lived well above their means. "If my dad had to choose between paying his credit card back or going on vacation, he'd go on vacation," she recalls. Her parents went through a bitter divorce when she was in her teens and fought constantly about money. Her father was a gambler who lost his profession because of his habit. A few years ago, he took out two credit cards in her name and forged her signature. She realized what was happening when a credit card company she'd never heard of called to ask about unusual activity on her card. "He has never apologized—he's a gambler, so in his mind he says he was always planning on paying it back," she says. "But you still feel very violated, whether it is someone you know or a stranger."

Jeanne, who is married, has no debt and is aggressively saving to buy a home. She has intense feelings about the importance of managing money responsibly—and equally fervent beliefs that money is not the source of happiness, or freedom, or power. "I don't think that someone can define her life by money," she says. "I've grown up seeing people do that with money they didn't even have—and they're not powerful, they're not happy, and they're not loved. It's not often you have children who don't follow in their parents' footsteps. But I erred on the side of not doing what they were doing. When it affects your life so much, you go in the opposite direction. You say, I can't be that person."

As Jeanne's experience demonstrates, we have the power to alter our worldviews so that money does not dictate our state of happiness. Here's the truth: Money only has the power over our lives that we are willing to surrender to it. Consider a story told by Sister Maria José Hobday, a Franciscan nun and author who has written and lectured internationally for 30 years on Native American spirituality, prayer, and simplicity. In the 1930s, her family was living on the edge of poverty: "One Saturday evening I was working late on my homework. I was in the living room, my brothers were outside with their friends, and my parents were in the kitchen, discussing our financial situation. It was very quiet, and I found myself more and more following the kitchen conversation rather than attending to my homework. Mama and Daddy were talking about what had to be paid for during the week, and there was very little money—a few dollars. As I listened, I became more and more anxious, realizing there was not enough to go around. They spoke of school needs, of fuel bills, of food. Suddenly the conversation stopped, and my mother came into the room where I was studying. She put the money— a couple of bills and a handful of change—on the desk. 'Here,' she said, 'go find two or three of your brothers and run to the drugstore before it closes. Use this money to buy strawberry ice cream.' I was astonished! I was a smart little girl, I knew we needed this money for essentials. So I objected. 'What? We have to use this to pay bills, Mama, to buy school things. We can't spend this on ice cream!' Then I added, 'I'm going to ask Daddy.' So I went to my father, telling him what Mother had asked me to do. Daddy looked at me for a moment, then threw back his head and laughed. 'You mother is right, honey,' he said. 'When we get this worried and upset about a few dollars, we are better off having nothing at all. We can't solve all the problems, so maybe we should celebrate instead. Do as your mother says.' So I collected my brothers and went to the drugstore. In those days, you could get a lot of ice cream for a few dollars, and we came home with our arms full of packages. My mother had set the table, made fresh coffee, put out what cookies we had and invited the neighbors. It was a great party! I do not remember what happened concerning other needs, but I remember the freedom and fun of that evening. I thought about that evening many times, and came to realize that spending a little money for pleasure was not irresponsible. It was a matter of survival of the spirit. The bills must have been paid; we made it through the weeks and months that followed. I learned my parents were not going to allow money to dominate them. I learned something of the value of money, of its use. I saw that of itself it was not important but that my attitude toward it affected my own spirit, could reduce me to powerlessness or give me power of soul."[11]

We started this book with the idea that true wealth comes from consciously aligning your values and your money. We have examined the sources of our values—family, community, personality—and how those combine with life experience to create a unique worldview. We've looked at how those belief systems result in action that can help us achieve our goals or hinder us—and the importance of challenging worldviews that limit our growth. With this foundation in place, make a list of your top five values. How are they a priority in your life? Start to think about the relationship between your values and your actions—the amount of time and money you give to them. See if you can begin to set goals by making connections between your values, your money, and your behavior:

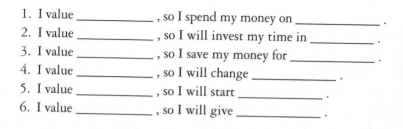

1. I value _____ , so I spend my money on _____ .
2. I value _____ , so I will invest my time in _____ .
3. I value _____ , so I save my money for _____ .
4. I value _____ , so I will change _____ .
5. I value _____ , so I will start _____ .
6. I value _____ , so I will give _____ .

Now that you have an idea of the values by which to steer your course, it's time to ask a fundamental question: How much money do you need to be happy? How important is money in the broader scheme of things that make us happy? We'll answer those questions in the next chapter.

How Money Relates to Your Happiness

Who is rich? He who is satisfied with his portion in life.
                                                    —The Talmud

On a crisp winter night in London, Kathy K. floated out of her office feeling like she'd won an Academy Award. The diminutive brunette—one of nine women among 360 men toiling on the trading floor of a major investment bank—had just landed a hugely profitable deal. The chairman himself phoned to congratulate her. "He said, 'Whatever you're doing, keep it up,'" Kathy recalls. She flung on her fur coat and settled into the supple black leather of her silver BMW, Big Ben chiming in the distance. She called a relative in Asia on her cell phone to tell him about her triumph. When she hung up, she burst into tears.

"I was feeling totally cool and empowered, and from the outside it looked like I had it all," she says. "But then I thought: '*This is it?*' When you achieve a certain level of success in that environment, it's incredibly thrilling. And then you find it's just you, all by yourself, and this big pile of money."

Nearly 2,500 years ago Aristotle wrote, "The happy man will need external prosperity." But how much prosperity do we need to be happy? Fortunately, the answer is no longer just a philosophical debate. Over the past three decades, researchers have devised rigorous empirical methods to test theories of happiness, prompting reams of data—more than 3,000 different studies, according to the World Database of Happiness. The relatively new field of "subjective well-being" has probed the relationship between happiness and factors like health, education, marital status, religious belief, and, of course, cold hard cash.

Although the studies offer intriguing, sometimes conflicting insights into money and happiness, one conclusion is universal: A certain amount of money does indeed make people happier. People who live in wealthy nations are happier than those who live in poor ones.[1] No bombshell there: Everyone enjoys life a little more when they've got enough to eat, clothing, and a warm place to sleep. But then it gets a little sticky. Excessive wealth seems to raise the happiness bar only slightly. Over the past few decades, big jumps in economic growth in developed nations like the United States and Japan have been accompanied by only marginal increases in happiness. Even the obscenely wealthy—the *Forbes'* 100 richest Americans—scored only slightly above the average Joe on the happiness scale, according to a study by psychology Professor Ed Diener at the University of Illinois, Urbana-Champaign.[2] And the wretchedly poor—people surveyed in the slums of Calcutta, India—reported positive feelings, especially about their friends and religion.[3]

In a now-classic study, researchers surveyed lottery winners who had won $50,000 to $1 million within the previous year. Compared with a control group who lived in the same geographic area, the jackpot winners reported only slightly higher levels of life satisfaction—4.0 on a scale of 5, versus 3.8 for the control group. Moreover, the lottery winners took less pleasure in routine daily activities.[4]

So what factors determine our ability to be happy about money? Before we reveal the scientific secrets of money and happiness, take the quiz that begins on the bottom of this page and continues on pages 61–62 to find your money-happiness quotient. Don't dwell on each question—go with your immediate response, and be as honest as you can.

Money-Happiness Quotient Quiz

1. How much do you earn?
   A. Less than $14,999
   B. $15,000 to $34,999
   C. $35,000 to $54,999
   D. $55,000 to $74,999
   E. $75,000 to $94,999
   F. $95,000 to $114,999
   G. $115,000 or above
2. How much more do you need to earn to be happy?
   A. 6 to 10 times my current salary
   B. 2 to 5 times my current salary
   C. I don't need to earn more to make me happy.
3. Think about your most satisfying experience of the last month. Did it relate to money? (Did you get a windfall, a raise, or enjoy a costly treat?)
   A. Yes
   B. No
4. Have you ever taken a job primarily for the money?
   A. Yes
   B. No
5. If yes, did you regret it?
   A. No
   B. Yes
6. Has your opinion of someone ever changed because you discovered how much they make?
   A. Yes
   B. No
7. Have you ever spent money you didn't want to spend just to keep up with friends or acquaintances?
   A. Yes
   B. No

(continued)

Money-Happiness Quotient Quiz *(Continued)*

8. Do you have more or less than most of your friends?
   A. More (see 8a)
   B. Less (see 8b)

8a. If more, which best describes your feelings about the situation?
   A. I feel guilty about earning more than my friends do.
   B. I don't think much about it.
   C. I deserve what I have.

8b. If less, which best describes your feelings about the situation?
   A. I feel resentful of friends who have more money.
   B. I don't think much about it.
   C. My friends deserve their success.

9. The more money I make, the more I spend.
   A. Agree
   B. Disagree

10. Money helps me buy things that define who I am.
   A. Agree
   B. Disagree

11. I frequently put other things I like to do on the back burner because I have to work.
   A. Agree
   B. Disagree

12. The most important reason I work at my current job is:
   A. The money
   B. It offers qualities that help me balance other priorities (i.e., close to home, appealing hours, flexibility)
   C. It is in the field/career I want to pursue; I enjoy it.

13. I always have something in mind I am looking forward to buying.
   A. Agree
   B. Disagree

14. I dream about things I do not own:
   A. Frequently
   B. Sometimes
   C. Never

15. Money is my top goal in life.
   A. Agree
   B. Disagree

16. Financially, I am better off than most people in the world.
   A. Disagree
   B. Agree
   C. I never think about it.

17. I have set firm goals and expect to meet them.
   A. Disagree
   B. Agree

(continued)

Money-Happiness Quotient Quiz (Continued)

18. Your fairy godmother agrees to grant your dream job. You ask her for three things: your ideal salary; freedom/autonomy on the job (i.e., you decide how you spend your time); and supportive colleagues. She says you can either choose *two* of those attributes, or you can have everything you asked, but at 60 percent of your ideal salary. You choose:
    A. The money and the autonomy
    B. The money and the supportive colleagues
    C. Both the autonomy and supportive colleagues at the lower salary

Score: Skip questions 1 and 8. For questions 2–7 and 8a/b–18:

A = Zero points

B = Two points

C = Three points

Analysis

36–43 Very happy about money

28–35 Happy about money

20–27 Sometimes happy/sometimes unhappy about money

12–19 Unhappy about money

0–11   Miserable about money

The Secrets of Money and Happiness

Did you score at the top or bottom of the scale? Does it accurately reflect your feelings about money and your experience with it? The quiz is designed to give you insight into the key areas of scientific research related to money and happiness: Aspirations; priorities; comparing; competing; and managing materialism. To help you understand your score, here are the highlights of the research, and some specific suggestions to improve your sense of financial well-being.

✔ Aspirations: The More We Have, the More We Want

When it comes to money and stuff, humans are hard-wired to want more. Richard Easterlin, professor at the University of Southern California, pioneered happiness research in the 1970s. "The problem is, people don't realize that as their incomes go up, their aspirations also go up," Easterlin explains. "When people are in good health, that doesn't lead them to aspire to *better* health. If people have a good marriage and children, they don't aspire to have *two* families. But in the case of material goods, people have this idea that they're going to be happier if they get more. They end up pursuing a goal that's biased toward money at the expense of other aspirations in life. They get caught on the 'hedonic treadmill.'"[5]

The phrase *hedonic treadmill* means *we adapt to the improvement in our circumstances, and then seek more.* The more money we make, the more we demand from life, and the more dissatisfied we become when we don't get what we want. Money and material goods become like a drug high—quickly gone, replaced by the desire for another fix.

As Liza D., a 38-year-old medical writer and mom of two in Georgia, puts it: "Not having money doesn't mean you can't do things, but having money makes it easier. It's a lot easier to travel the world when you have money—unless you're 20 and want to carry a rucksack and hitchhike—but that gets old. When you have money, you don't have to volunteer to be an usher to see the play. You just buy the ticket. You don't have to go to library to get books, you just order them from Amazon. There are a lot of things you don't need money for, but it's a lot easier if you have it." The problem is, we tend to work harder and harder with the idea that it will give us the money to make things easier and easier. Meanwhile, a stroll to the library is free, pleasurable, and won't fill up the house with a lot of books (or require more money to buy bookshelves).

Think of a positive money experience, like getting a bonus for the first time at work. Maybe you felt euphoric—and then, it's over. You begin to expect a bonus, desire a heftier one, and feel deprived if the company has a bad year and gives you nothing. I distinctly remember the pleasure I felt when we finished renovating the kitchen in my home, running my fingers across the silky stone countertops, admiring the soft blue ceramic tile floor and gleaming maple cabinets. We even opened a bottle of champagne to celebrate. Within a year, I caught myself thinking how nice it would be to have a *larger* kitchen.

In one study, Easterlin analyzed the results of a Roper-Starch survey that asked adults about their material aspirations and achievements. The survey was conducted twice—once in 1978 and again in 1994.[6] Roper asked respondents the following:

1. We often hear people talk about what they want out of life. Here are a number of different things. When you think of the good

life—the life you'd like to have, which of the things on this list, if any, are part of that good life as far as you personally are concerned?
2. Now would you go down that list and call off all the things you now have?

The Roper list included items such as a home, swimming pool, vacation home, cars, televisions, travel abroad, really nice clothes, and a lot of money. Because the two surveys were conducted 16 years apart, Easterlin was able to analyze whether people's aspirations shift as they age and their circumstances change. He found that as consumers moved through each stage of the life cycle—early, mid-life, and older years—they generally acquired more of the consumer goods on the list. But as they accumulated more, he found their *aspirations for material goods also rose, in proportion to the amount of things they owned.* "There is clearly a suggestion in these data that new material aspirations arise as previous goals are reached . . . the greater the increase in possessions, the greater the increase in desires," Easterlin concludes.

Why do we get stuck on the hedonic treadmill? One theory is that we're poor predictors of our own happiness. In 2002, Daniel Kahneman, a Princeton University psychology professor, won the Nobel Prize for his work integrating psychology and economic decision making. A fundamental theory of economics suggests people are motivated by self-interest. They consider their options and make rational decisions to maximize their own welfare. Surely we know what we like, we can imagine the most desirable outcome, and choose that course of action? Well . . . no. Kahneman and others psychologists who study well-being found we don't act rationally in a lot of cases. "The evidence suggests people may not have the ability to predict their future tastes . . . with the accuracy that the economic model requires," Kahneman writes.[7]

On the personal level, our failure to accurately predict how we will feel in the future can lead to poor choices—choosing the wrong spouse or the wrong career. When it comes to money, "we think that if we were richer than we are and we're able to consume things that we're denying ourselves now, that somehow would make life better," Kahneman said in a published interview. "But the indications are that when you take the whole population and you improve their ability to make economic choices of consumption, it does absolutely nothing to their life satisfaction."[8]

So if there's no great leap in happiness from making extra money or buying more stuff, why are we working so hard? Scientists have found people have a potent psychological immune system, a powerful mental capacity to transform, invent, or ignore information. At the same time, most people are largely unaware of the mind's ability to put on rose-colored glasses.[9] In other words, we will conveniently overlook the long commute, stressful assignments, or back-stabbing politics in a potential new job because we're convinced more money will make us happier than it actually does.

Even if we attempt to make rational decisions by basing them on previous experience, chances are the memory will be biased. As Kahneman's work has found, there are two people involved in our decisions—the self that actually experiences events, and the one that remembers them. "The remembering self keeps score and is in charge," Kahneman explains.[10] When we recall events, we tend to craft a narrative about our experiences, paying closest attention to the peak and the end of the experience—and that results in a limited representation of what actually happened.

Psychologists discovered this phenomenon by having subjects do both real-time and global evaluations of an experience. The subjects rate minute-by-minute what they are experiencing; and then describe the event after the fact. What they say afterward doesn't always match what they expressed during the episode. For instance, Kahneman did a study of patients receiving colonoscopy exams, a painful medical procedure, that lasted anywhere from four minutes to an hour in length. Patient A went through a build-up to sharp pain, and then the exam was over. Patient B went through a longer procedure—a build up to piercing pain that then declined to slight discomfort before the exam ended. Patient B, whose experience ended on a less-painful note, rated the experience better—even though they suffered the same level of pain Patient A did, and the event lasted for a longer period of time.[11]

"What really mattered was the peak pain they had experienced and how much pain they had experienced at the end," Kahneman says. "This tells you that there are really two ways of looking at experience . . . the experiencing subject who was actually living through the colonoscopy, and the remembering subject was passing judgment on the colonoscopy later, and saying, 'How much did I suffer?' So, if we have people whose memories work in this way, it can cause (them) to make rather foolish judgments or judgments that clearly are not in their own best interest."[12]

Another reason we make predictive errors is something scientists call "the hot/cold empathy gap."[13] When people are in a "cold," or neutral emotional state, they often have trouble imagining how they would feel or what they would do if they were in a "hot" state—angry, hungry, in pain, or at a Prada sample sale with 200 other women. On the other hand, when we're experiencing a hot state, we have difficulty imagining that we will cool off at some point. (Which is why, in the heat of the moment, knocking down the woman tussling with you over a Prada skirt at the sample sale seems like a reasonable move.) "Such 'hot/cold' empathy gaps can lead to errors in predicting both feelings and behavior," write researchers George Loewenstein of Carnegie Mellon University and David Schkade of the University of Texas, Austin. Human memory "seems to be well suited to storing visual images, words, and semantic meaning, but ill suited to storing information about visceral sensations." We can talk about the objective details related to a painful event or a craving, but can't re-experience the pain or craving itself. As a result, one study found that people who are not in a shopping situation underestimate the emotional "urge to splurge" that occurs once they enter a mall.[14] It may also be why people don't save for retirement when it's obviously in their best interest—it's impossible to imagine what it would feel like to be old and poor.

If the hedonic treadmill is ingrained in our biology, how can we let go and be happy with what we have, and stop ourselves from constantly aspiring to more? One solution: Don't stop—advance in a new direction.

Consider Sharon C., a 40-something mom of two in suburban New York. At the moment, Sharon is annoyed by a crack in the ceiling of her living room. She had a leak that was fixed long ago, but can't afford to have the ceiling repainted. "I'm not very handy," she sighs. "I'd get myself into one big mess if tried (to paint it myself). Some things I'll attempt, but some things are meant for professionals."

Since Sharon's husband started his own business in 2002, money has been tight. For the first time in their lives, they are carrying credit card debt—$20,000—and it feels oppressive. It was an unexpected turn; as Sharon puts it: "Going backwards. Ugh!"

After a merger at work, her husband decided to take a one-year severance package and trade in his 14-hour workdays for a different life— one that would give him more time with the family. His decision turned out to be fortuitous: A few months after he quit, Sharon developed breast cancer. He was able to take care of her and the kids while she recuperated. "We knew he could take a few months off to chill out and get our lives back together and take care of me—so as far as that goes, the timing was perfect," she says.

Then the timing was perfectly awful. Sharon's husband got back in the job market a month before the September 11, 2001, terrorist attacks. With the local economy devastated, he tried working on his own. His first consulting assignment lasted 18 months, but the client failed to pay for some of the contracted work and the matter ended up in court—adding legal fees to their looming debt. Sharon's friends ask her to come to New York City to see a play or go out to lunch and she refuses. She longs to move to a better school district, to travel again, to trade in her practical Buick for the sporty 4 × 4 she used to drive.

"I know I'm very lucky—I have my house, my kids are healthy, they're the joys of my life, I have a great husband. I do consider myself very happy," Sharon says. "But when people say money doesn't buy happiness, I think that's a load of crap. Does it buy you total happiness? No, but it helps. I think I could be a lot happier now if I had money— the bills would be paid; I wouldn't be frustrated and stressed."

Managing Your Aspirations

Sharon's frustration and stress are legitimate—the inability to pay bills can be a major source of anxiety. But just as we can aspire and adapt to luxury, we can aspire and adapt to a life that is both simpler (and richer) in many ways. Sharon started by shifting her activities away from money. She's focusing on her health, spending more time at the gym. She's simplifying her space, tackling long-standing clean-up projects at home, and clearing out things she doesn't need. She volunteers as a class mom at her kids' school. Most importantly, she visits breast cancer patients in a local hospital and raises money for research.

That's a particularly powerful technique to improve happiness and well being, according to Professor Sonja Lyubomirsky of the University of California—Riverside.[15]

Lyubomirsky conducted a study in which students were asked to practice altruism, doing five acts of kindness a week for six weeks. "The notion that being kind can make you happy has deep roots in probably every culture," Lyubomirsky explains. "There's a fairly well-known Chinese proverb that says, 'If you want happiness for an hour, take a nap; for a day, go fishing; for a month, get married; for a year, inherit a fortune; for a lifetime, help somebody else.' The first two are really kind of momentary pleasures . . . the second two are circumstances to which you adapt, and the last one is an intentional activity. Kind acts foster a sense of interdependence, cooperation. They make you perceive others and yourself more favorably. And I think most important, being kind has really a host of social consequences . . . where you can inspire some friendship."

Sharon should also create low-cost ways to spend time with her current group of friends, like starting a book club or meeting for coffee. The University of Chicago's National Opinion Research Center found that people with five or more close friends (excluding family members) are 50 percent more likely to describe themselves as "very happy" than respondents with fewer friends.[16]

Another way to boost happiness is to be conscious of how you talk about money. The way we explain things to ourselves has a huge impact on our happiness, according to author David Myers, professor at Michigan's Hope College.[17] Middle-class people can gain a healthier perspective on their situation by cutting the poor talk, he says: " 'I need that' can become 'I want that.' 'I am underpaid' can become 'I spend more than I make.' And the most familiar middle-class lament, 'We can't afford it,' can become, truthfully, 'We choose to spend our money on other things.' For usually, we *could* afford it—the snowmobile, the CD player, the Disney World vacation—*if* we made it our top priority; we just have other priorities on which we choose to spend our limited incomes. The choice is ours. 'I can't afford it' denies our choices, reducing us to self-pitying victims."

If you're facing a difficult money situation like Sharon, train yourself to be optimistic. Martin Seligman is a University of Pennsylvania psychologist and best-selling author of 20 books, including *Learned Optimism: How to Change Your Mind and Your Life.*[18] His book, based on 20 years of clinical research, explains that optimists view setbacks in their lives as temporary, rather than permanent; specific, versus universal; hopeful, versus hopeless; and external, versus internal—that is, optimists find an explanation for the misfortune that blames external forces rather than themselves. Sharon, for example, could boost her happiness by viewing her current financial situation as:

Temporary: This rough patch in the road that will be over soon and the bills will get paid.

Versus Permanent: We're going broke.

Specific: Everyone has career ups and downs; look at all the other great things we have going for us—our kids are healthy, we have a supportive extended family, we own our home, we love each other.

Versus Universal: Our financial troubles are wrecking our lives.

External: Lots of technology businesses are still feeling the effects of the recession; my husband is a talented professional whose company is going to flourish.

Versus Internal: He's not cut out to be an entrepreneur.

And Hopeful: Maybe the situation is an opportunity for me to explore fulfilling work I would really enjoy.

Versus Hopeless: I'm going to be forced to get a job to pay the bills.

Sharon believes earning two to five times her current income would make her happier. What's your magic number? Review your answers to questions 2 and 9. If you feel you need 2 to 10 times your current salary to be happy, ask yourself:

- Can I realistically achieve that number in the future?
- Do other people in my field earn that amount?
- What do I need to change to make that happen?
- Am I willing to commit to those goals, set up a plan and a timeframe to achieve them?

Most importantly, think about *why* you need to earn two to 10 times your current salary. If you're making poverty-level wages and can't cover your basic needs, working toward a larger salary is a natural response. But if you already earn enough to cover basic needs, make a list of exactly how you would spend the extra money. Do you genuinely value consuming the things on your list? (See Chapter 1.) What would you have to give up in your life to earn that higher salary? If earning 2 to 10 times your pay is *not* a realistic goal in your current field, you either need to jump ship or adjust your expectations. Consider a different career with better pay, which may require upgrading your skills. But before you do any of that, understand that decades of research have found all of your exhaustive effort will make you wealthier, but probably not a whole lot happier.

As for question 9, if you agree that with the statement "the more I earn the more I spend," you're not usual. Try to shift your thinking. Don't consume your treasure—bury it! When you get a raise or bonus, give yourself a cost-of-living increase of 10 percent, and have the rest automatically swept from your checking account into a fund reflecting your deeper values—whether that's a secure retirement, a home purchase or a trip to Tahiti. (For specifics on how to do this, see Chapter 6.) So if you get a bonus of $1,000, splurge with the first $100, and make the other $900 disappear into the long-term goal fund.

✔ Priorities: The Pursuit of Money Can Overwhelm Other Priorities

Money has the uncanny ability to hijack our time. The tension between pursuing money and our other values represents a "positional externality" in research-speak: We make trade-offs that short change our other priorities. Professor Easterlin sites a survey by sociologist Norval Glenn to illustrate his point: Americans were asked about their likelihood of taking a more financially rewarding job that would reduce family time because it would require longer office hours and more travel. None of the 1,200 respondents said they would be "very unlikely" to take the job. One in three said "somewhat unlikely." The majority—about two-thirds—said they were either "very likely" or "somewhat likely" to take the job. In other words, most Americans are ready to sacrifice family life for what they think will be richer monetary rewards from their jobs—

not realizing that these potential rewards are likely to be an illusion, at least in terms of overall happiness, Easterlin points out.[19]

The pursuit of short-term material gains, relative to other goals, means you have less time and energy to devote to things that make you happy in the long run, like hanging out with friends and family, exercising, hobbies, or volunteering. Question 11 looks at our priorities. Do you frequently put your other goals on the back burner because of work? Investment banker Kathy K., who we met at the beginning of the chapter, says she sacrificed everything for her job. "You become harsh; you almost don't understand the level other people are at," she says. "You think, why *wouldn't* you give up Thanksgiving with your family to go do a deal in Uruguay? That's a no-brainer!"

Everyone is given 24 hours a day to pursue her life. Money sometimes crowds out other priorities because it's easy to keep score—success is strictly by the numbers. We can prove we're thriving because the numbers in our bank account are going up. If this is you, figure out a way to quantify your other goals, so you can measure your success in less tangible areas. If you value spending time with someone you love, be specific about what that means—two lunches a month; dinner twice a week; two long vacations a year. Second, we think money will facilitate all of our other desires—we'll be able to afford the beach house where we'll have space and time to play. But how much time does it take to earn what you need so you have the time to play?

That's the dilemma Diane C. faced. A diligent student who worked her way through college, she joined an international accounting firm in her 20s and vaulted to partner at a time when fewer than 5 percent of partners were women. "To do the job really well, you had to live, eat, and breathe it, and that was fine with me—I loved it," she says. "I wanted to be the best, and money was kind of a way of keeping score."

In the mid-1990s, Diane began reflecting on a course she'd taken at work, in which participants were asked to visualize their lives at age 65. "Almost to a person, they described a scene where they were secure financially and surrounded by kids and grandkids," Diane recalls. "I thought, if you spend all your time working, what makes you think you'll have any family who care when you're ready for them? It takes a lifetime to build those relationships." A light bulb went off. Diane asked to be relocated to her hometown to be closer to her family. Her firm agreed, as long as she was willing to travel more often on business. A few years later she adopted a baby girl from China, and then a second girl. Her aunt moved in to help care for the kids while Diane kept running on the treadmill of long hours and frequent travel. "When I was home I was so tired and stressed," she recalls. "My oldest daughter got into preschool, and then kindergarten, and I felt I was missing out on too many of the special moments. You don't get second chances with this stuff." Diane quit, downsized her expenses and began consulting part-time. "These are special years when my girls are young," she says. "Having time with them is more important than funding 100 percent of what they want to do."

✓ Comparing: How Am I Doing?

When people make relative-income comparisons, they frequently look at those who have more—and get upset when their income compares unfavorably, according to a study by Andrew Oswald of England's Warwick University and David Blanchflower of Dartmouth. Oswald also found that even if our incomes are rising, we tend to become less happy if the incomes of others are rising even more.[20]

That happened to Molly D., a California marketing consultant, when she worked for a public relations firm. A year after Molly was hired at a comfortable salary, the firm brought in a new associate who was given 20 percent more. "I actually found out about it through a weird, unexpected way—an e-mail appeared in my box that wasn't supposed to be for me," she recalls. "That kind of pissed me off. I liked her—my anger was more directed at the people who hired her. This person was from a different industry and did not have a lot of relevant experience, but her resume looked good. My salary was adequate, and normally I would have never known, and would have been fine." Molly quit a short time later.

Envy seems to come naturally in a society as consumer-oriented as the United States. We look around and see people with a bigger homes, a better set of wheels, a season's worth of stylish clothes, jetting off on fabulous vacations. And we covet. As Claudian, the fourth-century Roman poet wrote, "He who covets is always poor." Most of us know this instinctively. But we can't help wondering about the people we envy: How do they do it? Stephanie V., 27, works for an East Coast real estate firm. She is engaged to be married and is funneling all of her extra cash to credit card debt and student loans, so she and her fiancé can begin their life together debt-free. "I just think about my friends and sometimes I wonder how they can afford certain things," she admits. "A couple I know, one is in graduate school, one is working and they just bought a new car and a new house—and I don't know how they're doing it. I think, 'Do they know something I don't? Am I doing something wrong?'"

Because talking about money is taboo in most circles, we never know the whole story. Maybe Stephanie's friends received a family inheritance; maybe they bought shares of Microsoft in the mid-1980s; or maybe they're drowning in debt. The image is bright and glossy—the reality may be much darker. Just ask East Coast attorney Lara P. "I have a friend who lives in a beautiful house," she says. "She has a kitchen to die for, she's beautiful, her husband is handsome, she wears a four-carat diamond ring, they have perfect kids. You look at them and it's the textbook perfect family. We went shopping and she spent $300 on stuff for herself and I spent $20 on a sweater for my daughter and felt guilty about it." Lara says she curbed her envy by focusing on her own treasures—her strong marriage, wonderful children, her own smaller, but still charming, home.

A few weeks later, her friend confessed she had been unhappy for years and was getting divorced. "I was right all along when I reminded myself about everything that I have," Lara says. "Watching my friend go through this made me think a lot about the idea that money can't buy happiness. It really is just a tool, and we place a lot of value on it, when ultimately the much more important things in life are personal relationships."

Review your answers to questions 8a/b and 16. How do you feel about earning more or less than your friends, or than most people in the world? If you want to be happy with your money, never measure your financial achievements against anything except your own goals. We can banish envy by returning to values—thinking about what you really desire in your own life, and organizing your financial house to get those things, or at least the most important of them. Because when you get what you truly want, why would you want what someone else has?

In the meantime, if you can't help comparing, then look down, rather than up, and be grateful for your abundance. That's what Gillian D. does. The 35-year-old communications executive lives in New York City, where envy is practically a contact sport, but her outlook on money comes from her childhood in South Africa. "My parents are very simple people and we really struggled for many years, so we learned to appreciate things," she says. "I come from a place where you experience unbelievable poverty every day of your life. Unemployment is 40 percent. I see people living in Shantytowns, people begging all the time. It has a profound affect on a person—you realize how much you actually have compared to other people."

Thich Nhat Hanh, a Vietnamese Buddhist monk, describes a technique for appreciating the well being we already enjoy in our lives. "When I have a toothache, I discover that not having a toothache is a wonderful thing," he writes in *The Heart of the Buddha's Teaching*. "That is peace. I had to have a toothache in order to be enlightened, to know that not having one is wonderful. My nontoothache is peace, is joy. But when I do not have a toothache, I do not seem to be happy. Therefore, I look deeply in the present moment and see that I have a nontoothache, that can make me very happy already."[21]

If comparing is your pastime, get some perspective by focusing on a difficult time you experienced in the past—and stop for a moment to savor your quality of life now. Rejoice in your "nontoothache" by starting a gratitude journal. Professor Lyubomirsky of UC Riverside conducted an experiment in which subjects wrote down five things they were thankful for. One group wrote on a weekly basis, the other group three times a week; and a control group didn't write at all. "Being grateful for what you have prevents you from thinking about what other people have. So I think it might inhibit some comparison," Lyubomirsky explains. "Gratitude also seems to be incompatible with some negative emotions. It's hard to feel envious or greedy or bitter when you're grateful." Interestingly, only the group that did the exercise *once a week* experienced a significant rise in gratitude. Lyubomirsky surmised that for the group writing three times a week, the activity became a routine chore.[22] So count your blessings, but choose a timetable that keeps the exercise meaningful.

✓ Competing: Keeping Up with the Joneses Leads to Misery

If comparing creates negative feelings, getting down and dirty with the Joneses is even worse. Dr. Shaun Saunders, an Australian researcher at the University of Newcastle in England, studied more than 1,000 people and discovered materialistic people who try to keep up with others are more likely to be angry, depressed, frustrated, and anxious.[23] This is something we've known instinctively for at least 3,000 years, ever since the story of Adam and Eve was written down. Think about it: One of our great classic narratives focuses on a couple that lives in total abundance and complete happiness (the Hebrew *Eden* means "delight"). They literally have everything they need, including good jobs and a compassionate boss. Then their next-door neighbor, the snake, eggs them on, implying he's had a taste of the tree that's off-limits, and it's a mind-blowing experience. Adam and Eve, stylish early adopters of the highest order (Adam *named* the animals, for God's sake) share in the booty. Then everything goes to hell.

Once upon a time, status was conferred upon people by their class and birth. Nowadays, we tend to use money to compete for rank. Immersed in a consumer culture of mind-boggling choice, we define ourselves by style and aesthetics. As Virginia Postrel explains in her book *The Substance of Style:* "Identity is the meaning of surface. Before we say anything with words, we declare ourselves through look and feel: *Here I am. I'm like this. I'm not like that.* . . . Aesthetic identity is both personal and social, an expression both of who we are and with whom we want, or expect, to be grouped. Do you want to be thought of as a practical, frugal person who sees fashion accessories as frivolous and vain (or perhaps a person who'd rather put his aesthetic dollars into his car or furniture)? Or do you want to seem like someone who pays attention to every detail, including personal appearance? Either way, you'll tend to attract the like-minded while alienating those who disagree. . . . Because others make similar selections, for similar reasons, *I like this* becomes *I'm like this*"[24]

What we buy does send a message about who we are, and what we value. Amy K., an East Coast psychotherapist and mom of four, recalls a style decision she made on a whim that she later regretted: "My brother in law was going to Europe and my sister asked him to bring her back a Louis Vuitton backpack and I asked him as well," she recalls. "I thought I would have it as my birthday present. He brought it back and I ended up feeling so uncomfortable about it. I could not bring myself to wear it and I still haven't worn it. It's sitting in a cashmere pouch—it's got little LVs all over it and cost $700. The store, of course, wouldn't return it, they'd only give me store credit. But I realized I don't want anything from the store. I couldn't wear it—it didn't feel right, it felt very ostentatious. It's kind of a joke—all my friends know about it and they say 'Just wear the thing already!' But somehow it symbolizes something I don't like—an overindulgence or showiness—a flashiness I'm just not comfortable with. From an aesthetic perspective I didn't like message it sent."

Even drinking your Starbucks coffee sends a message, according to an ad that fell out of my newspaper: "What does your drink say about you? The old saying is, 'You are what you eat.' But at Starbucks, we think what you drink reveals more about who you are. We've noticed for example, that triple, grande, decaf latte people aren't the same as iced caramel macchiato drinkers."

There's nothing wrong with the aesthetic pleasure of a $4 cup of coffee. But if you are drinking it to express how much more sophisticated you are than the people who drink instant Nescafe, you've got a problem. Review your answers to questions 6 and 7. When we compete, we alienate ourselves from others and base our self-worth on something extrinsic. Without your designer coffee, Jimmy Choo slingbacks, tree of knowledge—what have you—you're worthless. If you find yourself running step for step with the Joneses, take the competitive energy and turn it inward. Focus on who you want to be from the inside, instead of reacting to what others are doing. Otherwise, it will be hard to resist the luxuries, both big and small, that your friends and acquaintances own—a potentially disastrous detour on your road to riches.

A final point on competing: I love style. It's fun. I like to make an aesthetic impression. But I have worn shoes that cost $10 and gotten compliments on them. Style can have everything or nothing to do with money. That's up to you. But more importantly, style doesn't have to be some great competitive divide. When I see someone with cool shoes, I think, 'cool shoes.' I don't think, 'Gee, I really want to be your friend.' If I see someone in a white tee-shirt and jeans, I don't think, 'How bland. You must be a bland person inside.' What kind of friend judges you based on your shoes?

✔ The Downside of Materialism

People who make the pursuit of money a significant goal score lower for mental health, according to a variety of studies conducted over the past decade by Dr. Tim Kasser, associate psychology professor at Knox College, and Dr. Richard Ryan, psychology professor at the University of Rochester. "Relatively few people claim money is their very top goal," Kasser explains. "The problems are evident as money becomes more important relative to other goals. The problems are there if money is fourth, fifth, or sixth out of 11 goals, as opposed to closer to the bottom."[25]

What kinds of problems does Kasser encounter in materialistic people? They suffer a greater risk of depression; they have more anxiety and lower self-esteem; they experience more physical, behavioral and relationship problems; and they score lower on indicators testing for vitality (feeling alive and vigorous) and self-actualization. The problems were not caused by being affluent—but by making money a primary goal in life. In studies done by Kasser and Ryan and others, the findings were similar across a variety of age groups, income levels and countries.

The question is: Why would chasing money result in lower well being? It's possible that the people who are most likely to seek money are unhappy to begin with. But Kasser and Ryan speculate that the time spent pursuing material goals causes lower well-being because it detracts from experiences that might be more fulfilling, such as building relationships. "Research shows that what makes you happy is being connected to others and free to express who you are," says Kasser, author of *The High Price of Materialism.*[26]

In fact, money scored last on the list of psychological needs that create happiness and fulfillment, according to a study by Kennon Sheldon, psychologist at the University of Missouri-Columbia.[27] The four most essential needs? Autonomy—feeling your actions are self-chosen and self-endorsed; competence—feeling effective in what you do; a sense of closeness with others; and self-esteem. One problem is that people who pursue money are often chasing something deeper. As we discussed in Chapter 3, money can be an enigma—a powerful blank canvas for the psyche, a shape-shifter that assumes whatever meaning we apply to it based on our worldview. Money substitutes for a deeper intrinsic need. Kathy K., for instance, can pinpoint the exact moment she began to equate money with respect. She was eight years old, standing on a field in Connecticut where her father was coaching a team in Irish football. "I kicked the ball really high. He looked at me and said, 'What a waste you're a girl,'" she recalls. "I thought, I'm going to show him girls can do anything boys can do." Kathy muscled her way into Wall Street, impressing her father with every promotion. But the euphoria always faded, because she wasn't confronting the underlying emotional issue—the demon that said her father didn't respect her for who she was.

Review your responses to questions 3, 4, 5, 10, 12, 13, 14, and 15. Is money what you work for, what brings you the most pleasure? Look at your answer to question 18, about your fairy godmother and your ideal job. Did you go for the guaranteed ideal paycheck and sacrifice a quality that would make your work life happy? Did you consider that if you went for all of the qualities you desired, with the lower paycheck, you'd like the job so much you could earn promotions and eventually *reach* your ideal salary? (Okay, trick answer—but why not think *way* outside the box?) The research shows you'll have more well-being if you have autonomy and positive relationships in your life. So go for the qualities that will enhance your day-to-day work experience, and be optimistic and open to the possibility that your pay will rise with your enthusiasm and commitment to the job.

Finally, is the stuff of your dreams—*stuff*? It's okay to enjoy the finer things in life. In fact, another study on luxury-seekers found one group in particular scored high for happiness: *people wealthy enough to afford what they desired.* But don't make materialism your highest priority, and reflect on whether you're shopping to address emotional needs (see Chapter 5). If luxuries are important to you, find a career that will finance them. Otherwise you'll either be constantly frustrated or wallowing in debt. Meanwhile, close the catalog and reflect on the bigger picture. As Gandhi said, "Be the change you want to see in the world." Dedicate a slice of your life to improving someone else's, and you may discover the kind of happiness that doesn't come in a Prada bag.

✓ Values and Goals

Research shows people find happiness when they work for goals that are consistent with their values—even if the effort involves some short-term pain. A 1993 study by German psychology researcher Joachim Brunstein discovered that a strong commitment to goals, and measurable progress, resulted in higher levels of happiness.[28]

Dale M., a 40-something data center manager on the East Coast, consistently writes down her goals in a notebook she keeps with her at all times. "I am a list maker, I check off accomplishments as I complete them," she explains. "Sometimes you may feel discouraged, and at least you can look at what you've accomplished. You may have a short-term memory and not remember things you've done if they're not staring you in the face. When it's on a list, you don't feel bad, or say, 'Oh where did the money go?' At least you can justify where it went. It gives me a sense of accomplishment that these are things I've aspired toward and planned for."

Lila G., 43, a paralegal in New York City, agrees that writing down her long-term goals boosts her happiness. Her practice has been particularly helpful as she shoulders the burden of educational loans for her oldest daughter, who is in college. "It gives me more peace of mind. I can see light at the end of the tunnel," she says. "If I looked at things piecemeal I'd go crazy. I'll tell myself, it's tough now, but later it will be okay." Just keep in mind, researchers have found goal-setting can actually result in unhappiness if you strive for something that's unlikely to happen. Declaring you want to become CEO of a Fortune 500 company in the next five years probably isn't going to happen if you're 22. But maybe you could be CEO of a smaller firm, or your own business, in that time frame. Look at your answer to question 17. If you haven't set goals yet, review Chapter 1. If you have, stay positive and stick with your plan. Carry a copy of your goals with you, and be deliberate about celebrating milestones on the way to success.

Finally, a philosophical word on money and happiness: In the Bible, Jesus says, "Where your treasure is, there your heart will be also" (Matthew 6:21). The Greek word for treasure *thesanros* is derived from a storage box or chest. The Greek for heart is *kardia,* meaning emotions, wishes or desires. In other words, whatever you store up will lay claim to your emotions. Store up an insatiable hunger for money and material goods, and your heart will be hollow and restless. Store up status symbols, and you get insecurity and a yearning to connect in the bargain. Store up competition and elitism, and you'll reap a soulful of envy. Store up what you genuinely value, and your heart will find freedom, fulfillment, and peace.

So let's close where we began, with investment banker Kathy K. She experienced an epiphany when a friend suggested she describe her perfect day. Kathy visualized being happily married, strolling along the beach with her family, doing work that helped others—and realized her perfect day looked nothing like her current life. She quit her job and began volunteering, teaching life skills to formerly homeless drug addicts and alcoholics. Then she met Rick, who is now her husband, and trained to become an executive coach.

Fast forward several years: Kathy was walking along the beach near her Connecticut home, holding hands with her husband and talking about the baby they were expecting. "All of the sudden it occurred to me: This is my perfect day! All we need is a dog!" she laughs. Now Kathy coaches others on how to get the most out of life. "Life is about happiness, pure and simple, and I was not happy," she says. "All it takes is a decision to change. You can always get back to the essence of who you are if you decide to do it."

MANAGING SPENDING AND BANISHING DEBT

Sydney K., 24, and Christa S., 30, both live and work in New York City and earn between $50,000 and $75,000. They are both single, with bachelor's degrees. Both women would like to earn two to five times more than their current salaries, although they agree money doesn't buy happiness. The two women list family as a top value and describe themselves as "happy."

That's where the similarities end.

Christa says the purpose of money is "to live and pay my expenses, without being in debt." Sydney says the purpose of money is "to spend it." Christa rides the subway. Sydney takes cabs. Christa wears flip-flops and sneakers. Sydney sports $300 Manolo Blahniks. Christa grew up in the northeast, the daughter of a police officer and a teacher. Sydney was raised in the south, a debutante whose father works in finance. Christa says most of her money goes to "monthly bills." Sydney says most of her income goes to "shoes and clothes."

Christa rented an apartment after college and then decided to move back home. She scrimped and saved over five years to put a down payment on a one-bedroom co-op apartment in Manhattan. "I know people in their mid-30s living with their parents to save up a little money, so I didn't feel like a complete loser," she says, adding, "I couldn't fathom renting for a year, paying $16,000, and having nothing to show for it. If I did that for five or six years, what would it add up to?"

Sydney lives in a luxury studio apartment "that there's no way I could afford on my own," she says. "When I was in school, my parents took care of education and living expenses and a few hundred a month in spending money. They still pay half my rent and everything else is my responsibility. I can walk into a store, and something can be $400 or $500, and I have no perception of whether that's considered expensive or not. If the funds are there, I'll buy it. I kind of act on impulse."

Aside from her mortgage, Christa has no debt. Sydney thinks she has some debt, but admits, "I could not put a dollar figure on it." Christa says when it comes to spending, "I try to live on only cash so that I am always aware of where my money is going." Asked to describe her spending style, Sydney says, "I am completely reckless; I do not really have a true concept about the value of money."

Knowledge Is Power

Sydney and Christa seem to live on diametrically opposed planets. But their differences boil down to two things: knowledge and control. Christa knows exactly what she has to live on and spends accordingly. She pays herself first: Savings has always been a regular part of her budget, something she learned from her dad. "We would always make fun of my dad for being super cheap," she says. "He brown bagged it and saved receipts for years, and it was 'every penny counts, save it.' He was a big investor. It's also good to know if you want something you can get it, which I learned from my mom. You can save up and have the good feeling of buying within reason." For entertainment, Christa goes to yoga classes with friends or unwinds with a bottle of wine at someone's apartment. "I don't know anyone who lives the *Sex and the City* life here," she laughs. "That's a myth. We're all sitting in our apartments knitting, looking at the tube. 'Stitch and bitch' clubs are very trendy."

While Sydney knows what she earns, her life does include a hefty dose of Carrie Bradshaw-style glamour. "My mom grew up in the fashion industry, so she's always said, 'If it's a good piece and you like it, buy it; if you're going out with friends, do it, don't worry about it, you only live once.'" Sydney's father makes up the gap between her salary and her lifestyle, and that creates conflict. "We fight about money all the time," she says. "My dad wants to know who I'm trying to impress: 'Why do you care about this season? It doesn't have to be this season. You can wear something old.' It's not about the season; it's something I wanted. He gets so mad about my spending on clothes and shoes and art."

Christa says managing her money makes her feel "independent." Sydney says, "It really stresses me out to think about money." Money can be a source of empowerment or anxiety, depending on how we use it. Here's the secret to money confidence: Know exactly what's coming in and exactly what's going out, and have some ability to control both sides of the equation. That's what Christa does, and she also understands relative value: She bought her apartment because she realized that five years of renting in New York would leave her $80,000 poorer with nothing to show for it. Sydney doesn't completely control what's coming in—her father could lose his job, or decide he doesn't want to subsidize her anymore. She acts on impulse, without a firm grasp on the relative cost of things, so she doesn't have control over what's going out either. Sydney does save; in fact, she's put money aside since high school, when she started working part-time. But she delegates the responsibility for investing to her dad, so she doesn't know where she stands.

How does managing your money make you feel? Among the women surveyed for this book, 84 percent had positive feelings. They use words like in control, competent, secure, safe, calm, proud, responsible, organized, strong, smart, empowered, accomplished, and knowledgeable.

Want to feel that way? Figure out where you stand, and where you want to go. This chapter explains exactly how to start. The first four steps to achieving money competence are: (1) track your spending, (2) live within your means, (3) eliminate debt, and (4) maintain a high credit rating.

Track Your Spending

Let's start with your income. Write down your monthly take-home pay, after taxes. This is obviously a little trickier if you work on commission, freelance, or get a year-end bonus that comprises a good portion of your annual pay. (Do your best to ballpark monthly income based on your previous tax return.) Then write down any other regular monthly income you receive—alimony, disability check, interest on investments, and so on.

Get a small spiral notebook, a pen, a letter-sized envelope, an 8 × 10 notepad and a box of highlighter markers in different colors. Start your expedition on the first of the month. Keep the small spiral notebook, pen, and envelope in your purse; use one page of the notebook for each day. Every time you pull out your cash, debit card, credit card, or checkbook to pay for *anything*, grab your notebook and write down what you spend, to the penny, where you spent it, and what it was for:

September 1

    $40 Water bill

    $72 Electricity bill

    $200 Vintage little black dress—so Audrey Hepburn!

    $90 Three rounds of martinis with the girls at Italian restaurant

    $20 Tip for cute Italian bartender who makes killer martinis

    $59.95 Berlitz Instant Immersion Italian language 4-CD set

    $12.29 *Roman Holiday* with Audrey Hepburn and Gregory Peck, Special Collector's Edition DVD

    $3,000 Vespa scooter in fire-engine red

    $15 Gas

    $3 Parking

September 2

$60.20 Cell phone bill

$27 Groceries

$25.99 Amarillo Western Straw Hat with Horsehair braid

$19.99 Patsy Cline Ultimate Collection, the 2-CD set

$5.95 *Cowboy Roping and Rope Tricks* by Chester Byers

$276 Round-trip airfare New York to Dallas, Texas

$25 Rodeo entry fees

You get the idea. Save receipts that cover multiple categories of spending. Let's say you go to a discount store and pick up a package of muffins, pantyhose, running shoes, and laundry detergent. Put that receipt in your envelope, because you'll need to separate those purchases into different categories later. (And put back the muffins! Do you know how many carbs are in those things?) Meanwhile, you don't need to save records of other spending—such as your cell phone bill—because you already recorded it in your notebook. Just start on the first of the month and stop on the last. Don't say—"Well, I pay for everything with my debit/credit card, so I'll just look at my statement at the end of the month." The idea is to feel the visceral reality of the spending, to acknowledge the exchange of energy taking place—the dollars floating away, and the stuff you need or desire coming into your life. So stop after each transaction and write it down.

Some of your expenses won't have receipts or involve physical transactions. Maybe certain bills are deducted automatically from your checking account, such as a student loan payment; or automatically billed to your credit card, like a gym membership or newspaper subscription. If these are consistent expenditures, get out last month's checking account and credit card statements and make a list of those automated payments in your notebook on a separate page. (Alternately, you may have to wait until you receive those statements to finish your 30-day experiment.)

You may feel an internal resistance to this exercise. That's normal. The task can trigger fear and dread, because you're getting closer to a money truth you may not want to face. (*No more martinis with the girls?*)

Who wants to think about the possibility that she is spending way more than she earns, or carrying a whole lot more debt than she thought? Denial is so much easier. But is it *really*? The women I talk to who don't know where their money goes seem pretty unhappy about it. If you're one of those women, take 30 days, track your spending, sit with the discomfort, and tell yourself that getting to this truth puts you a step closer to being in control, calm, secure, empowered. (It's only four weeks.) At the end of the month, pull out your notebook and dump out your receipts. It's time to organize your spending.

Put each expense into one of the Spending Categories listed on the next page. Take out your 8 × 10 notepad, write one spending category at the top of each page, then list all the expenses underneath. For instance:

Page 1: Food

$60 Groceries
$6 Salad from Deli
$2 Vending machine at work
$4 Quart of Ben & Jerry's Chunky Monkey
etc.

Page 2: Clothing

$35 Banana Republic blouse
$10 Sweats at Old Navy
$250 Fendi purse at Macy's
$3 Pantyhose from Wal-Mart
etc.

Page 3: Entertainment

$8 Subscription to *Bon Appetit*
$25 Dinner and a movie
$17 Novel *Tall Island* by Bill Powers
$14 Collective Soul CD
etc.

Obviously, a few of your 8 × 10 pages will have only a single expense listed under the category, for example, Rent: $800. But most categories will have multiple expenditures listed, so use a page for each category.

Spending Categories

Rent or mortgage

Food

Utilities:
  Heat/electric
  Cable
  Internet connection
  Phone
  Cell phone
  Water
  Garbage pickup

Car loan/lease payment

Credit card payments
  Minimum due
  Total balance
  Amount paid

Gas

Auto maintenance

Public transportation

Tolls/parking

Cabs

Insurance
  Home/renter's
  Auto
  Health
  Life

Daycare

Student loans

Other education costs

Clothing/shoes

Drycleaning

Exercise/health (gym, trainer)

Entertainment

Newspapers/Magazines/Books/
Subscriptions

Personal services (hair, nails,
waxing, massage, facials, etc.)

Toiletries/cosmetics

Home furnishings/yard expenses

Professional services (therapist,
accountant, lawyer, cleaning person)

Household supplies (detergent,
toilet paper, batteries, etc.)

Medical expenses/prescriptions/
vitamins

Charitable donations

Vacations, travel (flights, hotels,
etc.)

Gifts

Postage

Savings

Miscellaneous

You may have to add your own categories as needed—personal astrologer, fencing lessons, poodle groomer and other pet care, and so on. You'll also have to make some judgment calls. If you swing into a friend's party with a chilled bottle of Korbel, is that entertainment or gifts? If you eat in restaurants most of the time, maybe you want to create a new category called "what, me cook?" or the more conventional "dining out." Then there are those other pesky expenditures that bring no discernable joy but must be dealt with nevertheless on an annual, or quarterly basis—auto insurance, life insurance, real estate taxes, or sewer fees. They may not show up in your 30-day survey. The best thing to do for the purposes of this exercise is to look through your checkbook, find the annual or quarterly payment, and break it out into monthly payments. So if you pay $600 a year for auto insurance, add it into your budget as $50 a month. Keep an eye on utilities as well—if your heating bill is $50 in the summer and $200 in the winter, you may want to look at what you paid for the past 12 months, and take an average (total the bills and divide by 12).

The beauty of writing down every penny is that you suddenly become aware of how much of your outflow is unconscious. Because the truth is, for most people, wealth is like good health: You get it by making small, intentional decisions every single day—exercising, eating vegetables, passing on a social cigarette—that add up over time. If you receive a cash windfall, more power to you! But for most of us, financial success tends to be the product of seemingly minor decisions made about marginal amounts of money that grow into large sums over many years.

Analyze Your Spending Patterns

Now reflect on your spending over the 30 days. First, total the amount of money you spent on each category (each 8 × 10 page). Then, rip out the pages from your 8 × 10 notepad. You're going to put each page in one of these piles: either Fixed Expenses or Fun Money. Fixed expenses are the necessities of life, such as housing, food, heat, and transportation. These can certainly be tweaked—you can get a roommate to share the rent, read by flashlight to cut your power bill, eat Ramen noodles instead of steak, ride a Skateboard to work instead of driving. But you have to spend *something* on your fixed expenses. Fun Money is everything else.

Next, let's look at the pages you put in your Fun Money pile. Where is the money going? Look for patterns across categories. Maybe you drop a large chunk of cash on vitamins, yoga apparel, charitable donations, meditating with a Swami, and working with a life coach on how to vaporize your rivals with kindness. Those kinds of activities indicate that perhaps spiritual growth is a strong value. Use a highlighter, and highlight these expenditures in one color. Are your big bills coming from Bloomingdale's, Sephora, Power Pilates, the seaweed facial scrub and manicure at Elizabeth Arden, the latest cut and color at Frédéric Fekkai? Then personal appearance is obviously a priority, so highlight those categories in a different color. Perhaps your biggest expenses are off-off-off Broadway theater tickets, foreign movies, historical biographies, a subscription to *Daedalus: The Journal of the American Academy of Arts & Sciences,* and cable television. Entertainment and culture are clearly important to you, so highlight those in a third color. Total up the spending for each highlighted category and give it a name that's meaningful to you ("Spiritual Growth," "Lookin' Hot," "Brain Food," etc.).

Turn to your other pile: Fixed Costs. Add them up (rent, utilities, food, etc.). Divide that number by your total expenses for the month. Multiply by 100. That's the percentage of your spending going to life's necessities:

Example

Total monthly spending: $3,400

Total fixed costs: $1,530

$1,530 divided by $3,400 = .45

45 × 100 = 45 percent

Do the same for the Fun Money categories you created. When I tracked 30 days of my own spending, 90 percent fell into four categories:

1. 50 percent fixed expenses (food, health insurance, mortgage, real estate taxes, homeowner's/auto insurance, utilities, transportation/gas)

2. 20 percent kids' education—school tuition, extracurricular activities, and college savings

3. 10 percent retirement savings
4. 10 percent entertainment (dining out, sports tickets, cable, video rentals, etc.)

The rest was roughly divided among clothing, household supplies, home furnishings, charity, and gifts. I could easily reduce my fixed expenses by moving further away from Manhattan, or by trimming our grocery bill, which is bloated by my husband's love of cooking. But I won't negotiate on either point, because I love my neighborhood, and gourmet family dinners mean we avoid eating out at restaurants (and getting thrown out of them, since my two-year-old has a habit of hurling steamed pork dumplings at unsuspecting diners). I routinely look at how to cut other fixed expenses, whether that means finding a less expensive drycleaner or reviewing phone plans to see if there's a better deal to be had. (More on cutting expenses in Chapter 6.)

Now you know where your money is going. How much spending came about because of lack of time or poor planning? Late fees, fast food bought on the run, a party gift purchased last minute (*Oh, the Clapper! I've always wanted to clap-on and clap-off my lights!*) when you could have found something less tacky for half the price if you'd had the time to shop? A lot of cash disappears for lack of proper planning and maintenance. (I bought my first car for $300 in college, and blew out the engine two weeks later because I didn't realize when the "oil" light went on, you really have to pour a little Pennzoil in there, pronto!) (For more ideas on how to plan ahead, see Chapter 6.)

But more importantly, what does your spending say about your priorities? Did you truly want or need everything you bought? *Was it worth it?* The only way to answer that question is to think about what you had to do to pay for your spending, according to Joe Dominguez and Vicki Robin, authors of *Your Money or Your Life*. As they explain: "Money is something we choose to trade our life energy for." [1] Divide your weekly earnings by 40 hours (or biweekly paycheck by 80 hours) and think about what you earn in one hour of working. Let's say you take home $14 an hour after taxes (the rough equivalent of a $40,000 a year job). You buy a $140 designer handbag. You had to work 10 hours to get it. Were the energy and the time worth it? Do this exercise for your major categories of spending. How long and how hard do you have to work to pay for things that don't necessarily create lasting happiness? Think about the values you identified in Chapter 1. Are there any less meaningful categories of spending that you can eliminate, and shift money into things that matter more to you? (*Your Money or Your Life* includes an excellent discussion of how to break out your *real* hourly wage, particularly if you work at a job you despise. Dominguez and Robin explain how to figure out the cost in time and energy of commuting, clothing, meals, escape entertainment, decompression, and so on—so you have a proper fiscal reason for telling your boss to *take this job and shove* . . . well, never mind.)

Retail Therapy

Now consider this: How much of your spending is retail therapy? Did you shake off a bad morning at work in the dressing room of your favorite store? Did you find solace on eBay after a fight with your spouse? People use money to satisfy a host of emotional needs instead of addressing those issues in a more direct way. "You've heard the cliché, 'when the going gets tough, the tough go shopping.' But it's true," said Karen McCall, founder of the Financial Recovery Counseling Institute in San Anselmo, California. "People think money will do something it won't. So many people are susceptible to emotional drivers." A survey by Myvesta.org, a credit counseling firm in Maryland, found 43 percent of women reported a mood change before or after shopping. Women tend to hit the mall to deal with boredom, disappointment, or loneliness.[2]

But retail therapy can be hazardous to your financial health. Just ask Marcia K., 45, a real estate manager in the southeast. "The only role model I had was my mother," she says. "If you had a good day, you spent money. If you had a bad day, you spent money. I was taught by my parents to just spend and not plan. When I went to college, my parents said, 'Now we have to give you a checking account,' and I thought, 'for what?'"

When she graduated from college, Marcia got credit cards and, as she put it, "went crazy." She would scour the Sunday newspaper ads and make a shopping list for her lunch hour during the workweek. "It was a panicky feeling: 'I still have to buy this at this place, that at that place,'" she recalls. "Shopping was supposed to make me feel better, but it wasn't working, so I had to keep working at it."

Marcia traces her compulsive shopping to her childhood. "Growing up in my household, there was no consistency. The rules were always changing—what worked one day with my mom didn't work the next," she explains. "I grew up with no self-worth or any kind of self-confidence. I always thought the next thing will make me right—if I buy this shirt, everyone will say, 'She looks good.' I was big on makeup—thinking, this will make me look attractive and somehow make me more loveable, because I wasn't good enough. Shopping therapy was a way to not feel the feelings; you could ignore them. If I didn't handle something well at the office that day, I could go shopping and pick out something really nice for myself and feel better. My dad showed mom love by spending money on her. By spending on myself, I was showing love I was not getting elsewhere."

Marcia eventually got into therapy, which helped her realize she suffered from depression. Her ex-husband taught her how to budget for what was important. "I learned that everything I see does not need to be mine," she says. "Just to learn to be self-sufficient is so freeing." Controlling her spending gave Marcia the option of leaving a well-paying but highly stressful job where she managed 30 people, for a lower-level position at a smaller firm. "I knew I was stuck in a job where I was getting burned out," she says. "Once I got rid of the credit card debt, I wasn't tied to that salary and I was free to choose the job I really wanted. That was the first time I realized I don't have to have tons of money. I didn't have much of a social life for a long time. Now I can read, garden, go out with friends, I served on the homeowner's board—I was even the treasurer for a while!"

Marcia now describes herself as "a very happy person" who doesn't need to earn more to be happy. She owns her townhouse and car and has no credit card debt. She saves 15 percent of her income for retirement. The importance of controlling spending hit home last year, when Marcia's father called with shocking news: Her parents, in their late 70s, had run out of money and owed $158,000 on their credit cards. Fortunately, they avoided bankruptcy because they owned two mortgage-free homes, one of them in a strong real estate market. By selling their primary residence, auctioning off most of their furnishings, and moving into their vacation home, her parents raised enough to pay off the debt. Marcia recalls her father, who worked as an accountant for 55 years, watching passively as movers dismantled his house. "It's extremely powerful to look at your father at that age and realize, 'Hey, planning for the future is a good thing,'" she says. "That man trudged to work every day no matter what." But years of compulsive spending ravaged her parents' savings, and they avoided confronting the issue until it was too late. "I guess the biggest thing that stuck with me is you need to be able to take care of yourself, to be responsible for yourself in all ways. It's only me that can make me happy."

Track Your Emotional Spending

The best way to eliminate compulsive spending is to try and deal with the feelings that caused it in a healthier way. California money therapist Judy Lawrence, author of several budgeting guides, helps clients become aware of the emotions driving their spending by "tracking and paying attention to where and when the money is being spent, and the feelings before, during, and after that spending."[3]

That's how Barbara C. got a handle on her budget. In her childhood, money was tight, Barbara recalls; she sewed her own clothes and rarely ate out. As an adult, her spending trail led to the trunk shows of a New York fashion designer and trendy restaurants. She shopped to distract herself from painful feelings. "My son's wedding was the hardest day emotionally because my ex-husband brought a lady friend and I was alone," she recalls. "I went into a little gift shop. I knew I was taking a hurt feeling and going into a store to make it better."

Barbara now calls a friend for coffee when she feels lonely. She traded in the trunk shows for affordable catalogs, and expensive restaurants for social gatherings with new friends at her synagogue. "I realized I could control my expenses without impinging on my happiness," she said.

If you have trouble keeping a lid on your spending, don't blame yourself entirely. The U.S. economy runs on the engine of shopping. Consumer spending accounts for two-thirds of all economic activity. We have an economy, culture, and political system built around the promises of mass consumption, as Harvard historian Lizabeth Cohen explains in her book, *A Consumers' Republic: The Politics of Mass Consumption in Postwar America.* You face a marketing and advertising onslaught your grandparents could never have imagined. For more than 50 years, some of the most creative minds in the world have focused on ways to separate you from your money. Cohen's book offers the story of B. Earl Puckett, the president of Allied Stores Corporation. In 1950, he told an audience of fashion executives: "It is our job to make women unhappy with what they have." Today, marketers focus heavily on emotional appeals sliced and diced to the perfect demographic.[4]

With temptation laid before you like a banquet at every turn, controlling spending demands a new level of consciousness. "We live in a money-addicted culture—it's really hard to stay grounded," said Karen Sheridan, an Oregon certified financial planner and author. "You have to be a total nonconformist to stay true to yourself." Sheridan has her clients write down what they want to buy in painstaking detail rather than purchasing it immediately. After waiting a week or so, they often find they didn't really need or want it. "The whole key to managing money without emotion is to understand that what you want is available to you," says Sheridan. "You just have to make choices."

By making value-driven choices, you can stay out of debt. Roughly 2,700 years ago, a biblical scribe writing what later became the *Book of Proverbs* lamented the "exorbitant interest" charged by lenders. The writer admonished the wise person to avoid the folly of debt, declaring: "The borrower is the slave of the lender." Today, we borrow for all sorts of reasons, sometimes to obtain things we value—an education, a home, a business. That's otherwise known as "good debt," since you're borrowing to invest in yourself, or in things that tend to increase in value. There's also what I would call "necessary debt": You need a car to get to work and don't have the cash to buy it outright; you charge business attire on a credit card because you're starting your first job out of college; you have medical costs that exceed your health insurance; or a family member is ill and you have to fly home to help out.

And then there's old-fashioned, well, naughty debt—the kind you incur because the jacket was just cut so beautifully, it took off 10 pounds when you put it on, and heck, it would be out of style by the time you saved up enough to buy it. Call it lifestyle debt, or maybe too-much-easy-credit debt, or the-world-is-my-oyster debt. That's the kind of debt Michelle R. is struggling with. Over the past year, the 27-year-old has racked up $9,000 on her credit cards. And she's no slouch when it comes to money management skills, either: She's a certified financial planner. Among the most prestigious of the planner designations, CFPs must pass an arduous test and work in the planning field at least three years. Michelle serves clients who have a net worth in the millions, helping them invest for the future.

Michelle recently moved closer to New York City from an outlying suburb, and her rent nearly doubled. "I live so close to the city, I feel like I should experience that," she explains. "Most of my friends make more than I do. It's hard to say, 'No I don't want to go out to dinner because that will hurt my budget.' I probably overspend on things that make me happy, such as concerts, clothes, going out, travel—to the point where I live outside of my means." She took a five-day trip to Florida with friends for a bachelorette party, and went on a 10-day sailing excursion with a boyfriend.

Michelle's dilemma is not unusual, according to the study by Myvesta.org. It found that while men overspend to impress other people, women get in financial trouble because they want to socialize with a particular peer group. "Whether it's your neighbors, people at work or friends—you will typically buy similar clothes, drive similar cars, have similar activities," says Steve Rhode, Myvesta.org. president and cofounder. "If someone identifies with a group who is able to spend more money than her, she will unconsciously overspend in order to stay with her friends. You can be very drawn to a group of friends or an experience or a neighborhood—and before you know it, you're in way over your head."

Michelle used to contribute the maximum to her retirement plan at work, but has cut back. "It doesn't seem to make sense to be saving somewhere when I'm continuing to borrow," she says. "I'm frustrated with my finances because I don't make enough. I've come to the conclusion that the best solution is not to drastically change things. I feel at some point I'll be able to overcome it, I just can't right now."

Maybe Michelle is right—she may get a raise down the road and conquer her debt. But what happens if she loses her job? Employment peaked in the United States in March 2001. Between that month and June 2004, the economy had a net loss of 1.2 million jobs.[5] The rebound from this latest recession has been excruciating for the unemployed—this is the longest it has ever taken to regain the jobs lost over a downturn. U.S. companies are delaying hiring full-time workers because of the skyrocketing costs of benefits, particularly health care. Employers are replacing workers with technology, or shifting jobs overseas where salaries are a fraction of the going rate in the United States. But unless you've been on the receiving side of a pink slip, you rarely think about preparing for the worst.

Julie H., 30, worked at a large financial services firm on the East Coast. Her company offered to pay for her master's in business administration, so she enrolled in classes at night and on the weekends at a nearby university. Then she was laid off. She managed to land another job two months later and continue her master's program, but had to pay for it out of pocket. A year after that, she was laid off again. She decided to go to school full time and graduated with her MBA the following May. "I went six months with no money, and it was strange to watch every penny that went out the door," she says, adding she's still cautious. "I only buy things on sale, and I don't buy it unless I know I'm going to use or enjoy it—there's nothing in my closet I don't wear. I look at friends who have more money than me and they have a ton of credit card debt. But after being laid off twice I think, you never know what's going to happen."

How much of your spending is going to revolving credit card debt? What are you paying in interest charges every month? The answer should be: Nothing. I interviewed many financially savvy women for this book, and some said they saw no problem with carrying a little credit card debt. Everyone's doing it, right? Actually, no—only 45 percent of American households carry revolving debt from month to month, according to the Federal Reserve.[6] The other 55 percent understand a crucial fact: Credit card debt drains away resources you could be using to enrich yourself, rather than your lender.

Here's a quiz: If you buy a $1,500 couch, put it on a credit card and pay the minimum on your card at 15 percent interest, how long will it take you to pay it off, and what will the couch cost you?

Answer: 10 years and 10 months, and $2,837—you'll pay $1,337 in interest. You've nearly doubled the cost of your couch. More importantly, there's this minor detail called *opportunity cost*. Economists have all sorts of fancy definitions for it—but it basically means, you paid interest to a credit card company and got nothing back! You not only gave up $1,337 to have the couch immediately, you sacrificed the money you could have made on the $1,337 if you had put it in an interest-bearing account. For instance, if you put the $1,337 away in a tax-sheltered retirement account for 35 years at 9 percent, you'd have $14,666, a sum that can buy you all sorts of fun in your golden years. But instead you gave it to a credit card company!

Okay, sorry to harangue you. I do use credit cards by the way. If you pay them off at the end of the month, they're an excellent way to rack up frequent flyer miles and go on free trips. But debt's greatest cost is the havoc it wreaks on your emotional health. Some 58 percent of women in debt reported signs of depression, and more than half said their stress level was "high" or "very high," according to a survey by credit counseling firm Myvesta.org.[7] Debt can be crippling. That's exactly how one woman described her debt situation to me: "I feel trapped, imprisoned by my debt."

Money itself isn't freedom, and it isn't independence. But you certainly end up with more of both if you're not mired in debt—or so desperate you have to declare bankruptcy, as a record 1.6 million Americans did in 2003. Debt is one of the toughest habits to break. But you are not your debt. You simply made a series of decisions (hopefully ones you really enjoyed at the moment) that resulted in debt. Don't waste time feeling guilty or trapped. Make a different set of choices and rid debt from your life. Hey, here's a brilliant idea: Set up a web site on the Internet and ask thousands of strangers to give you a dollar each to get rid of your debt! Whoops, never mind, some crafty chick named Karyn Bosnak already did that with her site, SaveKaryn.com (which incidentally led to a book and a movie deal, and a whole lot of cyber-beggars imitating her concept). You don't need a creative brainstorm to get rid of your debt. Here's how to do it the old-fashioned way, step by step:

1. *Prioritize your pay-down plan.* Make a list of all your creditors, the amount owed, and the annual percentage rate (APR) on each loan. Put them in order from greatest to smallest APR. Student

loans should be paid off last, because they generally charge the lowest interest, and up to $2,500 of that interest may be tax deductible. (For more information consult an accountant or search "student loans" at www.irs.gov.) Direct any extra cash you can generate toward the highest-rate card until it's paid off. Then take the amount you were paying toward that card, and apply it to the next one on the list, working your way down. If you're feeling completely overwhelmed, pick the card with the smallest balance and get rid of that first. It may give you the psychological boost you need to keep going.

2. *Pay on time.* For all of your loans, pay at least the minimum, on time, to avoid late fees, and establish a record of improving payment history. This sounds simple, but lenders aren't making it easy: Over the past few years, many have reduced the time between when they mail the bill to you and when it's due. Second, many companies now sock you with a late fee if your payment arrives just one day tardy—in some cases, if it arrives after 10 A.M. on the day it's due! And 85 percent of banks will raise the interest rate on your card if you pay late, according to the 2004 Credit Card Survey by Consumer Action in San Francisco.[8] Miss that due date twice in a row and watch your rate jump from the single digits to nearly 30 percent. But here's the real kick in the pants: Some credit card companies will now raise your interest rate if your payment to *another credit card company or even your mortgage lender* is late, Consumer Action found. This is fair, they argue, because, to quote one of my all-time favorite films, *Wayne's World:* You're not worthy! Their offer to you is based on your overall creditworthiness. Typically, if you pay on time for six months or several consecutive billing periods, your rate should readjust downward. In the case of student loans, some lenders will reduce your interest rate if you pay on time for a certain period, and cut it even more if you agree to have the payments automatically deducted from your checking account. Bottom line: Don't be late!

3. *Negotiate a payment you can afford.* If you can't come up with the minimum payments on your loans, call the lenders and negotiate

for an amount you can pay. Paying something, even $10 a month, will help you move closer to a clean slate, and may keep the lender from putting you in collection. Ask if they'd be willing to eliminate the late fee and interest for the month.

4. *Reduce your interest rates.* This can save thousands of dollars over time. The average APR is around 15 percent. If you have several cards that are well above that level, call the credit card companies and ask for a lower rate. In 2002, a group of consumer organizations had volunteers do just that. With a five-minute phone call, 56 percent successfully reduced their rates by an average of one-third—from 16 percent to 10.47 percent.[9] Translation: If you are making minimum payments on a $5,000 debt, you would save $278 in the first year; and nearly $5,000 in interest over the life of the loan. The volunteers in the study simply told the lenders they had received better offers from other companies for cards at less interest, and asked the lender for their best offer.

5. *Transfer your debt to a lower-rate card.* If you can't persuade lenders to cut your interest rate, apply to get a new card at a lower APR, and transfer all of your balances to the new card. Just watch out: Some companies offer their premium rates as a teaser, and then assign you a less attractive deal based on your credit score (see the discussion that follows). Verify the terms before you accept the offer. Just as important, watch out for fees on balance transfers. Some lenders treat these transactions as "cash advances" and charge a percentage. For example, if you transfer $5,000 to your new card, a 3 percent fee would set you back $150. So read the credit card offer carefully. Try to open the new account with a credit union or community bank—they tend to be less aggressive about fees and penalties. You can research credit card offers from banks around the country at www.cardweb.com and www.bankrate.com.

6. *Commit to paying 10 percent of the balance every month.* Over the years, credit card companies have gradually reduced minimum monthly payments from 5 percent of the balance to 2 percent, according to the Massachusetts Public Interest Research Group.[10]

This can *triple* the amount of time it takes to pay off your debt. Commit yourself, as soon as possible, to paying 10 percent of the balance each month. Let's say you have a $5,000 debt on a credit card at 16 percent. If you pay the 2 percent minimum, the loan will cost you $8,350 in interest over 26 years. Boost your monthly payment to 10 percent of the total (or $50), and you'll pay just $743 in interest and be finished with the debt in three years and eight months!

7. *Set specific goals.* Motivate yourself by connecting your debt reduction plan to a special milestone: Maybe you want to be debt-free by your thirtieth birthday, by your 10-year high school reunion, or before your wedding. Check out www .truthaboutcredit.org. It offers a credit calculator that shows how much you need to pay each month to eliminate your balance within a certain time frame. It can also tell you how long it will take to pay off your debt if you continue to pay the same amount each month.

8. *Consider credit counseling.* If you really can't manage your debt, visit a debt counselor. Be careful: The field is rife with fraud and scams, even by so-called nonprofits. Any firm that asks you for money upfront is breaking the law. Contact one of the following organizations, which can steer you to a local chapter or affiliated agency in your area:

The National Foundation for Credit Counseling at www.nfcc .org or (800) 388-2227

The Association of Independent Consumer Credit Counseling Agencies at www.aiccca.org

Consumer Credit Counseling Services at www.cccs.org or (800) 388-CCCS

American Consumer Credit Counseling at www.consumercredit .com or (800) 769-3571

These organizations offer information and structured programs to help you negotiate with creditors. Be sure to ask about fees, the time commitment required, and how the program will affect your credit rating (see the following discussion). If you can't control your spending, consider joining Debtors Anonymous for support (www.debtorsanonymous.org).

9. *If you've been ripped off, file a complaint:* If you believe you are the victim of unfair credit card fees or penalties, contact your state Attorney General's office and the national Office of the Comptroller of the Currency Customer Assistance Group at (800) 613-6743 (www.occ.treas.gov/customer.htm).
10. *Eliminate temptation:* If your mailbox in stuffed with promotions offering you new lines of credit, call (888) 5-OPTOUT. This will remove your name from prescreening lists at the three major credit bureaus, and greatly reduce your credit card junk mail.

Finally, be positive. Don't beat yourself up for being in debt. Act as if someone else is taunting you, intent on making you unhappy, suggests University of Pennsylvania psychologist and author Martin Seligman, and fight back. If you hear an internal voice say, "you'll never dig your way out of this," imagine it's a stranger saying it to you, and defend yourself! Seligman's book *Authentic Happiness* is an inspiration if you find debt clouding other aspects of your life.[11]

Improve Your Credit Rating

Paying down your debt can do wonders for your credit score. This is a numerical system developed by Fair, Isaac & Co. that makes a huge impression on the people who count, financially speaking. Banks, insurers, landlords, and even potential employers all examine your credit score to decide if you're reliable—and in the case of loans, what they'll charge you. Investing a little effort to boost your score can save you thousands of dollars. Here's how it works: About one-third of your score is based on payment history, including number of accounts that are on time versus past due, how long they've been delinquent, and so on. Another 30 percent is based on how much you owe to creditors. Other factors include how much credit you have available to you, what percentage of that credit you're currently using, how long you've had particular accounts, number of accounts opened recently, and the mix of credit used (auto loans, mortgages, credit cards of various type, etc.). It also includes any negatives from public records, such as bankruptcies, liens, or court judgments against you. The score does *not* include your address, age, gender, race, religion, country of origin, salary, occupation, or your employment history.

You actually have three credit scores, which are calculated by the three largest credit bureaus—Equifax, Experian, and TransUnion—and reported to lenders who request them. Your FICO score ranges from 300 to 850 points. Let's say you applied to get a $150,000 mortgage to buy a home in fall of 2004. If your FICO score was on the upper end of the scale—720 or higher—many lenders would have given you a 30-year mortgage at 5.62 percent—a monthly payment of $863. If your score was below 560, the exact same loan would soar to 9.29 percent—or $1,238 a month, a $375 difference. The best way to improve your score is to pay your bills on time and pay down your credit cards. Aim to get your debt down to 50 percent of the maximum credit available on each of your cards—the lower the debt, the better the score.

Credit history is something you have to build, slowly. Perhaps you've paid all your obligations throughout your life with cash. You may be surprised to discover you have a low score. It's because the credit agencies have no information on which to judge your financial reliability. Start building a history by opening a credit card (one with no annual fee) and paying in full and on time each month. Don't apply for a bunch of new cards simultaneously; it will hurt your score. Here's another technique to build your credit history: Get a trusted relative who has good credit to issue you an additional card from one of her existing accounts. Her history of wise use on that card will show up on your report.

Order your credit report from all three bureaus every year to check for mistakes. Consumers in most states can now order them for free, as part of the Fair and Accurate Credit Transactions Act passed by Congress in 2003. You can request the reports by visiting www.annualcreditreport.com; by calling (877) 322-8228; or by sending a written request to Annual Credit Report Request Service, P.O. Box 105281, Atlanta, GA 30348-5281. The program expands to the entire country by September 2005. Although you will receive a free report, you still have to pay a fee to get your actual credit score. Be sure to obtain these reports directly from the bureaus; do not provide personal information to any third parties who offer to get free reports for you. (You need to give the bureau your name, address, date of birth, and social security number to retrieve the report.) Nearly 80 percent of people have at least some negative information on their credit reports, and one in four reports contains errors significant enough to cause consumers to be denied credit, a loan, an apartment, mortgage, or even a job, according to a Masspirg survey.[12] Any inaccuracies should be disputed in writing with the credit bureau. (That site also has good tips on how to build a credit history.) It also makes sense to review your score at least six months before seeking a loan, so you'll have time to enhance your score before approaching a lender.

According to Bob Hammond, author of *Repair Your Own Credit*, the basic techniques to improve your score are simple. "If you can read and write, that's basically as much knowledge as you need," he says. "You just need to know how to contact the credit bureaus, look at report, determine what things are inaccurate. Those things can be disputed directly with the bureau. If, on the other hand, there's some (negative) things that are accurate, you can deal directly with the creditors and try to work out something with them."[13] Make a settlement offer of pennies on the dollar to creditors who have written off your debt, in exchange for deleting negative information from your report, Hammond advises. Also close high-interest charge accounts you don't use, especially those you've had for a few years or less.

But manage old accounts and defaults with care. Don't close a charge card you opened five years ago and used only once—you may wipe out favorable credit history. By the same token, if you defaulted on a debt six years ago, you may want to let bygones be bygones. Defaults are removed from your report after seven years. A six-year-old delinquency has already done damage to your report. If you begin paying it back now, it will renew as a fresh item on your report—showing that you paid a collection agency many years later, versus having it fall off your report altogether. Morally, I would pay it, because I incurred it. But from a credit-scoring perspective, paying it off may do more harm than good. Finally, never pay a company that claims it can immediately fix your credit score. These are often scams. You're better off contacting one of the counseling firms listed earlier and working with them to pay off debt and improve your credit score.

Congratulations! If you made it this far, you've got what it takes to control your spending, pay off your debts, and improve your credit score. It's time to move on to the next step: Saving for what you value most.

6

How to Save

Money is something you should make first and then make last.

—Anonymous

What does it take to become a saver? For some people, it's natural. Maybe they're smart shoppers, or choose interests and hobbies that aren't expensive. Maybe their parents were successful savers and the old cliché "pay yourself first" hits home with them. As Georgia medical writer Liza D. put it: "I saved money starting at my first job out of college. I was making $16,000 a year, and on payday my boss would say, 'Go right now to the bank on the corner and buy a savings bond.' I had great respect for him and listened to him; so I'd buy a $50 bond every single week. I could never understand how people say they don't make enough money to save. You just save first, spend second— otherwise you end up with nothing. You just do it. You don't want to be fat? Stop eating and exercise. You want to save? Stop buying things! Here's my money motto: If you need public storage, you've got too much crap."

If the straightforward argument doesn't do the trick, a little reflection on the future might motivate you to save. Lisa B. is a nurse practitioner in Wisconsin. In her early 30s, she left her career in corporate sales to work in geriatric case management, caring for people at the end of their lives. "Money means security for me—because I know how expensive it is to be an elderly person in this world," she says. "I'm lucky I'm really healthy, but you never know down the road. I don't want to end up in a one-room boarding house waiting to die. I've seen that happen to people who worked hard their whole lives, who didn't have the ability to plan or put away—or but maybe they did but didn't do it."

When you're starting out financially, you need to take three steps:

1. Find a low-cost checking account.
2. Open a savings account at the highest interest you can find and build an emergency fund.
3. Start saving for retirement.

This chapter covers the basic knowledge you need to save effectively—why time is your most powerful ally, how compound interest works, how to get the best deal on a checking account, build an emergency fund, and plant the seeds for your longer term investing goals—plus 50 ways to save money. The specifics of how to start saving for retirement are in the next chapter. If you have already established this financial foundation, you may want to skip Chapter 7 and go on to Chapter 8, which discusses investing in more depth.

Making Money on Your Money

If you take away anything from this book, take this: The sooner you start saving, the more options you'll create for yourself later in life. Imagine you've just graduated from college and landed your first job. You've got school loans, rent, a car payment, an appetite for adventure, and memories to make. Who can possibly think about saving?

You can. At age 22, you have an incredible economic power in your hands—even if you haven't got a dime in the bank. It's called *time.*

Consider this: Would you trade $5.50 a day, for nine years, for financial independence later in life? Give me $5.50 a day, and I'll give you *half a million dollars* for retirement. And I only want your daily donation for *nine years!* Here's how it works: You set aside $5.50 a day starting at age 22 and stop at age 30. That's $2,000 a year in a Roth IRA, an individual retirement account that allows your money to grow tax-free (see the next chapter for details on IRAs and other investments). You don't touch the money until retirement. You'll have more than $500,000 by age 65. And get this—you'll have a bigger kitty than someone who starts at age 31 and contributes for 35 years!

That's right. Just nine years. $5.50 a day. $38.50 a week or an average of $167 a month. You decide. What will you trade? I say "trade" rather than "give up" because it's about choices, not sacrifice. If you have enough discipline to get out of bed and go to work every morning, you have what it takes to make this happen. Here are a few ideas for some trade-offs you can make that could change your financial life:

- Cook two to three times a week instead of eating dinner out.
- Brown-bag your lunch daily instead of buying it.
- Get a roommate.
- Quit smoking.
- Brew your own coffee and read the paper online instead of buying a daily Starbucks and a newspaper.
- Do your own manicure/pedicure instead of purchasing a weekly professional one.
- Check out three books a month from the library instead of buying; rent three videos a month (and pop your own popcorn) instead of going to the movies and hitting the concessions stand.
- Pass on one Banana Republic pinstriped suit jacket.
- Pass on one pair of Ferragamo black pumps (purchased on sale at eBay).
- Choose a haircut that doesn't cost a fortune to maintain and enjoy your natural color, or color your hair yourself. (See the end of the chapter for 50 more ideas.)

Let's look at the example of Jane and Jill. Jane gets a job out of college at age 22. She makes $27,000 a year in public relations. She values time with family and friends, good health, and creative expression. She lives with her parents for a year, then gets an apartment and splits the rent with a friend. Instead of going to the movies, she joins Netflix for $12 a month and has potluck DVD parties ("come dressed as your favorite *Godfather* character"). She drags her friends to free poetry readings and concerts, and rides her bike in the park. By doing her own pedicures, shopping vintage stores, making tuna fish club sandwiches for lunch and babysitting occasionally for a couple in her building, she manages to stash away $38.50 a week—or $2,000 a year. She puts it into a Roth IRA, and does this every year. One day she crashes her bike into a guy named Steve, marries him, and at age 30, leaves her job to stay home with their newborn daughter. Jane eventually goes back to work, but never contributes to her IRA again, leaving it untouched until age 65. It grows at 9 percent a year.

- Jane's total contribution over 9 years: $18,000
- Jane's account value at retirement: $531,622

Now meet Jane's cousin, Jill. Right out of college, Jill lands a job in retailing, earning $27,000 a year. She also values time with family and friends, good health, and creative expression. She goes out to dinner and drinks, movies, and plays with friends; buys a fresh salad for lunch daily; and works out on the rock-climbing wall at a Reebok Sports Club. She tackles a new mountain on vacation with her sister every year, putting the bill on her credit card. She buys new work clothes every season at a discount from the retailer that employs her. At age 31, rappelling down the side of Mount Washington in New Hampshire, she gets her harness tangled up with a guy named Bob, whom she marries. Their combined income is $80,000, and Jill feels she finally has enough income to begin saving for retirement. She puts $2,000 in an IRA, and does so every single year until she retires at age 65. It grows at 9 percent a year.

- Jill's total contribution over 35 years: $70,000
- Jill's account value at retirement: $431,422

Jane ended up with $100,000 more than Jill—and saved for just nine years. In fact, Jane's results were actually better than that: If you take the value of each account, and subtract what each woman contributed, Jane ends up with $152,200 more than Jill. Time and interest: Pretty powerful stuff. In fact, Albert Einstein once said, "There is no greater power known to man than compounding interest."

Here's how compounding works: You deposit $1,000 in an account that earns 5 percent, compounding annually. At the end of the year you have $1,050 ($1000 × .05 = $50; $50 + $1,000 = $1,050). The next year you receive interest again, but this time you get interest on $1,050 (the money you originally put in, plus the interest you already earned). At the end of year two, you'll have $1,102.50. To take advantage of compounding, you want to save as early as possible and simply let the money grow for you. But even if you're 30, or 40, you should still take advantage of the opportunity to save when you can, and let compounding work its magic. Some accounts offer annual compounding (the example above). Some compound your interest on a semi-annual basis (every six months), on a monthly basis or even a daily basis. For instance, if you have $1,000 in an account earning 5 percent that compounds daily, on the second day you'll have $1,000.14. The third day builds on that amount, and so on. It doesn't make a huge difference in one year—with daily compounding you'll have $1,051.27 at the end of the year versus $1050 for annual compounding. But over time this can add up. So the more frequent your rate of compounding, the better. Two words to remember in the world of compounding: rate and yield. The annual percentage rate (APR) is quoted as a percentage of your investment—in the example above, 5 percent. The annual percentage yield (APY) depends on how often the account pays interest; in the previous example, in which your account compounds daily, the yield would be 5.127 percent.

Want to be a millionaire? There are two ways to accomplish this: Number one, keep saving. If Jane continued to put away that $167 a month until age 65, she'd have $1 million for retirement. That's assuming she made an average of 9 percent on her money every year. The second way to become a millionaire is to get the best possible return on your savings, without taking on so much risk that you end up with an ulcer. Let's look at Jane's example again: Between age 22 and 31 she put away $18,000, and it grew at 9 percent until she retired at age 65. She ended up with $531,622. Now what if she did exactly the same thing, but had earned an average of *11 percent* on her money? She would have more than $1.3 million dollars at retirement.

In Chapter 7, we discuss investments that offer a higher rate of return than traditional savings. Want to figure out how to become a millionaire yourself? Try out a savings calculator online. You input how much you can afford to save every month, and the interest rate you get on your money, and it will tell you how much it will grow. (Be realistic about the rate of return you can achieve. More on this in the next chapter.) Some of the best calculators, for all aspects of your financial life, are at financenter.com. Click on "Calculators for Public Use" or go to www.financenter.com/consumertools/calculators. The calculators go beyond savings to budgeting, debt management, auto and home financing, and so on. This is an excellent resource to figure out instantly how to make progress toward your goals.

You may be thinking, where do interest rates come from? What determines how much interest a bank will offer? Interest rates are influenced by many factors, but one of the most important is the Federal Reserve, the nation's central bank. Founded in 1913, the Fed is charged with issuing the nation's currency and regulating the money supply and the banking system. The Fed works to keep the economy growing steadily, because bad things happen at economic extremes. Too much growth too fast, and prices spiral out of control (also known as inflation); too little growth, people lose their jobs (also known as recession). One of the ways the Fed stabilizes growth is by moving short-term interest rates up or down. Those adjustment affect the interest rates that financial institutions will offer for savings accounts, as well as what they charge for all types loans—credit cards, mortgages, auto loans, and so on. (Here's TMI—too much info—but in case you were wondering: There are two short-term rates—the federal funds rate and the discount rate. Banks must keep a certain percentage of their customers' money on reserve at all times. To maintain those required reserves, banks lend each other money overnight and charge interest—the fed funds rate. The discount rate is the rate charged by a Federal Reserve bank for overnight borrowing—which almost never happens in reality, because the banks turn to other banks first; the Fed is a lender of last resort.)

Choosing a Checking Account

Before you can invest, you need a bus station for your paycheck, a place it hangs out and eats bad fast food before embarking on a journey to pay your bills. That's the checking account, the lowest rung on the financial ladder. It's the club soda of cocktails: You can add ice, lemon or lime, a swizzle stick or two, but it's basically water and bubbles no matter where you go. You can get a checking account anywhere, so why not go local? I'd recommend opening one at a nearby bank or credit union. Knowing my personal banker has come in extremely handy. Case in point: When I was buying my house, I needed to bring a large certified check to the closing. I had to transfer the money from an investment account (where I'd been saving the down payment for the house) into my checking account. A few days before the closing, a bad storm snapped a tree and it crashed through the garage of the house we were buying. Distracted by the last-minute turmoil, I waited too long to transfer the money. When I arrived at the bank to get my certified check, the bank teller said I'd have to wait another day for the money to clear from my other account. This would mean missing the closing and incurring headaches too costly and numerous to mention. Fortunately, I'd banked at that local branch for 10 years. The branch supervisor knew me, called up the investment firm to verify I had transferred the money, and personally approved the certified check.

So find the best checking deal you can at a local bank, savings and loan, or credit union. These days, checking accounts range from "basic" to "super duper" with a confusing array of features. Here's what you really want: A no-frills, free checking account. Find one that has the following features:

- No minimum balance, or the lowest possible minimum.
- No monthly service charges.
- Unlimited deposits.
- Free online banking and online transfers to other accounts.
- Free use of the ATM as often as you need, and a wide ATM network; (some banks will even refund the fees you pay to other banks' ATM machines).
- No per-item service charges; the ability to write as many checks as you need (which won't be many, because you're going to do your banking online).
- Minimal fees for bounced checks.
- Balance alert e-mails; with this nifty feature, offered by some banks, you can get a daily e-mail from the bank stating your

balance, or an e-mail that's sent when you dip below a number you specify.

You may have noticed I didn't mention interest. Some checking accounts pay a little interest if you keep a sizeable sum in there. But you can usually earn more interest elsewhere, so forget about interest on your checking account, and think of your checking account as a wallet to pay for your basic needs. Keep the minimum balance in your checking account to avoid any fees, plus one month's living expenses. That amount, obviously, gets replenished each month by your paycheck (as long as you're living within your means). If your employer offers direct deposit, sign up through your human resources department at work— it's safe, secure, convenient, and *fast*—the money gets credited to your account on the same day you get paid.

Next, set up online bill paying. There are several ways to do this, but the easiest is to go through the bank where you opened the checking account. The bank will give you a login and password; sometimes you have to choose a new password when you login for the first time. Then it takes all of 15 minutes to set up. Just find your major bills from last month. For each bill you pay every month, you click "add a new payee" (or a button similar to this) and fill in the form that appears with the company name (Acme Electric, etc.), address, phone number, and your account number. When your bill comes in and says it's due in three weeks, you jump online, tell the bank what date you want the bill paid and click. (It's best to leave at least three days before the actual due date—not including weekends—to make sure the electronic payment goes through on time.) Write the date and amount of the bill in your checkbook register. You're done. No checks to write, no stamps to buy, no random utility bill diving into the bottom of your purse to be discovered floating there months later. (An important note on those few bills for which you do write paper checks: New banking legislation, known as Check Clearing for the 21st Century Act, went into effect in 2004. Checks you write now clear immediately—which means you better have the funds in the account. Unfortunately, it doesn't work the other way—banks are not required to clear the checks you deposit any faster. If you're someone who usually pays bills a few days before you get your paycheck, either ask those creditors to adjust the date your account is due, or consider getting overdraft protection from the bank. This may involve a fee.)

I used to balance my checking account to the penny. I don't anymore. This is because balancing my checkbook to the penny made me a little crazy, especially when I couldn't find the source of a $1 discrepancy. I'd spend an hour searching for it. Then I decided my time is worth more than that. Here's what I do instead: I'm extremely careful about recording all my deposits and the bills I pay in my checkbook register (whether I pay them online, write a check, use my debit card, or get cash from an ATM). Then every month (sometimes more often) I go online and compare my handwritten register to the transactions listed online, to make sure the lists match. How do I keep from overspending and bouncing checks? I have a really good handle on what my life costs every month, and that's the amount I keep in the account, with a few hundred dollars in slush money in case of an unexpectedly high utility bill or a spontaneous night out. If your expenses fluctuate wildly from month to month (by several thousand dollars), then it's worth the time to balance your checkbook to the penny. The key is to painstakingly record any inflows and outflows in your register. Add up all the money spent (checks written, bills paid online, cash withdrawn from ATMs, transfers made to your savings or other accounts); and inflows at the end of the month (your paychecks), and subtract one from the other. Take this total, and if you spent more than came in, subtract it from last month's balance. If you earned more than went out, add the total to last month's balance. It's pretty simple. The only tricky part is stopping to write all of these transactions in your checkbook. When using the ATM, try to take out the same amount of cash on a weekly basis only to minimize the number of transactions.

Setting Up Your Emergency Fund

There's an old skit by comedian George Carlin, in which he talks about oxymorons: Jumbo shrimp. Military intelligence. Plastic silverware. How about "job security"? A recent survey found that more than half of all workers and their family members have been laid off at least once during their lifetimes. Between 2000 and 2003, nearly one in five workers was laid off from a job—for those with only a high school education, it was about one in four.[1] Meanwhile, experts say the average worker will change jobs *10 times* and change careers *three times* in a working lifetime.

That's the purpose of the traditional "rainy day" fund. This account contains three to six months of living expenses in case you lose your job. (To figure out your monthly expenses, see Chapter 5.) Start your emergency fund even if you are paying off debt. Otherwise, some financial emergency may come along that will have to be charged to your credit card, starting the debt cycle all over again. Try this: For every $1 dollar you can save, funnel 75 cents toward reducing your debt and 25 cents toward your emergency fund. (So if you can save $100, put $75 toward your credit cards and $25 into your savings.) When you get two months' worth of emergency funds in place, you may want to switch back and put all your capital into paying down your debt. When the debt is paid off, return to building your emergency fund. Stash your savings in an account that you can access quickly and easily, where there is no risk of losing your money, and where you can earn some interest. By "no risk," I mean an account that's insured by the Federal Deposit Insurance Corporation (FDIC). In 1933, the government created the FDIC to provide stability to the banking system. You can deposit up to $100,000 in an FDIC-insured bank, and if the bank goes bust for any reason, you'll get your money back from the government. Three possible places to begin salting away your emergency dough: savings accounts or money market accounts, certificates of deposit, or savings bonds. I'll explain these no-risk vehicles first, and then discuss other ways to make your emergency fund earn more interest over time.

Savings and Money Market Accounts

Your first option is to open a savings account at the bank where you do your checking. There may certain benefits to having both accounts at one institution. For instance, some banks will add up what you have in all of your accounts to determine whether you meet the minimum balance required by checking (so if your minimum is $1,000 but you fall to a $500 balance in your checking account, you won't pay a fee if you have at least $500 in your savings). When you begin to grow your savings and start investing in other things like stocks, bonds, and mutual funds, it can be helpful to have everything in one place. Some institutions offer both banking and brokerage services—so-called "bankerage" firms, where you can do checking, savings, and more sophisticated investing at the same institution. If you are just starting out, this may be more than you need. (It's like buying one of those gadgets that slices, dices, chops, and makes julienne fries when all you really need is a butter knife.) I think it's important to keep money management as straightforward as possible in the beginning, so you understand it and gain confidence in your ability to control it.

Where should you open your savings account? Shop around. Get the best interest rate you can find. It's easy to open a savings account at a different institution and link it to your checking account electronically. Internet banks in particular offer higher interest on savings, mainly because they don't pay for bricks-and-mortar branches and friendly drive-through employees. They only exist in cyberspace. Weird concept, but they work, at least in their ability to offer superior interest rates (and they are FDIC-insured). Many of these Internet bank savings accounts have no minimum requirements either—you can open your account with $10.

Linking your checking and savings accounts electronically is an excellent way to automate your savings: You instruct the Internet bank to transfer a specific amount from checking to savings at a specific time (say $25 a week). Click—you're building your emergency fund without thinking about it, and earning interest immediately. Consider savings as a bill you must pay every month, to yourself, *first*—before you tackle the cable, power, water, or any other household bill. If you do it the other way around and wait until those bills are paid before you pay yourself, you'll fail. You'll find something else to do with the money before it makes its way into your savings. If you pay yourself first, and then find you're getting perilously close to nada in your checking account as you pay your other bills, you'll have to restrain your spending. You won't have the option of using the money you had planned to save to pay off a utility bill.

It's very easy to open an account with an Internet bank online or by phone. The best place to shop around for a savings account is www .bankrate.com. Some online banks are:

- INGdirect.com, (888) 464-0727
- virtualbank.com, (877) 998-2265
- bankofinternetusa.com, (877) 541-2634

Your other savings account option is a *money market account* (MMA), also known as a *money market deposit account.* On the upside, these accounts are FDIC-guaranteed, usually give you a higher interest rate than the standard passbook savings account, and you can write checks against them. (So if your emergency fund is in a money market account and your car's transmission dies, you can just write the $1,000 check to fix the damage right from your MMA; you don't need to transfer the money into your checking account first.) On the downside, MMAs require a minimum balance in most cases, and there's a limit to the number of checks you can write. Most importantly, don't confuse the MMA, which has the FDIC guarantee, with a money market *fund,* which is a type of mutual fund—a relatively safe investment but not a government-guaranteed one, explained in Chapter 7. (Just verify with the bank when you set up the account that it's FDIC-insured.) Money market accounts can also be linked to your checking online, allowing for easy transfers from checking into savings.

Certificates of Deposit

Certificates of deposit (CDs) are investments that allow you to lock in a specific interest rate for a certain period of time, usually three months to five years. The longer you are willing to lock in your money, the higher the interest rate you will receive. Of course, this limits your flexibility. If you buy an 18-month CD and your car transmission dies a year later, you'll have to pull the money out of the CD before it matures. You won't lose your principal, but you will forfeit a few months' interest.

Some people "ladder" their emergency savings in CDs with different maturities to get a better interest rate. Because, let's face it, six months of living expenses can add up to quite a bit of money. Let's say your monthly living expenses are $3,000. That means an emergency fund containing six months of living expenses would total $18,000.

Let's look at how two women—Emma and Jenny—invest in CDs. They both keep $4,500 (six weeks of emergency funds) in an MMA, where they can access it any time they want. That leaves $13,500 to invest. Emma takes the $13,500 and puts it in a one-year CD. When it matures 12 months later, Emma reinvests in another one-year CD. Another 12 months goes by, and she does it again.

By contrast, Jenny realizes if you're willing to commit to a CD for a longer period of time, you'll get a higher the interest rate. So Jenny takes the $13,500 and invests $4,500 in a three-year CD, $4,500 in a two-year CD, and $4,500 in a one-year CD. Then next year, when the one-year CD matures, she buys another three-year CD. By reinvesting in a three-year CD every time one of her CDs matures, she builds a ladder of CDs, with maturities one, two, and three years out.

Hopefully, the six weeks of emergency money she put in an MMA ($4,500) will cover financial bumps in the road while her CD ladder earns higher interest for her. She can still withdraw the money in case of emergency. But if you try the laddering strategy, ask about penalties for early withdrawal. In some cases, you'll lose three months' of interest, in other cases, six. (For example, if you invest in a one-year CD that has a six-month penalty for early withdrawal, and you pull the money out after four months, you'll actually lose some of your principal.) Aside from CD laddering, another way to boost returns on your emergency fund is to set aside two months of it in a liquid account, and invest the rest in a conservative mutual fund. (For details see Chapter 7.)

Savings Bonds

When you buy a savings bond, you're loaning money to the U.S. government for which the government pays you interest. Your best bets for a rainy day fund are Series I bonds or Series E/EE bonds. You can buy them from most banks, credit unions, and savings institutions. But the easiest way is to set up an account online and buy them direct from the U.S. Treasury at www.treasurydirect.gov. You can open your account for as little as $25 online ($50 if you go through a bank). Savings bonds are a great way to save on a regular basis: You can set up the account so a regular amount is transferred right to your account to buy more bonds. These bonds will never lose value and start earning interest on the first day of the month they are issued. The interest compounds every six months and is exempt from state and local taxes. You only pay federal tax on your earnings when you cash in the bond, or when it reaches maturity. (The "maturity" is how long you receive interest payments on the bond. It's 30 years for Series I and Series E/EE. That doesn't mean you *have to* hang onto them for 30 years. It's just that you won't get any more interest after that point, so you redeem them and move the money elsewhere.) Series I and E/EE are even free of federal tax if you use the money for college tuition (your own, your spouse's, or your children's). Note that even if you use them for a child's education, the bonds must be in a parent's name.[2]

There are some restrictions: You can't touch the money for one year. If you cash out and sell your bonds before five years, you lose the last three months of interest earned. (So if you buy a bond and sell it two years later, you'll get your principal back plus 21 months of interest, instead of 24 months.) Since the monthly interest on the bond accrues on the first day of a given month, time your sales accordingly. For instance, if you sell your bond on January 31, you won't get any credit for interest in the month of January. Wait until February 1 and you *will* receive interest for January.

Series E/EE bonds are different—you buy them at a 50 percent discount to face value—so you pay $50 for a $100 bond. They are guaranteed to reach face value in 20 years, and continue to earn interest up to 30 years. Series E/EE bonds offer a fixed rate of interest for the life of the bond. By contrast, Series I bonds are issued at face value—meaning you pay $500 for a $500 bond. Also, I-bonds have a unique feature: A portion of the interest you receive is a fixed rate that never changes; another portion is based on the rate of inflation. Inflation can be loosely defined as a rise in the cost of living. It is measured by a little tool called the Consumer Price Index (CPI). The government examines the prices of a basket of stuff—food, housing, apparel, transportation, education, various services, and so on—to figure out how much costs are rising. While the prices of some items, like prescription drugs, might be skyrocketing, the cost of others, like computers, may be falling. The government translates what's happening into a percentage measurement (or the CPI). Why should you care about what's happening to inflation when you invest? Think about it: If you're only getting 2 percent a year interest on your investment and the cost of living is rising 3 percent a year, you're actually going backward: You've lost 1 percent in terms of what your money can buy. The point of this rather long-winded explanation is to say that Series I bonds protect your earnings from inflation. The inflation-indexed part of your interest rate changes every May 1 and November 1; the other part stays fixed for the life of the bond.

Why do I like Series I bonds in particular for beginning investors?

- They're easy to understand—you pay $1,000, you get a $1,000 bond.
- There are no transaction fees or management fees on your investment. (I'll explain fees in the next chapter.)
- The rate of return is better than savings accounts, MMAs, and one-year CDs (at least at the time of this writing).
- The tax benefits allow you to keep a little more of the interest you earn for yourself, rather than handing it over to your state and local governments.
- You can go online and easily see your money growing.
- If you need the money for an emergency, you can cash out any time after 12 months.

Just one caveat: Even the safest investments have a risk. The risk for Series I bonds is if inflation goes in reverse—if the country experiences deflation. This is when the prices for goods and services are dropping. It's great for your shopping cart, but bad for your Series I bonds. Since the inflation-indexed portion of your interest rate adjusts every six months, the rate would adjust downward if the cost of living moves down. (Presumably if that happened, you could sell your bonds and move into an MMA or a CD paying a more attractive interest rate.)

Short-Term versus Long-Term Goals

MMAs, CDs, and savings bonds are great places to stash your "slush fund"—leave off the "d" and you have "fun"—as in, great vacation, new car, holiday gifts, home furnishings, and so on. For example, for vacations, we use a savings account at an Internet bank. I'm a planner personality: I like to map out vacations a year in advance and put a little money aside every month for them. For me, psychologically, paying for it all at once would feel like a big extravagance. If I did it that way we'd probably never go anywhere, or I might feel guilty about it. Think you can't afford to save for short-term goals like vacations? Try this: When you pay for something in cash, only use bills. (So if the groceries come to $10.04, don't hand over the four cents. Take the change.) At the end of the day, throw your change in a jar. We put other random cash in our jar, too—product rebates, coins we find in the clothes dryer, stupid $5 bets I've made with my husband on the outcome of Bears-Giants football games. If we avoid a regular expenditure, that goes into the jar, too. For instance, we often eat brunch out as a family on Sundays. It costs about $25. If for some reason we eat brunch at home, we throw the $25 in the jar. We empty the jar monthly, deposit the money into checking, and then transfer it electronically to the vacation savings account, where it earns interest. A year later, this little jar covers most of our getaway. As a bonus, the exercise helps my children understand the value of money, and how to reach a financial goal.

For longer-term goals, you want to choose different kinds of investments. The investments I described earlier are completely safe and very liquid—you can get your cash out at any time. But you pay a price for this safety and liquidity: The interest rates are rock bottom. In other words, your money is working for you, but it's only getting the minimum wage. When you have time on your side, you can afford to take more risk—which means more reward (a higher return on your money). The longer you are able to put your money away, the more time it has to navigate the ups and downs inherent in every investment.

Chapter 7 discusses saving for retirement; how to figure out how much risk you can tolerate; and some good places to invest the money to boost your return. Chapter 9 looks at educational savings accounts and what to think about when buying a home. Meanwhile, here are 50 tried and true ways to start saving money. Many of them relate to the Internet; if you are not online at home, you can take advantage of most of these tips by using a computer at the public library.

50 Ways to Save

1. *Grocery shopping:* Control your spending by shopping alone, with cash, and following a list. Never shop when hungry. The most profitable items are at eye-level on the shelf; so look down for better prices. Buy extras of butter, bread, meat, and poultry when they're on sale and freeze them.

2. *Grocery coupons:* Download coupons from the web at MyCoupons .com, smartsource.com, coolsavings.com, or thefrugalshopper .com. Just click and print. For more coupon sites, visit epinions .com and search "coupons."

3. *Discount clubs:* You can save a huge amount on regular staple items and even home office equipment by shopping at Costco or Sam's Club. But make sure you're saving enough to cover your annual membership fee; and that you're not purchasing items you don't really need just because the deals are so hard to resist.

4. *Cook in bulk and freeze:* Allrecipes.com has free recipes for meals that freeze well; cook in bulk on the weekend, trade dishes with friends, freeze. Cook a whole month's food ahead of time. Deborah Taylor-Hough, author of *Frozen Assets: How to Cook for a Day and Eat for a Month,* says she cut the monthly food bill for her family of five from $700 to $300.[3]

5. *Consignment shops:* A great place to sell those impulse buys you never wore and get a little cash back; a great place to find a deal on other people's impulse buys.

6. *Shop at a factory outlet center:* Outletbound.com lists centers near you.

7. *Research prices online before you buy:* Web sites such as bizrate.com or epinions.com allow you to search by product or manufacturer and compare store prices.

8. *Get the insider's deal:* Sometimes an online store will offer a discount or promotion to an exclusive segment of customers. Make sure you're not missing out by visiting naughtycodes.com, edealfinder.com, and dealhunting.com. They locate special deals and list the codes on their sites.

9. *Get cash back:* Ebates.com is a site you join for no fee and receive cash back from literally hundreds of online merchants. Simply by clicking through Ebates to get to my favorite online stores, I got about $25 cash back in the first year. (I would have shopped these stores anyway.)

10. *eBay:* More than 50 million people are registered on eBay. Always check here before you buy the item for full price from a store. I had my eye on a specific Pottery Barn rug; I found it new on eBay for half the catalog price. (Just look at the seller's feedback rating and make sure you're dealing with a party you can trust.) Meanwhile, chances are someone wants your old junk. To get the edge when selling your goods, time your sales to eBay's "Merchandising Calendar," which lists when specific categories will be promoted on eBay's home page.

11. *Designer on the cheap:* Sites like overstock.com and bluefly.com offer discounts of up to 80 percent on designer goods.

12. *Earn extra cash as a mystery shopper:* Stores and restaurants pay consumers to shop their establishments anonymously so they can check up on how the service is performing. To find out how to become a mystery shopper, visit the Mystery Shopping Providers Association online at mysteryshop.org.

13. *Water:* Don't buy bottled. Buy a Brita pitcher and filter your tap water a gallon at a time. Bring your own container to the gym.

14. *Magazine subscriptions:* Compare prices on magazinepricesearch .com, budgetmags.com, magazines.com, or magazinesfinder.com.

15. *Furniture:* Avoid buying it new. Furniture has one of the highest mark-ups of any consumer product. Check out estate sales or garage sales instead, or buy floor models.

16. *Film:* Develop your photos for a discount at an online store such as snapfish.com. Or invest in a digital camera and never buy film again.

17. *Prescription drugs:* Ask your doctor for free samples when the drug is prescribed. Always ask for generic drugs and comparison shop pharmacies. A survey by the New York Attorney General found the retail price of one popular drug ranged from a low of $250.19 to a high of $372.97. Some pharmacies will price match if you ask. (If you live in New York, comparison shop drugs at nyagrx.org.)

18. *Cars:* Find out what you should be paying and how much your trade-in is worth at sites like Kelley blue book (kbb .com), Edmunds.com, or nadaguides.com. *Consumer Reports* publishes a *Used Car Yearbook* for $5.99, which includes a list of the best values in used cars (it may be at your library as well).

19. *Tune up:* Keep your car engine tuned and tires inflated to the proper pressure and save up to $100 a year on gasoline.

20. *Auto insurance:* If you're a safe driver and have an older vehicle, consider dropping both collision and comprehensive coverage and raising your deductible. If you have a safe driving record for three consecutive years, you may also be able to negotiate a discounted rate.

21. *Home insurance:* Raise your deductible to $1,000 and save up to 25 percent on your premium, according to the Insurance Information Institute. You can also save by buying your home and auto policies from the same insurer. Safety features such as smoke detectors, burglar alarms, dead-bolt locks, or other systems can also win you a discount.

22. *Heating and cooling:* Buy a programmable thermostat, a gadget that costs from $30 to $100. You can save up to 10 percent a year on your heating and cooling bills by adjusting your thermostat by 10 to 15 degrees for the eight hours you're at work. Keep it at 68 degrees when you're home and lower it to 60 when you're out or in bed.

23. *Insulation:* About one-third of your home's energy leaks out of ceilings, walls, and floors. The fastest and cheapest solution is to insulate your attic. Insulation is measured in R-values (the higher the number, the better). Figure out what kind of insulation you need by entering your zip code on the web site www

.ornl.gov/~roofs/Zip/ZipHome.html. Get a staple gun and install it yourself.

24. *Water:* You use most of your water in the shower—about 37 percent. Replace your old showerhead and faucet with low-flow aerating models. Lower the thermostat on your water heater to 115 degrees.

25. *Lighting:* Replacing just 25 percent of your lights in high-use areas with fluorescents can save about 50 percent of your lighting energy bill. Fluorescent lamps last 6 to 10 times longer than incandescent bulbs and are much more energy efficient.

26. *Phone service and other bills:* Visit Lowermybills.com and enter your area code and the first three digits of your phone number. The site spews out a list of the lowest cost services in your area.

27. *Cell phones:* Save by buying a second-hand, refurbished phone for little or no money. Providers including AT&T Wireless, U.S. Cellular, Cingular, and TracFone offer online deals on pre-owned phones as a way to sell their service, especially if you're buying prepaid minutes.

28. *Cell phone plans:* Before you choose a plan, consider where and how often you plan to use your phone. Understand when the off-peak hours begin and end on your plan. Ask for any promotions available. Visit web sites such as www.letstalk.com to learn about the best-priced plans in your region.

29. *Drycleaning:* Sweaters, even cashmere, with labels that say "dry clean only" can be machine washed in cold water on gentle/delicate (turn them inside out for safety); hang up and air out suits and spot clean to reduce your dry cleaning bill.

30. *Foreign ATMs:* Never use another bank's ATM. Those $1 charges add up. Instead, go to the grocery store, buy one item, and use the "cash-back option."

31. *Shorten your mortgage:* If you have a 30-year, fixed loan, make one extra payment on your mortgage a year. If you can't afford the lump sum, just take your mortgage payment, divide by 12, and add that extra principal amount to each monthly mortgage payment. You can cut five or more years off the life of a 30-year

mortgage and save thousands of dollars in interest payments. (The exact number of years depends on the size of your mortgage and the interest rate. Check out the home financing calculators— "how advantageous are extra payments"—at www.financenter .com.) Don't sign up for a biweekly mortgage program. You will pay thousands of dollars in fees over time to have a service do what you can easily do yourself.

32. *Get the best deal on savings and checking:* You can find the best rates for savings, lowest fees for checking, and other deals on the web site bankrate.com.

33. *Bank checks:* Find out what your bank charges you to reorder checks. Comparison shop at online sites such as checkworks .com.

34. *Get the best deal on credit cards:* Search for the lowest interest rates, fees, and other features at cardweb.com, bestcardvalue .com, or quicken.com.

35. *Flexible spending accounts (FSAs):* If you have medical or child-care expenses you pay out of pocket, find out if your employer offers flexible spending accounts for these costs. They allow you to have tax-free money taken out of your paycheck and put in the account, which then reimburses you for these costs. Let's say you take a prescription that costs $30 a month and isn't covered by insurance. That's $360 a year. If you put that amount in an FSA, you will only spend $180 to $200 for your prescription, depending on your tax bracket. The savings are even greater for child-care or private preschool costs. (Just be sure to estimate your costs carefully—if you don't use the money in your FSA during the year, you lose it.)

36. *Flights:* All of the airlines offer low-cost weekend getaway fares. Go to their web sites and sign up to have the deals e-mailed to you weekly. Other good discount travel web sites include Orbitz.com, Travelocity.com, Expedia.com, and hotels.com. Sometimes you can search these sites first to determine the price, then book that rate directly with the airline or hotel (and save on the booking fee charged by the travel sites). If you do not mind not knowing which hotel or car rental agency you are

using, try Hotwire.com for even better rates. At Hotwire, you accept and pay for the deal and then are told the name of the hotel, airline, or car rental agency.

37. *Last-minute getaways:* Skyauction.com is a web site that lets you bid on vacations—cruises, flights, all-inclusive packages. If you have a lot of flexibility, you can score cheap last-minute deals. (If you're planning ahead, be sure to price out your vacation before you bid so you don't get caught up in the heat of the moment and overpay.)

38. *Fly as a courier:* If you have a hankering to travel and a lot of flexibility, travel as a courier. There are certain shipping brokers that expedite packages for the major freight companies such as FedEx. They contract with an airline to use one seat per flight for their time-sensitive packages. You, as a courier, use that seat and give up your checked luggage space to the courier firm for their package. You pay 50 percent or less for the flight. (It's ideal for people who travel alone, because it's difficult to coordinate schedules with another courier.) See couriertravel.org for more details.

39. *Drive a new RV cross-country for free:* While most automobiles are shipped on flatbed trucks, there are certain vehicles that don't fit, such as recreational vehicles. According to roadrat.com, you can actually make money driving a new RV from the manufacturing plant to the dealership selling the vehicle. Your airfare home may be covered, too. Start by asking your local recreational vehicle dealer how they get their stock.

40. *Check out government benefits:* Are you eligible for a government program offering low-interest mortgages? What about educational scholarships for your children? How about a business loan? You can find out at a web site called benefits.gov. You fill in a survey (it does not ask for any identifying information) and the site lists all the government programs for which you are eligible.[4]

41. *Time your investment buys in taxable accounts:* If you're interested in purchasing a stock mutual fund, don't buy it in the last six weeks of the year. That's when mutual funds usually give out dividends and capital gains to shareholders of the fund.[5] You'll

end up paying taxes on an investment you've only owned for a short time. (This does not apply to savings in tax-deferred vehicles such as 401(k) plan or individual retirement account IRA.) For more on mutual funds and tax-deferral, see Chapter 7.

42. *Frugal web sites:* Sign up to receive e-mail newsletters with more tips on saving money at cheapskatemonthly.com and stretcher.com.

43. *Time your retail purchases:* The most obvious tip is to buy decorations and wrapping paper in the days and weeks directly *after* the major holiday—outdoor summer stock in September, and so on. But other goods have specific seasons as well: refrigerators tend to go on sale before Memorial Day; washers and dryers in September; and bicycles in the fall, according to *Consumer Reports*.

44. *Swap babysitting time with the neighbors:* Babysitters charge $10 an hour in my area; by switching Friday/Saturday evenings with my neighbor, we save a small fortune, which we can spend on the night out instead of the sitter.

45. *Get creative with entertainment:* Hold a monthly potluck dinner, poker night, Scrabble championship, or book club with friends; go to author readings at the bookstore; visit the museum on its free day; play tennis or toss a football in the park.

46. *The Library:* Your tax dollars pay for it—use it for books, videos, music, and computer games for the kids.

47. *Get creative with gifts:* Think personal and priceless, not manufactured and pricey. For my cousin's birthday, I spent six months ambushing her family, friends, and acquaintances with my video camera, asking for their happy birthday messages. Then I set up a board with photos from her childhood and other big events and videotaped them to music. She was blown away. It cost almost nothing but time and was fun to put together.

48. *Don't lose money to a scam artist:* If it sounds too good to be true, it probably is. If you receive a financial proposal that smells like a fraud, research it on scamvictimsunited.com or scamorama .com. If it's a work-at-home offer, check with the Better Business Bureau.

49. *Stop telemarketers:* Hang up on offers coming into your home selling everything from chimney cleaning to vacations. Put your name and number on the national Do Not Call Registry at (888) 382-1222 or donotcall.gov. Registration is free.

50. *Before you buy anything, ask:* Do I truly value this? Make all of your decisions value-driven and saving will become a regular part of your life.

7

GET YOUR RETIREMENT PLAN IN GEAR

Chicago marketing executive Barbara J., 40, earns well into the six figures. But she managed to save even during her first job out of college, when she made $15,500. "I was dirt poor and would not spend more than I made—it was ingrained," she says. "The more I make, the more I spend, but I always keep the same proportions of spending and saving. As my income has increased, my spending has increased, but so has my savings."

Barbara writes down the goals she wants to achieve in various aspects of her life. They include being a well-rounded, kind person; education; building her savings; and having a nice home. "I do things proactively to improve in each area," she explains. "For education, I went back and got my graduate degree, I try to read the news, read classic books—those are some of the things I throw in that bucket. I reevaluate what the buckets are based on my priorities in life, and I make sure they are in line with my values."

Barbara connects her money to her values by spending and saving to achieve her goals for each area of her life—and by rewarding herself for accomplishing a particularly difficult task. For more than three years, while working full time, she went to school to get her master's degree in business administration. "I promised myself that I would go to Italy for two weeks when I graduated, so I'm planning that right now," she says. "Sometimes I give myself that motivation."

It is time to motivate yourself to save for retirement. By the end of this chapter, you should be able to take seven important steps that will get you on the road to retirement wealth. This chapter focuses on the nitty-gritty of investing. It's not exactly a light read but stick with it, because knowledge of investing basics is power over your financial future. Read the chapter and then get going! Follow these steps within the time frames suggested (in some cases, you can accomplish a step in a day but an average time is suggested at the end of each step):

1. Decide which retirement account is right for you and open the account (one week).
2. Decide how much risk you can take (one week).
3. Choose an allocation strategy (one week).
4. Evaluate specific investments for your retirement account (two to three weeks).
5. Invest in one or more funds for your retirement account (one week).
6. Set up an automated investment plan for your retirement account (one week).
7. Ballpark the amount of money you need to retire (within six months of finishing step 6).

Reward yourself each time you accomplish one of these steps to keep yourself motivated (I'm talking about a music CD or a bottle of wine, not Italy). By the end of this chapter, you'll be able to answer the following questions:

- Where do I invest my retirement money?
- Where do I open these accounts?
- What do I need to know about taxes in retirement planning?
- What's "dollar-cost averaging" and why should I do it?
- What are stocks, bonds, and mutual funds?
- Why should I invest in to the stock market?
- What are index funds and what are their benefits?
- How much risk is involved in investing, and how much can I tolerate?
- What does it mean to "diversify" my retirement savings and why is it important?
- What does it mean to "allocate" my retirement savings and how do I do it?
- What is "rebalancing" and why is it important?
- How do I evaluate and choose mutual funds to invest in?
- Why are fees and expenses important considerations in investing?

You probably noticed that the last of the seven steps is figuring out how much money you need to retire. I realize this is a little unorthodox. Usually we start planning by stating a specific goal. But before you figure out the goal, lay the groundwork. Get into the habit of saving as early as possible, and choose specific investments. Once retirement savings is a natural, automatic part of your financial life, go back and determine how much money you'll need. This approach may seem backward, but if you start by figuring out you need a million dollars to retire, you may not save at all. You'll procrastinate, short-circuiting your savings plan. Get an automated savings plan up and running, and after six months, fine-tune the ultimate amount you are trying to save. It's as easy as flipping a light switch to tell your retirement fund to withdraw $200 a month from your paycheck instead of $25. But it takes time, focus, and research to get the retirement fund in place. If you start by thinking, *How can I possibly save a million dollars for retirement?* you may decide you can't be bothered right now. By focusing on steps you need to take today, tomorrow, and next week, and ignoring the ultimate cost for a time, you take the fear factor out of the process. I'm not suggesting you wait forever to assign a price tag to retirement.

But if you're not retiring for 25 years or more, you can afford to give yourself time to lay the groundwork without worrying about the ultimate number. (Even if you want to retire in 15 years or less, you can still follow this plan. Just ballpark the number you need as soon as you finish the first six steps.)

There are countless ways to make your money grow for your golden years. But first you have to make two decisions: What vehicle do I want to use, and what investments do I want to make within that vehicle? Think of the vehicle as the container, and the investments as the beverages inside. Some containers do a better job than others for specific situations—the way a plastic travel mug is more suitable for a car ride than a delicate Wedgwood teacup. The converse is also true—some investments work better within certain vehicles, the way champagne is more appropriate for a crystal flute than, say, Kool-Aid.

Where Do I Invest My Retirement Money? The 401(k)

First, let's look at some containers for your retirement money. (Later, we'll cover how to choose the investments that fill the container—such as stocks, bonds, and mutual funds.) The government wisely created certain vehicles to encourage people to save.[1] On the upside, these vehicles shelter your savings from taxes, which allows your money to grow faster. On the downside, these benefits are meant to boost *retirement savings,* so you can't really spend the money until you are 59½ years old. If you do withdraw the cash before that time, you will likely pay a penalty. But there are a few important exceptions to that rule—including money used to buy a home and pay for college. (More on that in a moment.)

Once upon a time, big companies offered "defined benefit" plans—or traditional pensions, based on salary and length of service with the company. The employer provided the money and took care of all the investment decisions. These are an endangered species, however. Between 1992 and 2001, the number of heads of families participating in a defined benefit plan fell from 59.3 percent to 38.4 percent.[2] Many companies that used to offer pensions have switched to something known as a *cash balance plan,* in which the employer puts away a certain amount of money for you based on your salary and guarantees a certain return on the money every year. That's still a pretty good deal, since you didn't have to save the money yourself.

However, it's far more likely your company offers a *defined contribution plan.* The most common are 401(k) plans, a 403(b) if you work for a nonprofit, or a 457 if you're a government employee. Companies love these plans because you are the one who has to put the money in them. Sometimes your employer will kick in a little scratch (known as matching funds), but in a defined contribution plan, *you* have to put away the money, plus choose and manage your investments. That can be intimidating, which may be why a lot of people—an estimated one-third of those eligible—ignore this fabulous benefit.

The government allows you to contribute up to a certain amount of your income to a 401(k) plan. For example, for 2005 the limit is $14,000 (for people over age 50, $18,000). In 2006, the limits are $15,000 and $20,000, respectively. One in 10 people contribute the maximum to their 401(k) plan, according to a 2003 study by Fidelity Investments. Meanwhile, your company may match your contribution up to a certain amount—an automatic salary raise for you! Here's why you should enroll in your plan as soon as you can:

1. *It's a mindless way to plan for retirement.* Your contribution dollars are automatically taken out of your paycheck before taxes. Saving is effortless, and you don't miss what you can't see.

2. *Contributing to your 401(k) reduces your taxable income.* Uncle Sam wants to encourage people to save for retirement. For that reason, the money you set aside in a 401(k) is deducted from the income you report for tax purposes. Uncle Sam pretends you never earned it at all. Let's say you earn $31,000. You put $3,000 away during the year in your 401(k). You subtract that from your gross income ($31,000 − $3,000 = $28,000). For tax purposes, you only made $28,000. This cuts down on what you pay to the government on April 15.

Example 1

Contribution: $3,000 of your $31,000 salary

Company match: $1,500

401(k) savings at the end of the year: $4,500, plus whatever interest you earned on your money during the year

Federal tax bill: $4,915 on $28,000 in income

(If you pay state and local income tax, you will save on these taxes also.)

Example 2

Contribution: 0

Company match: 0

401(k) savings at the end of the year: 0, plus 0 investment returns, equals 0.

Federal tax bill: $5,462.50 on $31,000 in income (or $547.50 more than Example 1).

3. *Money in a 401(k) grows tax-deferred.* You pay no taxes until you take it out at retirement. We talked in Chapter 6 about the power of compounding. The power of compounding combined with *tax deferral* is dramatic.

Example

Investment: $250 per month (or $3,000 a year)

Time frame: 30 years

Average Annual Return on Investment: 9 percent

Account value in a 401(k): $461,368.

Account value in a taxable account: $349,616 (assumes a tax rate of 15 percent on capital gains)

4. *A 401(k) is a great way to get your money working harder for you immediately.* Through your company retirement plan, you can invest in stocks or stock mutual funds right away. This is a big advantage over someone who opens an individual retirement account (IRA) on their own (see below); in many cases you must have at least $1,000 to invest before they let you in the door. Why do you want

to invest in stocks? Over a long period of time, exposure to the stock market offers potentially higher investment returns. For example, between 1926 and 2003, stocks returned an average of 10.5 percent a year on investment, while government bonds averaged 5.45 percent, according to Ibbotson Associates, a research and consulting firm.[3] (Stocks and bonds are defined next.)

5. *Matching funds, aka free money.* According to Fidelity, 80 percent of employers who operate 401(k) plans offer matching funds, covering 69 percent of workers.[4] Repeat after me: This is free money! For example, I once worked for a company that matched 50 cents for every dollar I contributed up to $3,000. So if I put in $3,000 during the year, they put in $1,500. Think about that: Is there anything else in the world that will give you a *guaranteed 50 percent return* on your money? Imagine you saw $1,500 lying on the sidewalk. Would you walk by? One important tip: If you decide to quit your job before a certain amount of time has passed, your plan may limit how much of this match you get to take with you. No matter when you leave your firm, you take all of the money *you* contributed to your 401(k), plus any investment returns. But the matching funds from *your employer* may have a "vesting" schedule. For instance, my firm's 401(k) plan had a five-year vesting period: If you left after one year, you only got to take 20 percent of the matching funds; two years, 40 percent; three years, 60 percent; four years 80 percent. After five years, you were 100 percent vested. (Game over! Winner takes all!)

6. *The money isn't necessarily locked in a vault until age 59½.* If you're concerned that you might need the funds before that age, you can borrow from your 401(k) savings if you really need to. But I don't recommend it. (For details, see Chapter 9.)

Once you sign up to participate in your firm's plan, you have to choose among the investments offered. I'll explain how later in the chapter. First, let's look at your options if your company does not offer a retirement plan, or if you're an aggressive saver who has already contributed the maximum to your 401(k), and wants to save more.

Individual Retirement Accounts

If your company doesn't offer a 401(k) or other plan, the traditional Individual Retirement Account (IRA) is your next option for retirement savings. (Some people call them Iras, as in "Ira" your friend from the fish store; I personally prefer the initials "I.R.A.") Anyone younger than age 70½ who has earned income during the year can put in up to $4,000 in an IRA (or $4,500 if you're over age 50) in 2005. In 2006, the limits are $4,000 and $5,000, respectively; they rise again in 2008. But you can't put in more than you actually earned. So if you made $2,000 working part time, that's the most you can contribute. The exception is the *spousal IRA* for married women (or men) who don't work, and file jointly (that means one tax return between the two of you). Uncle Sam wised up a few years back and decided that even though you might be a student, parent, caretaker for an elderly relative, or lounging by the pool while your spouse works at a paying job, you still need to save for your own retirement. So if you are married and filing jointly and have little or no income, you can still contribute up the maximum to a spousal IRA.

Where Should I Open an IRA?

You can set up an IRA with a variety of organizations—banks, mutual fund companies, life insurance firms, stockbrokers. I would suggest a mutual fund company that has a reputation for low-cost investments, such as:

- Vanguard Group, www.vanguard.com (877) 662-7447
- Fidelity Investments, www.fidelity.com (800) 343-3548
- Charles Schwab Corp., www.schwab.com (866) 855-9102
- T. Rowe Price Group, www.troweprice.com (800) 225-5132
- TIAA-CREF, www.tiaa-cref.org (800) 842-2888

Many fund companies require a minimum IRA investment of $1,000 or $3,000. However, there are some funds that will allow you to open an account with as little as $250. Later in the chapter, when we discuss how to invest in mutual funds, we'll look at how to find funds that allow you invest with less than $1,000, so you can get started immediately.

Dollar Cost Averaging

When can you put the money in your IRA? Anytime! But if you want to apply the tax benefit to this year's tax return, you have until April 15 of the following year to contribute (i.e., April 15, 2006, is the deadline for the 2005 tax year). But don't just plop a lump sum in the account on April 14. The ideal way to contribute to an IRA—or any investment— is to save small amounts week after week or month after month. This strategy is known as *dollar cost averaging.* For example, let's say you invest your IRA money in a mutual fund (if you don't know what this is, I define it shortly). You can't "time" the market. No one knows when that mutual fund will rise or fall in value. That's why you contribute a little bit of money at a time; sometimes you might pay $10 a share for the fund, sometimes $15 a share—averaging out to $12.50 a share. Dollar cost averaging reduces the risk of paying too much for an investment. (A fund rises and falls in price from day to day; if you have the bad luck of putting all your money in the investment when it hits its peak, your investment will fall in value. Think of a roller coaster—if you hop on the ride at the top of the hill, there's no place to go but down.) A 401(k) plan is already structured for dollar cost averaging, because the plan invests a little bit of your salary in the market every time you get paid. To achieve dollar cost averaging with an IRA, just fill out a form at the institution where you open your IRA, establishing a regular transfer from your checking into the IRA, so you are buying shares on a steady basis.

Taxes, Penalties, and Using an IRA for More Than Retirement

A traditional IRA is similar to a 401(k) in that the money you contribute is deducted from your gross income, so you pay less in taxes. However, Uncle Sam hates double dipping on retirement savings tax benefits. So if you or your spouse is covered by a 401(k) or other employer retirement plan—even if you don't contribute—you may not be able to deduct your IRA contribution from your gross income. You can still put the money in the IRA. You just can't use it to reduce your taxable income in many cases. It depends on how much you make. (Check with an accountant or visit www.irs.gov.) If you already max out your contributions to your firm's 401(k) or other retirement plan, and you *also* want to contribute to an IRA—rock on! You're a saving maniac! But keep reading: A Roth IRA is a better bet for a disciplined retirement saver who already contributes to a 401(k).

As mentioned, IRA money is supposed to be for retirement, so if you withdraw your savings before age 59½, you'll pay a 10 percent penalty to Uncle Sam. However, there are some exceptions to that rule. For instance, you can tap $10,000 of the money penalty-free (one time only) to buy or build your first home, pay for qualified higher education expenses; or pay for big medical bills that aren't covered by insurance. (See Chapter 9 for more details on saving for a home down payment or college expenses.) You can also tap the money if you become disabled. You won't pay the 10 percent penalty in those cases, but you will have to pay some tax on the money in the year you withdraw it because you didn't pay any tax on it when you put it in the account.

You can start to withdraw your IRA money at age 59½, and you *must* begin taking something called "required minimum distributions" by age 70½ or Uncle Sam will slap a penalty on you. This is because Uncle Sam is a bully who enjoys slapping people, especially the elderly. Just kidding. It's because the whole point of an IRA is to save money for *retirement*—and, here's a radical concept—actually *spend it* while you're retired. Remember, when you put this money away, you didn't pay tax on it. You think Uncle Sam is going to let you get away with that? Nope. He's going to make you withdraw it so he gets his cut!

What kind of tax do you pay on withdrawals? When you take the money out of the traditional IRA, the government considers that income (imagine your IRA is your boss handing you a paycheck with no taxes taken out of it). So you pay ordinary income tax on the money. Why does Uncle Sam wait until you're retired to tax you? Because, theoretically, you'll probably be in a lower income tax bracket. As you know, income taxes rise with earnings—the more you make, the more taxes you pay, as a percentage of income. Example: A single person making less than $29,050 is in the 15 percent tax bracket; the same person making over $146,751 is in the 33 percent tax bracket. Here's the whole IRA concept in a nutshell: You put the money away in an IRA tax-deferred while you're young, carefree, working hard, and making the big bucks. Your big-buck salary vaults you into a higher tax bracket. So you contribute to an IRA, which helps lower your tax bill every year. Then you become old, carefree, and make the little bucks. Your little bucks drop you into a lower tax bracket, so you pay *lower tax* on the money you withdraw from your IRA.

This is the theory; but it may not be true for everyone. Imagine you're a fine art painter your whole life, and can't even sell your stuff at garage sales. Then a celebrity art dealer discovers you in your 60s. Your masterpieces are flying out the door, going for tens of thousands of dollars. Boom! You're in a higher income bracket. You decide to live large, spend all your art earnings and withdraw some savings from your IRA to go to Paris. Uncle Sam is delighted about your success because now that you're in a higher income tax bracket, he gets a bigger chunk of your IRA money. My point is this: You never know what your circumstances will be in retirement. For that reason, you don't want to put *every penny* of your retirement money into *tax-deferred* vehicles like 401(k)s and traditional IRAs, because you may get an ugly tax surprise in retirement. You want to consider other savings options that are taxed differently, like a Roth IRA (see the discussion that follows). Before we get into the Roth, though, let's finish up this conversation about traditional IRAs. As stated earlier, you must begin taking distributions at age 70½, because IRAs are supposed to be for *your* retirement, not a tax-free savings vehicle to pass along money to your heirs after you die. The minimum distribution rules are extremely complicated, and there actually *are* techniques that help you pass along your account to your heirs when you die. But I'm not going to describe them here, because thinking about death depresses me, and "How to Spend Your Money in Retirement" would make a mighty fine sequel to this book. Most importantly, who knows what the world will be like when you're 70½? No doubt you'll still be in touch with your sexy inner babe, but the rules for IRA distributions may change between now and then, because politicians love tinkering with tax laws. So let's move on. (If you *are* close to age 70½, or helping someone who is with their IRA, see an accountant or financial advisor before selecting a method for taking distributions.)

The Roth IRA

The Roth IRA is similar to a traditional IRA in many respects, but if you're looking for versatility, this is the vehicle you want to drive. The contribution limits are the same as a traditional IRA ($4,000 or $4,500 for age 50 and over in 2005) and the money grows tax-free. (There are limits on who can participate; you can't contribute to a Roth if you earn $110,000 or more as a single, or $160,000 or more as a couple filing jointly.) Now here's the big difference: In a traditional IRA, you get the tax break now, and pay Uncle Sam later when you withdraw the money in retirement. In a Roth IRA, you get no tax break upfront—you pay tax on your contributions *now,* before you put the money in the account. But here's the best part: You get to withdraw both your contributions *and your earnings on the money* tax-free at age 59½. Repeat after me: "This is awesome!" Why? Because there are very few vehicles in the world of investing that allow you grow your money and enjoy your profits, completely free of taxes.

Remember the painter who starts making the big bucks in her 60s? A Roth IRA would be ideal for her, because she would pay no tax on her savings when she withdrew them in retirement, regardless of her income bracket. The Roth is probably a better choice for you, too, because it offers so much flexibility. For instance, it's easier to get your money out of a Roth than a traditional IRA, in the event you need it before retirement. (Although you shouldn't really think about retirement assets as anything but retirement assets. When you tap the money for other goals, you may hear a giant sucking sound; that's the fun—and possibly the ability to pay for food and shelter—disappearing from your senior years.) Here's what you need to keep in mind: There are two components to your retirement savings: the money you put in (contributions) and the interest you earned on that money (profits or earnings). Because you've already paid the tax upfront on your *contributions,* Uncle Sam will let you take them out of your Roth anytime after five years, for any reason, without taxes or penalties. After age 59½, you can take out both contributions *and profits* tax-free (you must have maintained the account for five years). However, if you decide to tap the *profits* from your account before that magic age of 59½, Uncle Sam won't stop you—but he will slap you with income tax on your profits plus a 10 percent penalty. On the other hand, Uncle Sam recognizes there are legitimate reasons why you may need your profits before age 59½. So he has carved out some exceptions that allow you to take the profits early. You will still pay income tax on the profits, but you can avoid the 10 percent penalty if the money is used:

- To put a down payment on a home (one time only, up to $10,000)
- To pay for qualifying college expenses
- To pay for big, unreimbursed medical expenses (more than 7.5 percent of your adjusted gross income)
- To buy health insurance in the event you are unemployed (you have to be out of work for 12 weeks or more)
- If you withdraw a series of equal payments for at least five years until age 59½ (For details on this, see www.irs.gov.)

Example: Rebecca is 25. She wants to save for retirement and would like to buy a home in a few years. She opens one savings account to save money for her home, as well as a Roth IRA:

Rebecca's Roth IRA contributions: $2,000 a year for seven years ($14,000 total)

Profits on her contributions: $4,000 in interest

Total account value: $18,000.

At age 32, Rebecca manages to accumulate $7,000 in her home down payment savings account. That's a substantial sum, but not enough to buy her home. She decides to tap the money in her Roth for a down payment for her first home.

Here are her options for her Roth IRA:

- Withdraw all of her contributions—$14,000 (no tax or penalty) *and* $4,000 in profits (pay ordinary income tax on them)

Here is her option if she invested in a traditional IRA:

- Withdraw $10,000 only, and pay ordinary income tax on it.

As you can see, she has more money available to her by investing in the Roth. Now Rebecca's a smart gal. She knows she needs that money in her Roth for her retirement. So she only withdraws $10,000 to help cover her house down payment, and leaves $4,000 in the account to continue growing. Now you might be thinking, what's the big deal? In one case (the Roth), she paid income tax on the money *before* she put it in the account. In the other (the traditional IRA), she paid income tax on the money *after* she took it out. But here's why the Roth is superior: Over seven years of working, there is a strong possibility Rebecca's salary has gone up, putting her in a higher tax bracket. That means higher taxes on the money she withdraws from the traditional IRA to put down on her home. Because the Roth is so flexible, it also requires discipline. I would discourage you from using your Roth for anything other than retirement. (Suppose Rebecca loses her job and can't make her mortgage payments. She would have to sell her home, possibly at a loss, or even wind up in foreclosure. That would mean she not only lost her home, but a big chunk of her retirement savings just went down the toilet, too.) Table 7.1 shows the differences between the traditional IRA and the Roth IRA.

Retirement Plans for the Self-Employed

If you are self-employed, certain retirement savings plans apply specifically to your situation. You can sock away much more money in these vehicles than in typical IRAs. Part of the reason is that these are considered "company" retirement plans—and in any company retirement plan, you have an employer-employee relationship. But if you're the only person in the business, you get to be both people, and you get to take advantage of both sides of the equation. You can even take advantage of these plans if you moonlight part time—in some cases, even if

TABLE 7.1
Differences between Traditional IRA and Roth IRA

	Traditional IRA	ROTH IRA
Contributions	$4,000 ($4,500 over age 50)	$4,000 ($4,500 over age 50)
Affect on income	Reduces taxable income	Does *not* reduce taxable income
How contributions are taxed	When you withdraw them in retirement at age 59½	When you contribute the money
How profits are taxed	When you withdraw them in retirement at age 59½	Never, unless withdrawn before age 59½
When I can tap my contributions	At age 59½, with some important exceptions	Anytime
When I can tap my profits	At age 59½, with some important exceptions	At age 59½, with some important exceptions
When I must take distributions	At age 70½	Never
If I take the money out before age 59½	Pay income tax on the money + 10% penalty	Pay income tax on the earnings only + 10% penalty
The most important exceptions that allow you to withdraw money early with no penalty are	Home downpayment Qualified higher education expenses Unreimbursed medical bills that are more than 7.5% of adjusted gross income	Home downpayment Qualified higher education expenses Unreimbursed medical expenses that are more than 7.5% of AGI Health insurance if you are unemployed (and have been for 12 weeks)

you are already part of a retirement plan at your full-time job. Among the most popular plans for the self-employed are the Simplified Employee Pension Plan (SEP-IRA); the Self-Employed 401(k); and the Savings Incentive Match Plans for Employees (SIMPLE IRA). This is a brief overview; talk to an accountant to help you choose which one of these plans is right for your business.

The SEP IRA is the most straightforward of these options. You can open one through a mutual fund company and contribute 25 percent of your income up to $41,000. Consider a freelance graphic designer who earns $60,000 a year; she can put up to $15,000 into her SEP in a single year, and deduct that amount from her taxes. Money in a SEP IRA can be taken out at any time but the withdrawals will be hit with income tax and a 10 percent penalty if this occurs before age 59½.

Business owners with no employees (except a spouse) can take advantage of the *Self-Employed 401(k)*. If you are not far from retirement, it's a fantastic opportunity to put huge amounts of money away. This 401(k) was created as an unintended side effect of a bill passed by Congress a few years ago to encourage retirement savings. Congress raised the maximum amount employers can contribute to 401K plans on their employees' behalf to 25 percent from 15 percent. At the same time, Congress decided the money workers contribute from their salaries *won't* be counted toward that 25 percent limit. The result: As the business owner, you can put away 25 percent of your compensation or 20 percent of your self-employment income (up to $205,000), and as the employee you can put away $14,000 in salary ($18,000 if over age 50, according to 2005 limits; and $15,000 and $20,000, respectively, in 2006). Let's return to our graphic designer. She earns $60,000. As the "employer," she can put 25 percent of her compensation—or $15,000—in her self-employed 401K. As the "employee," she can set aside another $14,000—for a total of $29,000. Mutual fund companies have jumped right on this bandwagon, so you can open a one-person 401(k) without all the headaches and paperwork that normally go with these plans. The self-employed 401(k) is an excellent option if you're nearing retirement and have nothing put away. The plan has a number of administrative requirements, including IRS filings. Unlike an IRA, you cannot take withdrawals except at retirement or under other narrow conditions. Given the restrictions involved, don't opt for this plan unless you're certain you won't need the money before retirement.

The *SIMPLE IRA* is designed for companies that have no other retirement plan in place and employ up to 100 workers. But you can open a SIMPLE IRA even if you're the only employee. As employee, you can put in up to $10,000 in 2005, $12,000 if over age 50. As an employer, you can match those contributions dollar for dollar up to 3 percent of salary. Let's take our graphic designer again, who earns $60,000. She can put in $10,000 as an employee of the company, and another $1,800 (3 percent of compensation) as employer, or a total of $11,800. So you can you double-dip in SIMPLE—but the benefits aren't big enough to justify choosing this plan over a SEP. Money in a SIMPLE IRA can be taken out any time but will be subject to taxes and penalties if withdrawn before age 59½.

Overview of Key Investments

Now that you have an overview of the tax-advantaged vehicles available to save for retirement, it's time to look at the investments you'd like to put inside them. Think of the vehicle as a restaurant; inside the restaurant is a whole menu of items (investments) to choose from. Here are some of the most important.

Stocks

When you buy a stock, you're buying a small piece or "share" of the company. Stocks are quoted as "price per share." If the stock is trading at $10, and you want to buy 100 shares, it will cost you $1,000 (plus a fee you pay to a brokerage firm to make the purchase for you). The company uses the shareholders' money to grow the business and increase earnings, which usually makes the stock go up, or "appreciate" in value. You make money—capital gains—when you sell your stock at the higher value. Another way to make money is through dividends—some companies pay shareholders a piece of the earnings each quarter as a return on their investment. On the downside, the company, and its stock, may decline because of poor management decisions, competition, dishonesty by executives or the person who sold you the stock, or a host of other reasons. That's why it's essential to understand exactly what you're buying. A stock is represented by a ticker symbol, under which it trades, that is, MSFT for Microsoft; GM for General Motors, and so on. Stocks trade in what is essentially an auction: When there is great demand to buy a particular stock, the price goes up; when demand falls, the price of the stock falls as well. A whole array of factors can affect demand, and subsequent price, for a stock. U.S. stocks trade on a centralized exchange such as the

New York Stock Exchange, the American Stock Exchange, or the Nasdaq stock market.[5]

Bonds

When you buy a bond, you're making a loan to a corporation, a municipality, the federal government, or other entity, called the *issuer*. They use your money and promise to return your principal at a specific time when the bond comes due, or "matures"—say, in 10 years. In return for the privilege of borrowing your money, the issuer promises to pay you a specified rate of interest over the life of the bond, and repay you the face value of the bond when it matures. Unlike a stock, bond offerings tell you upfront exactly how much money you'll get back on your investment if you hold it to maturity. For that reason, bonds are considered safer than stocks; also, if a company goes belly up, bondholders get paid before stockholders. Independent agencies, such as Moody's, rate the quality of a company's bonds from highest—Aaa, Aa, A, Baa, Bb, B, and so on—to lowest—C. The rating gives you a good idea of how likely you are to get your money back as promised. You can hold a bond until maturity (the full 10 years in our example) or you can sell it before that time into a secondary market in which bonds are traded. If you sell before maturity, there's no guarantee you'll get the price you paid for the bond—bond prices rise and fall depending on what's happening with interest rates. You can also buy someone else's bonds in the secondary market. Another important aspect of bonds: Some bonds are "callable"—meaning the company can decide to pay you back before the bond matures (i.e., you invest in a 10-year bond from Acme Soap, and it decides to pay back its debt in four years). The risk of callable bonds is you may have to scramble to find somewhere else to put your money (and it's possible other investments won't be as attractive at the time).[6]

Mutual Funds

When you put your money in a mutual fund, you're pooling your resources with other investors and turning them over to a professional fund manager, who invests in a basket of different investments. Mutual funds are an excellent way to get started investing, because instead of spending all of your time researching, evaluating, and tracking individual stocks and bonds, you choose a fund and its manager to do that work for you. Mutual funds spread your risk because the manager invests in a basket of stocks or bonds, rather than betting your whole kitty on one investment. Because this manager must be paid to supervise the pool of money, there are *management fees* that come with investing mutual funds. There may be other fees as well; for example, sometimes a mutual fund will charge you a sales commission to get in the door, or when you cash out of the fund. This is known as a "load." (More on fees follows). In 2003, there were 261 million shareholder accounts with $7.4 trillion invested in mutual funds, according to the Investment Company Institute, an industry lobbying group.[7] Unless your mutual fund is held in a tax-advantaged account such as the 401(k) or IRA, you pay taxes on the fund's distributions in any year the fund makes such distributions; and you are taxed on any capital gains when you sell the investment.[8]

What Makes One Mutual Fund Different from Another?

Funds are separated primarily by type of investment and style of investing. Here's an overview of the kinds of mutual funds you might consider:

A. U.S. Stock funds, also known as *equity funds*
   1. By *size:* Large-, mid-, or small-capitalization (see later discussion)
   2. By *sector:* Focuses on a specific industry, such as biotechnology, utilities, or financial services
   3. Or by *style* (from aggressive to conservative):
      a. Growth (invests in stocks where sales, earnings, and stock price are growing quickly, often in cutting-edge industries such as technology)
      b. Value (invests in stocks that are out of favor, undervalued by the market for some reason, or on the verge of a turnaround; tend to be dependable performers that chug along steadily rather than zoom ahead; also tend to be in more traditional industries, such as utilities or construction)

    c. Index (invest in the same stocks that are held by a particular market index such as the S&P 500—details later)

    d. Blend (invest in a mix of growth and value stocks)

    e. Income (invest in bonds and/or stocks that pay dividends, so the investor can count on a stream of cash; very conservative, often favored by retirees and others who need steady income)

B. U.S. bond mutual funds, also known as *fixed income* funds:

    1. By *sector:* Corporate; government; high-yield or "junk" bonds

    2. Tax-exempt (federal or municipal) or taxable

C. Hybrids, also known as "balanced" mutual funds (invest in both stocks and bonds)

D. Foreign mutual funds:

    1. Invest in stocks, bonds, or other instruments

    2. Invest in developed nations or "emerging markets"

    3. Focus on a region or specific country; global funds may also invest in U.S. stocks

E. Money market mutual funds: Similar to money market accounts discussed in Chapter 6. They are a good place to keep cash, they pay a relatively low rate of return, and are not guaranteed by the federal government. But they are extremely conservative and it's unlikely you'll lose your principal.

    1. Taxable or tax-exempt

What Makes a Stock "Big-Capitalization" or "Small-Capitalization"?

Capitalization is just the price of the stock multiplied by the number of shares outstanding. So if a stock is $5 and there are two million shares floating around in the investment universe, its market-capitalization is $10 million. Morningstar, the essential resource on mutual fund investing, defines large caps as the top 70 percent of companies in the market by capitalization; mid-caps are the next largest 20 percent; and small-caps are the smallest 10 percent. They define it this way because sometimes the value of the market swells as more investors jump in (like in 1999 when everyone was going crazy for stocks) and sometimes the overall value of the market falls. In March 2004, for instance, Morningstar's definition of big-cap stocks were those with capitalization above $8.5 billion; mid-caps were those with capitalization of $8.5 to $1.5 billion; and small-cap were those below $1.5 billion. Obviously, a stock can start out as a small-cap (Microsoft in the early 1980s) and blossom into a big-cap over time (Microsoft in 2004, with more than $305 billion in market capitalization). Mutual fund managers who run small-cap stock funds tend to sell a company's stock when it mushrooms into a medium- or large-cap.

What's an Index Fund and Why Is It a Good Place to Start?

With so many different types of funds to choose from, where do you begin? An index fund is a great choice for beginning investors with a medium to long-term time frame for their goals (five years or more). An index fund holds the stocks that are in a particular market index, such as the S&P 500. What's an index? It's an instrument that takes the temperature of a certain part of the stock market. Here's an analogy: Before an election, pollsters will interview a sample of people in, say, New Hampshire, to determine which candidate the state is favoring. A stock index does the same thing: It checks on how certain stocks are doing in a particular area of the market to determine how that group is faring, whether it's the stocks of small companies, large companies, foreign firms, and so on. Example: The S&P 500, an index created by the firm Standard and Poor's, tracks the stock performance of a representative sample of 500 leading companies in leading industries. These stocks are chosen for their size, the industries they represent, and their liquidity. (Liquidity means millions of people own shares of the stock, so it trades quite easily. If you, me, your mom, and the postman are the only ones who own a particular stock, then there aren't a whole lot of people for us to sell it to, making it *illiquid.*) So the S&P 500 represents what's happening to large company stocks as a whole within the broader stock market, the way the poll of certain people in New Hampshire represents what's happening in that state within the broader United States. How does an index fund mimic the performance of a particular index? It simply buys and holds each of the stocks in the index. Other index funds track different parts of the market—such as the Russell 2000, which represents what's happening with the stocks of smaller companies. Here is why I like index funds for beginners:

- *Higher returns:* Index funds offer broad exposure to the stock market, which generally means better returns than savings accounts or savings bonds.
- *Low minimums:* You can get started investing in index funds with as little as $250 in some cases if you agree to continue to automatically invest a certain amount electronically (i.e., the money is transferred directly from your checking account every week or month).
- *Sales charges:* The majority of index funds are "no load"—which means they do not charge sales commissions to invest in them.
- *Minimal fees and expenses:* Index funds also have very low management fees, because they are considered "passive" instead of "active" investments. The funds simply hold the stocks in the index they are trying to mirror, and companies in an index tend to change very rarely. Compare this to a high-powered mutual fund manager who "actively" invests in foreign companies, and has an army of researchers looking for investment opportunities. Management fees are paid out of the fund's assets. So the more money that gets siphoned off to pay an active manager, the less money there is working for you in the fund.
- *Performance:* Studies show index funds beat the returns of actively managed funds most of the time.

Your Investment Strategy: Understanding Risk

Before you choose an index fund or other mutual fund, you have to think about risk. Remember those savings accounts in the previous chapter? The government guarantees all of them—you can't lose your principal. But even those guaranteed savings accounts pose a risk because the interest you receive may not keep pace with the cost of living, in which case your money will lose buying power. By contrast, all of the investments I just described carry risk. You can lose money investing in stocks, bonds, and mutual funds. This raises an essential investing question: How much risk can you take? Investors range from ultra conservative—you can't bear the thought of ever losing a single dollar you save for retirement—to ultra aggressive—you're okay with the risk of losing your principal for the possibility of huge gains. When you invest in the market, you take the chance that your money might not grow as you had hoped, or worse, you could lose your principal. In its best year ever, the S&P 500 skyrocketed nearly 54 percent; in its worst year, it dropped about 43 percent, according to Ibottson Research.[9] However, "In the history of the stock market, there is not one investor, who has left their money in the market for more than 20 years, lost any money," according to the National Endowment for Financial Education.[10] Nobody knows what's going to happen in the future, but studies based on the past performance of the S&P 500 have found since 1925, the chance of losing money over one year is 28 percent; over five years, 10 percent; over 10 years, 3 percent; and over 20 years, 0 percent. And consider this little factoid from Jeremy Siegel, a Wharton School professor of finance who directs the Securities Industry Association Institute: For every rolling five-year investing period from 1802 to 2002 (that means 1802 to 1807, 1803 to 1808, 1804 to 1809, etc.), stocks have outperformed bonds 80 percent of the time.[11]

In other words, the most important factor in deciding how much risk to take with a particular investment is your *time frame.* The more time you have, the more risk you can afford to take, because your investment has the opportunity to ride out the market's ups and downs. For example, we put 100 percent of my two-year-old's college fund in stock mutual funds and individual stocks, because we won't need to tap the money for 16 years. In 12 years, when she starts high school, we'll shift her college money into a more conservative mutual fund, because at that point we don't want the risk—we want "capital preservation"— to make sure the money is secure and available to cover the tuition bills. So we'll settle for lower returns on the money in the final years before we need to spend it.

Identify your goal, put a time frame on it, and make a decision about risk: These are the essential first steps to investing. Many financial services companies and financial web sites offer question-naires to help test your risk tolerance, including:

- Kiplinger.com at www.kiplinger.com/tools/riskfind.html
- Fortune.com at www.fortune.com/fortune/quizzes/investing /riskquiz.html
- Rutgers University Cooperative Extension at www.rce.rutgers .edu/money/riskquiz

Bottom line: The more risk you are willing to take in terms of losing the money you invest, the more reward you might receive. But this is the "sleep-at-night" factor. Only you can determine what kinds of in-vestments you should avoid because they keep you awake at night.

Diversification, Allocation, and Rebalancing

Once you've discovered your risk tolerance, you may think: Can't I just throw all my money into one mutual fund and be done with it forever? Well, picking one fund is a good way to start, but you don't want to keep all your eggs in one basket, or your retirement fund may end up scrambled. You want diversification—with some of your money in stocks and some in bonds—because this reduces the risk of losing money. The stock market tends to move in cycles. Stocks may be up while bonds are down. Also, different types of stocks move in and out of favor as well: At one point, investors might be hot for small company stocks and their prices go up, while demand wanes for large-cap stocks, and they decline in price. Then it might reverse. Or, sometimes foreign stocks are popular, and other kinds of stocks are duds. So you want ex-posure to all different kinds of stocks and bonds, so your portfolio is like a fleet of aircraft carriers, solidly navigating rough seas, rather than the Titanic, sunk by a single iceberg.

Big, small, growth, value, U.S., foreign—how do you choose which areas of the market and which funds to invest in? This is the art of in-vesting. It's called *asset allocation.* You allocate your money into different areas of the market to spread around your risk and smooth out the ups and downs of your portfolio. In 1990, Harry Markowitz won the Nobel

Prize in economics. He developed a theory that suggests almost 92 percent of your investment returns come from asset allocation. In other words, the *kinds* of investments you choose are more important than the specific *choices* you make within each category.[12] That's why we're first going to look at how to choose your categories, then how to choose specific mutual funds within those categories.

A classic rule of thumb suggests you subtract your age from 100, and invest that amount in stocks, the rest in bonds. So if you're 35, you should put at least 65 percent of your money in stocks. Personally, I always put more in stocks than that model suggests for my long-term goals, because I feel comfortable with the risk. I may end up disappointed, but I gotta be me! Risk tolerance is a very individual decision. Once you decide how much of your portfolio you want to put in stocks, you need to choose among the equity mutual funds available. One classic scenario suggests your portfolio mimic the makeup of the market itself, by investing:

- 70 percent of your stock allocation in a large-cap fund
- 20 percent in a mid-cap fund
- 10 percent in a small-cap fund

Under this model, here is what a $10,000 investment would look like:

- $2,500 in bonds
- $7,500 in stock funds, with:
  —$5,250 (70 percent of stock allocation) in a large-cap fund
  —$1,500 (20 percent of stock allocation) in a mid-cap fund
  —$750 (10 percent of stock allocation) in a small-cap fund

Investment advisors suggest you consider at least some exposure to foreign stocks for more diversity. So of the portion of your portfolio allocated to stocks, you might consider investing:

- 65 percent in a large-cap fund
- 15 percent in a mid-cap fund
- 10 percent in a small-cap fund
- 10 percent in a foreign fund

In dollar terms, a $10,000 investment in this portfolio would look like this:

- $2,500 in bonds
- $7,500 in stock funds, with:
  —$4,875 in a large-cap fund
  —$1,125 in a mid-cap fund
  —$750 in a small-cap fund
  —$750 in a foreign fund

Within each of those categories (big, medium, small, foreign) you can choose growth or value styles of investing; growth funds tend to be more aggressive, and carry more risk. Once you establish your allocation strategy you should revisit that strategy once a year—no more, no less, and realign your investments to reflect it. This is called *rebalancing:* It's like driving down a highway, and your car begins to drift to one side or the other. You want to correct the steering and get yourself back in the center lane. This means if one of your funds has zoomed in value, it will now make up a bigger percentage of your overall portfolio than it did a year ago. You would sell some of that fund to return to your original allocation. You would take the proceeds from that sale and use it to buy more of the fund that has slipped below the original allocation.

Example: Original Allocation Strategy
- 70 percent in Snow White Large-Cap Fund
- 20 percent in Bashful Mid-Cap Fund
- 10 percent in Happy Small-Cap Fund

12 months later, the funds rise or fall in value:

- 75 percent in Snow White Large-Cap Fund
- 20 percent in Bashful Mid-Cap Fund
- 5 percent in Happy Small-Cap Fund

To rebalance at the end of the year, you would sell 5 percent of the Snow White Large-Cap Fund, and buy 5 percent of the Happy Small-Cap Fund. You may have heard the classic investment phrase "buy low, sell high." It simply means you should invest in assets when they are low in price, and sell them when the price goes up. Unfortunately, many investors often do the opposite—they see the price of stocks decline and they panic and sell. Or they notice that everyone is buying a certain kind of stock, and they all pile in after one another. But you want to be the investor who is buying when everyone else is panicking and selling; and selling when everyone else is caught up in a buying frenzy. This takes a tremendous amount of discipline, and a realization that you're in this for the long haul. Choosing an allocation strategy and sticking with it by rebalancing once a year helps you stay the course, and shelter your investments from your emotional reaction to what's happening in the market.

How to Evaluate and Choose Mutual Funds

Remember, asset allocation is the most crucial factor in how your investments perform over time. But if you are a beginning investor, you have to start with a single fund in either your IRA or 401(k). Are you nervous about exposing all your money to stocks? Look for a hybrid fund that contains both stocks and bonds. If you like the idea of stocks, but want a less aggressive style, look for either a value fund, or a balanced stock fund that strikes a pleasant medium between the riskier *growth* category and the more conservative *value* style. For someone investing in a 401(k), your choice of funds is limited to the menu of investments offered by the plan. If you're an individual investor, you have more than 10,000 mutual funds to choose from. But don't panic! Fortunately, there are extremely nifty tools online called *fund screeners* that narrow down your choices in minutes. I'll discuss that a little later. First, let's look at how to evaluate mutual funds.

Performance and Management

When you are judging a mutual fund's performance, look at its *total return*. Sometimes a mutual fund pays out distributions—which may be dividends from the stocks it holds in the fund, or capital gains that result from selling a stock in the fund. Total return represents the change in the investment's value over a given period of time, assuming you reinvested any distributions back into the fund. (That's exactly what happens when you are investing for retirement—you leave the money in place for a long time, reinvesting any distributions along the way.)

Next, look at *relative performance*—how does the fund stack up against other funds of that kind, or against a particular market index in that category? For instance, if you were considering a large-cap stock fund, you would want to know where it ranks among all large-cap stock funds, as well as how it has performed compared to a large-cap benchmark, such as the S&P 500.

In addition, examine results over *different time periods*. What are the fund's returns over the past 10 years, 5 years, 3 years, and year-to-date? You want a fund that has performed consistently over 1, 3, 5, and 10 years. A fund that returns 12 percent year after year is better than one that is up 40 percent one year and down 25 percent the next.

Where can you find all this information on performance? At Morningstar.com, the indispensable guide to mutual funds. Let's assume you are trying to decide among the funds offered by your 401(k) plan. On the top of the Morningstar home page, where it says "Enter ticker, name or topic," type in the name of one of the funds offered by your 401(k), and hit enter. (Morningstar may reply with a couple different funds that sound like the name you entered, since many fund families have similar-sounding mutual funds. Just make sure to click on the one that matches the name of your fund exactly.) Morningstar will respond with a comprehensive report that describes:

- What category of fund it is, for example, Large, Growth, or Small Value
- Total assets (how much money the fund has)
- What kinds of stocks it invests in, and what its largest holdings are
- What fees and other costs come with the fund (expense ratio, front load, deferred load—explained next)
- Minimum amount you need to invest in the fund (minimums do not apply for 401(k) investors)
- The name of the fund manager and the date he or she started managing the fund. (Look for a fund manager with a long track

record; if the fund has had great returns over the past five years, you want to make sure the same manager produced those returns.)

Now take a look at the extremely helpful Morningstar rating, ranging from one to five stars. Morningstar ranks funds from worst (one star) to best (five stars) based on both performance and risk. The higher a fund's return, and the lower its risk, the more stars it receives from Morningstar. The report also features a chart showing how a $10,000 investment in the fund has performed over the past five years. It includes:

- The percentage the investment grew each year
- The average return for funds in the same category
- How the fund ranks in its category by percentage (i.e., "10" means it ranks in the top 10 percentile)
- How the fund's performance compares to an appropriate benchmark, such as the S&P 500 for large-cap funds or the Russell 2000 for small-cap funds
- How much the fund has returned year-to-date, over three years, five years, and 10 years

Next, click on "data interpreter" and you'll get a straightforward explanation of all the numbers.

Fees and Expenses

In the stock market's go-go years of the late 1990s, you almost never heard anyone talk about investment fees and expenses. That's basically because investment returns were so spectacular nobody cared about the cost of the investment. Then the market plunged. As the performance of mutual funds declined, people began to take a closer look at the fees and expenses—and realized they can quickly erode profits.

Why does a fund charge fees and expenses? Someone must be paid to manage the fund; there are costs related to marketing the fund to investors; sometimes you will be charged a sales commission when you buy or sell a fund. Sometimes the fees are fairly obvious, but some of them are sneaky—you don't discover them unless you carefully read the fund's *prospectus* (the detailed document put out by the fund that explains its investment strategy). Fortunately, Morningstar tracks fees closely; when you pull up a fund's report, just click "fees and expenses."

Table 7.2 shows an example of how fees can erode your investment. You invest $10,000 each in two different mutual funds.

Choosing Fund B would give you 18 percent more money over the 20-year period. In general, if you're comparing two similar funds, choose the one with the lowest expenses.

The most important item to look for is the fund's *expense ratio.* This represents the fund's total annual operating expenses (including management fees, distribution (12b-1) fees, and other expenses explained below) expressed as a percentage of average net assets. To figure out what the investment costs you every year, take your total investment and multiply by the expense ratio. In our example in Table 7.2, the person who invests $10,000 in Fund A will pay $150 a year, while Fund B will cost $50 a year. Morningstar recommends you pay no more than 1 percent for a stock fund, and 0.75 percent for a bond fund. According to the Securities and Exchange Commission, a mutual fund may charge the following fees:

- *A load or sales charge:* This can be a *front-end load,* charged to pay a broker upfront when you buy the fund; or you can get spanked with a *back-end load* when you sell the fund. Look for a *no-load* fund—but watch out for sneaky funds that call themselves no-load and then whack you with fees disguised under other names, such as *purchase or redemption fees.*

TABLE 7.2
Fees Erode an Investment's Value over Time

Fund A	Fund B
Annual return before expenses: 10 percent	Annual return before expenses: 10 percent
Annual operating expenses: 1.5 percent	Annual operating expenses: 0.5 percent
Value of investment in 20 years: $49,725	Value of investment in 20 years: $60,858

- *Purchase fee:* Similar to a front-end load but it is paid to the fund rather than the broker.
- *Redemption fee:* Charged when you sell or redeem shares.
- *Exchange fee:* Imposed if you transfer to a different fund within the same fund family.
- *Account fee:* Charged to maintain your account, sometimes levied if the value of your account falls below a certain dollar amount.
- *Management fees:* Paid out of the fund's assets to the investment advisor to manage the money; the fund may also pay a fund advisor or affiliates.
- *Distribution or service (12b-1) fees:* These are paid out of the fund's assets to cover the costs of marketing and selling the fund, or cover the costs of shareholder services. They include fees to pay brokers who sell the fund, advertising, printing, and mailing out prospectuses and sales material. Shareholder service fees go to cover the salaries of fund staff who respond to investor inquiries and provide investors with information.
- *Other expenses:* These are expenses not included under "Management Fees" or "Distribution or Service (12b-1) Fees." They can be any other shareholder service expenses, custodial expenses, legal and accounting expenses, transfer agent expenses, and other administrative expenses.

Fund Classes and Turnover

Finally, when you're considering the cost of your mutual fund investment, be aware that many funds have more than one class—such as Class A, B, or C. All of the classes invest in the same things, but each class may have different expenses, services, and distribution arrangements. Those factors will affect the performance. If you are choosing between Class A versus Class B shares, make sure you understand the difference between the two so you can select the appropriate class for your money. The SEC offers an online Mutual Fund Cost Calculator to help figure out the toll that fees and expenses can take on your investment over time. See www.sec.gov/investor/tools/mfcc/mfcc-int.htm.

Bottom line: Find a fund with as few fees and expenses as possible, but don't let the tail wag the dog. First find a fund that's a solid performer. A major part of that performance comes from the buying and selling of stocks in the portfolio. When a mutual fund manager buys or sells stocks it triggers tax consequences. The amount of buying and selling that goes on in a fund is called *turnover*. According to the SEC, more than 2.5 percent of the average stock fund's total return is lost each year to taxes—much higher than the amount lost to fees. If you are holding your funds in a 401(k), IRA or other tax-sheltered account, you are protected from the taxes related to high turnover—but the fund's shareholders do get hit with transaction costs related to lots of buying and selling. However, if you buy a mutual fund *outside of a tax-advantaged account*—let's say, to save for a home purchase, you will pay taxes every year on fund distributions—even if you reinvest those dividends in the fund, and don't sell any shares. In general, avoid funds where the manager is buying and selling like crazy. The Morningstar report includes a percentage that shows how much turnover a fund has each year. If a fund has turnover of 100 percent, that means, during the year, it sold all of the stocks it held and bought different ones. (If turnover is higher than 100 percent, that means it sold all of its stock during the year, bought others, and then sold some of those and bought others.) Obviously, an index fund, which buys and holds the stocks that are in a particular index, will have extremely low turnover—just one more reason to love index funds! According to Morningstar, the average turnover of managed U.S. stock funds is 130 percent. The National Association of Investors Corporation, an education group for individual investors, suggests its members look for turnover of 20 percent or less.

Fund Screeners

Let's review what we've covered in this chapter. By now you should know:

- Which retirement account is right for you
- How much risk you are comfortable taking
- How to choose an allocation strategy
- How to dollar cost average through a 401(k) or IRA
- What types of mutual funds are available

Now it's time to pick specific investments for your retirement account. Start by narrowing your parameters. If you are a 401(k) investor, get the list of funds offered by your plan. Print the Morningstar report for each fund. Join the premium membership on Morningstar. (Sometimes the site offers a two-week free offer, or you can join for a month for $12.95—well worth the cost!) Premium membership gives you access to any detailed reports Morningstar analysts may have written on these funds. Then start the process of elimination:

- Eliminate any funds that are ranked one or two stars.
- Eliminate any stock funds with an expense ratio above 1 percent.
- Eliminate any bond funds with an expense ratio above 0.75 percent.
- Eliminate any fund where the manager was not responsible for the past five year's of investment returns (i.e., the start date for the manager is less than five years ago).
- Eliminate any fund where the turnover is more than 100 percent.
- Eliminate any fund in which the percentile performance number is below 50 (those would be the funds performing in the bottom half of their category).

Of the funds that remain, make a decision about investing style:

- Choose a stock fund that is either most aggressive (growth), medium aggressive (value), or least aggressive (blend).
- Pick a fund where the returns over the last 1, 3, and 5 years have matched or outperformed the average for the category, and/or the relevant benchmark (i.e., S&P 500).

Hopefully, this process will leave you with two or three funds from which to choose. Call each fund, order the prospectus, and read it before making your decision. Then instruct your 401(k) to buy that fund, either by telephone or online, and to invest your future contributions in that fund. A final note on choosing funds in a 401(k): Your plan may allow you to invest in your company's stock. If you choose to do so, don't make it more than 5 percent of your total investment. (So if you invest $12,000 during the year, only $600 should be in company stock.)

Now what if the worst happens, and the process outlined above eliminates all the funds in your 401(k) plan? That's a possibility. Not every company offers an excellent plan. Go back through the process again step by step, narrowing your choices down to the funds that meet as many of the previous criteria as possible (i.e., look for the highest star ranking, the best returns, the best percentile performance number, the lowest possible expense ratio and turnover, the manager with the longest tenure). If your 401(k) plan offers five funds, and they are all ranked one star by Morningstar, march into human resources and ask why the company is offering such a mediocre retirement plan. It may be because the financial services representative who sold the plan to your company golfs with your CEO. You deserve better. Get out your Norma Rae blue jeans and enlist your coworkers in a crusade demanding a superior retirement plan!

Now let's look at what to do if you are choosing a fund for an IRA. Go to Morningstar.com and find the "Fund Selector" at http://screen.morningstar.com/FundSelector.html. This tool allows you to input certain criteria to narrow down your choices from the thousands of mutual funds available:

- Decide what type of fund you would like (stock or bond, domestic—meaning U.S.—or international).
- Decide what category of fund you would like by size and investing style (large-, mid-, or small-cap, growth, value, or blend).
- Choose manager tenure (meaning how long you want the manager to have been working at the fund; choose 5 years or more).
- Choose minimum initial purchase based on how much money you have to invest.
- Choose no-load funds only.
- Choose expense ratio equal to or less than 1 percent.
- For ratings and risk, choose funds with 3, 4, and 5 stars.
- The next five questions relate to the kind of return you would like from the fund; choose category average for all five.
- Choose turnover of less than or equal to 50 percent.
- For net assets and market cap enter "any."

Now hit "show results." Morningstar will respond with funds that fit your criteria. Get any detailed Morningstar reports on these funds by joining the premium membership (see above). Call each fund and order the prospectus; read it, make your decision, and then call the fund company (or go to its online web site) and get the forms to open an individual retirement account and purchase that fund. Never pay a broker a commission to open a fund for you. (Review the section on IRAs versus Roth IRAs to pick the right vehicle for your circumstances.)

Monitoring Performance

Once you have chosen the funds for your retirement plan, save all of the Morningstar reports you printed on your top choices in a folder labeled "401(k) Investment Research Conducted by the Savviest Investor I Know." Set up separate folders labeled with the name of each fund you ultimately chose. Then read and file the quarterly statements sent by your fund. When you receive your 12-month statement at the end of the year; keep this one (forever) for your files, and shred the four quarterly statements. Don't panic if you see a fund decline in value one quarter. You're in this for the long haul. However, if you see your fund decline over six consecutive quarters (that's 18 months), you may want to return to your original research folder, look at some other funds you liked, and see how they have performed over the last 18 months by visiting Morningstar. It may be prudent to make a switch.

Automatic Pilot

Earlier in the chapter, I spoke about the importance of diversification—allocating retirement money among different kinds of stock and bond funds, and rebalancing each year. Some fund companies realized that this is a difficult challenge for many of us. So they have introduced a different kind of mutual fund that does the allocation for you, rebalances, and responds to your needs over time. Think of these as a *fund of funds*—a short-cut to diversification. There are life-cycle funds, that allocate your money among both stock and bond funds; and target strategy funds that take your age into consideration, and then gradually change the investment strategy from aggressive to more conservative as you get closer to retirement, the way you would if you were managing your own portfolio. If you really don't have any time or interest in managing a portfolio for retirement, check out Vanguard Group's "LifeStrategy funds," the "SimpleStart IRA" from Fidelity Investments, or the "SmartChoice IRA" from T. Rowe Price Group.

Last Word: How Much Will You Need to Retire?

We've come full circle. Once you are invested in a 401(k) or IRA, it's time to think about the ultimate goal: How much money do you need to retire? Experts say you'll need at least 70 percent of your preretirement income to maintain your lifestyle, although you may want 90 percent or more if you plan to travel, dine out, and pay for other kinds of fun in retirement. The American Savings Education Council offers a Ballpark Worksheet to help you estimate how much money you will need in retirement to maintain your current lifestyle. It also helps you calculate how much you need to save each year between now and retirement to achieve 70 to 90 percent of your current income. You can find it at www.asec.org/ballpark/ballpark.htm. One caveat: The calculator does not include the equity you have in your home—which in many cases is an investor's biggest asset. The calculator presumes you are not going to sell your home and downsize to a smaller, less expensive dwelling when you retire, although this is fairly common practice. And keep in mind—this calculator only offers a rough ballpark figure. Once you have laid your investing foundation and are building savings month after month, it's wise to meet with a financial planner who can hammer out the details of how to achieve all of your savings goals.[13]

✔ Retirement Planning Checklist

1. Decide which retirement account is right for you (check one):
   _____ 401(k)
   _____ Traditional IRA
   _____ Roth IRA
   _____ Simplified Employee Pension Plan (SEP-IRA)
   _____ Self-Employed 401(k)
   _____ SIMPLE IRA

2. Take a risk-tolerance questionnaire to help decide your risk appetite:

www.kiplinger.com/tools/riskfind.html

www.fortune.com/fortune/quizzes/investing/riskquiz.html

www.rce.rutgers.edu/money/riskquiz

3. Choose an allocation strategy based on your appetite for risk.

_____ % in stock mutual funds

_____ % in bond/fixed-income funds

4. Choose specific types of stock and bond mutual funds within your allocation strategy. (These choices are traditional core holdings; review the chapter for other options.)

Stock fund allocation:

_____ % in a large-cap stock fund (choose an investment style: growth, value, or blend; also choose a management style: index fund or an actively managed)

_____ % in a small-cap stock fund (growth, value, or blend; index or actively managed)

_____ % in a large-cap foreign stock fund focused on developed, industrialized countries (growth, value, or blend; index or actively managed)

Bond fund allocation:

_____ % high-quality corporate bond fund

_____ % high-quality government bond fund

(Or you may choose one fund that invests in both kinds of bonds.)

If you want to start saving for retirement with a single fund, consider a life-cycle fund from such companies such as:

_____ Fidelity Investments

www.fidelity.com (800) 343-3548

_____ T. Rowe Price Group

www.troweprice.com (800) 225-5132

_____ Vanguard Group

www.vanguard.com (877) 662-7447

5. Evaluate each of the investments offered by your 401(k) plan. Go to Morningstar.com, identify the style of each fund, and choose the ones that fit your allocation strategy. Follow the steps outlined in the chapter to find the best funds. Save all your research in a folder. Sign up for your 401(k) through human resources. Allocate the maximum percentage of your salary possible—at least enough to get any match.

6. Choose mutual funds for your IRA. Narrow down your options at Morningstar.com, following the steps outlined in the chapter. Call the fund company, open the account, and set up an automated investment plan—so that the fund company transfers money from your checking account to your retirement savings every month. Not sure how much you can afford to set aside? Start with a nominal figure, such as $25 or $50. You can easily boost the amount later.

7. Keep one folder for each investment. File your monthly/quarterly statements. When you receive your 12-month statement, file it, and shred the monthly/quarterlies for that year.

8. Ballpark the amount of money you need to retire at www.asec .org/ballpark/ballpark.htm.

9. Rebalance once a year so your funds reflect your original allocation.

10. Celebrate! You are now a literate investor. You have the tools to achieve a successful retirement. Get out your calendar, and give yourself a deadline for accomplishing each of the steps on the checklist.

If you made it through this chapter, you've discovered that investing is not about magic or luck—in the same way that staying healthy is not about magic or luck. It's acquiring some basic knowledge, developing a strategy, taking action as early as possible, and sticking with your plan. You may not enjoy learning the difference between a stock and a bond or choosing from a menu of mutual funds—just as you may loathe counting calories or working out at the gym. But in both cases, that's what it takes to achieve your goal: knowledge and discipline. Chapter 8 is a cautionary tale about what happens when we throw knowledge and discipline to the wind, and rely on magic, luck, and emotion to make investment decisions.

8

FEAR, GREED, AND MONEY MISTAKES

It is a Wednesday night at 9 P.M. A woman I have spoken to only once, by phone, has invited me to listen to a secret conference call. I dial the number and enter the access code, which changes every week for security. A series of chimes are heard on the line as more women join the clandestine event. I feel a bit like an atheist hiding in the back row of a Gospel tent revival.

There is idle chatter as the first callers wait for latecomers to dial in. They discuss moving the conference call to a different hour the following week, and I realize the participants are spread across the country, because it appears that at least three different time zones are involved.

Finally, the woman who invited me joins the call, and asks a group member I'll call "Mary" to bring the meeting to order with a prayer.

"Conventional wisdom says that to get what we want, we must solve problems and conquer our adversaries," Mary intones. "In the circle, there are no adversaries, only energies that must be handled differently. The circle allows us to experience the state of being in which the solution is lived . . . when you are within the circle, obstacles present themselves as gifts to show you the way to the new reality."

"Wow," someone on the line responds. "That's beautiful. It really makes you realize that if you just shift your perspective and change old ways of thinking, anything truly is available to you."

What these women hope will be available to them is money—a lot of money. Each member of the circle sent $5,000 to a stranger, in hopes of reaping $40,000—an 800 percent return on investment. They are part of an underground women's movement that has proliferated across the United States in the past two decades. "It's not about making money, it's about pooling resources to help each other realize our dreams," my host says.

But according to federal and state authorities, those dreams of abundance will likely become the nightmare of financial loss, because the group is structured like an old-fashioned pyramid scheme. You can't move up and cash in unless you recruit other women to join. At a certain point, further recruiting becomes mathematically impossible. Moreover, the circles violate numerous federal and state laws.

These groups are called the *Dinner Party, Gifting Circles,* and *Women Helping Women,* among other names. "Regardless of the name, they are a pyramid in form," says Mary Simmons, the deputy district attorney who prosecuted a *Women Helping Women* group in Sacramento, California. In that case, police estimate 10,000 women lost a total of $12 million. "It's not like everybody has an equal chance to win; 90 percent basically will lose. The problem is the social aspect—the 90 percent who lose will be best friends and family members. That's the real evil—people suck in friends and family."

When I stumbled on the *Dinner Party,* I knew I had to include the story in the book, because it epitomizes what happens when we let emotions guide investment decisions. As we discussed in Chapter 3, money behaviors come from a specific belief system. In the case of the *Dinner Party,* the belief goes something like this: *By overcoming our fears of the unknown, pooling resources, and trusting in a supportive community of other people, we can achieve financial abundance.* This is not necessarily a bad belief system, and certainly not a radical new idea. It's what my own ancestors did. It took a dramatic change in thinking to get on a boat in Ireland and sail off to an unfamiliar country, not knowing where they would work or live. Instead of an "every man for himself" mentality, they stuck together; found each other jobs; built each other's homes. Certainly overcoming obstacles and relying on community showed them the way to a "new reality."

But that's not how the *Dinner Party* works. Imagine an inverted triangle with four rows, and circles lining each row. The widest edge of the triangle has eight circles—these are the "appetizers"; below it are four circles—known as "soup and salad"; then two circles, the "entrées"; then one circle—"dessert"—at the tip of the triangle. The rows represent the four levels of the *Dinner Party* process. When a new woman joins as an appetizer, she "gifts" the woman in dessert. Once eight new women have sent in their $5,000, the woman in dessert leaves, and the table splits into two. The two women who were in entrée position now move up to the dessert position at the tip of each new triangle. The four people in soup and salad move into the two entrée spots; the eight appetizers move into the four soup-and-salad positions. Each table now has eight empty seats to fill at the top of the inverted triangle. The four ladies in soup and salad must each draft two new "appetizers" to join.

The Pitch and the Math

That's what the conference call I joined is mostly about—recruiting. I hear the music of normal lives—barking dogs, the sweet sing-song of a toddler's voice—seeping into the telephones of people on the call. The host tells us we can press "6" to mute ourselves. I mute myself. I have agreed not to tape the call, so my fingers are click-clacking loudly as they fly over the keys of my laptop. The host proceeds to lay out the circle as I have described it, along with the "R&R"—the roles and responsibilities of each person in the group. This information is repeated in every call for invited guests, who listen in silence. "When you are invited to join the circle, you are thought to be of great integrity," says the woman in dessert, who has been involved in this process for 18 months. "We want women to join us who are really of a like mind. They are interested in a paradigm shift in their lives, where they are looking for a no-fear relationship with other women, and a relationship with abundance. That means we are support for each other, empowerment for each other, we work together as community."

"We are here to pool our resources not only monetarily, but spiritually and emotionally," she continues. "When it feels right, you send a $5,000 gift to the woman in dessert. It's a trust, it's a knowing. And when you send your gift, it's to say that you believe in this process, you trust in this process—that it's going to work, if I keep my agreements and everyone else keeps their agreements."

This is a seductive pitch, especially to a woman who may be unemployed, strapped for cash, mired in debt, or bewildered by the mechanics of money. But frankly, it's persuasive even to me, a personal finance columnist who deals mostly in rational concepts. Understanding how compound interest works does not make you immune from greed. Just by joining a sisterhood and "changing my old ways of thinking," I can turn $5,000 into $40,000 in a fraction of the time traditional investing requires. (Even with an optimistic 10 percent return on investment, it would take *21 years* to turn $5,000 into $40,000—and that's before taxes.) I get momentarily warm and fuzzy at the prospect of helping my soul sisters and trading in my 1995 minivan for a Lexus.

But then I look at the math—something you must do when anyone asks you to part with your hard-earned money. I have just as much math anxiety as the average person, but you only need grade school addition and multiplication to figure this out. I start adding up the cold, hard numbers this insatiable circle demands. Let's presume you and I, and six of our friends, join an existing circle of women in the appetizer position. In order for us to move into dessert, the table has to split four times. Remember those high school science videos of cells dividing? Same principle here: 1 into 2; 2 into 4; 4 into 8; 8 into 16. So at the fourth level, 16 tables are involved. For me to cash out, 32 women must join my table (eight women for each time it splits).

But who knows if you and I will both end up on a juicy table, with women dying to join? It's fairer to consider what it would take for *all eight members of our group,* who joined together, to cash out. Now the figure is 256 (32 × 8). So in order for all eight of us to move to the dessert position and cash in, 256 women must contribute $5,000 each or $1,280,000. Still with me?

As the circle goes on, you obviously need more and more people to join. Every time it divides, the number of tables requiring eight new recruits multiplies exponentially. Now let's look at what happens if the group goes on. What would it take for women who were recruited on the sixteenth cycle to cash out? That would require 8,338,607 women, and a total of $41.2 billion (roughly the entire budget for the Department of Homeland Security in 2005). See Table 8.1 for some sobering facts.

Circle participants argue that women who reach dessert join the party again and again. My host says she knows someone who has been through the *Dinner Party* four times. "You have to be really committed to the process," she says. "And with the commitment and trust and community that happens, the circle keeps going and going and going." The problem is, even with commitment, trust, and repeat customers, you'll eventually run out of participants, because there's no getting around that 1 to 32 ratio required for one woman to cash out.

Circle of Fear

"This is not like playing the lottery, where you have the same chance as others—only the first 10 percent of participants will win," says Robert FitzPatrick, coauthor of *False Profits: Seeking Financial and Spiritual Deliverance in Multi-Level Marketing and Pyramid Schemes.*[1] "If you come in later, you've just bought *yesterday's* lottery ticket." More than 500,000 women have lost money in gifting circles over the past 15 years, by FitzPatrick's count.

The Federal Trade Commission (FTC) agrees that roughly 90 percent of the people involved in pyramids will never get a dime back. "We've seen (circles) all over the country," says Jim Kohm, chief of staff for the FTC's bureau of consumer protection. "Many have a cult-like aspect to

TABLE 8.1
Dinner Party Progression

Appetizers	00000000		
Entrees	0000		
Soup and Salad	00		
Dessert	0		

Stage (in Cycles)	Get $	Get $ (total)	Recruited	Total Involved	Losers	% Losers
Founding	1	1	14	15	14	93.3
1st	2	3	16	31	28	90.3
2nd	4	7	32	63	56	88.9
3rd	8	15	64	127	112	88.2
4th	16	31	128	255	224	87.8
5th	32	63	256	511	448	87.7
6th	64	127	512	1023	896	87.5
7th	128	255	1,024	2,047	1,792	87.5
8th	256	511	2,048	4,095	3,584	87.5
9th	512	1,023	4,096	8,191	7,168	87.5
10th	1,024	2,047	8,192	16,383	14,336	87.5
11th	2,048	4,095	16,384	32,767	28,672	87.5
12th	4,096	8,191	21,768	65,535	57,344	87.5
13th	8,192	16,383	65,536	131,071	114,688	87.5
14th	16,384	32,767	131,072	262,143	229,376	87.5
15th	32,768	65,535	262,144	524,287	458,752	87.5
16th	65,536	13,1071	524,288	104,8575	917,504	87.5
17th	131,072	262,143	1,048,576	2,097,151	1,835,008	87.5
18th	262,144	524,287	2,097,152	4,194,303	3,670,016	87.5
19th	524,288	1,048,575	4,194,304	8,388,607	7,340,032	87.5

- Scheme begins with one person assembling 2 below and 4 below them. They recruit 8 paying members. 1 gets money, 14 have not gotten money, total of 15 are involved. One "winner" is 93.3% of total.
- Group then splits and each of the two groups now each recruits 8 more people or 16 total. 2 more people have now been paid, a total of 3.
  31 people are now involved.
  28 have not yet gotten any money, or a total of 90.3%.
- After this, the scheme progresses and soon settles out at a pattern of 87.5% of all who have ever participated being in losing positions. That percentage will remain for as long as the scheme continues. The longer it runs, the percent remains constant but the total number of losers grows geometrically. At just the 20th level, there will be over 7 million losers. With each investing $5,000, that would be $35 billion in losses.

Source: Courtesy of pyramidschemealert.org.

them—there's a strong undercurrent that if you fail, it's your personal failure, and not the failure of the system. I think a lot of people really don't understand the math." It's not that the women who join gifting circles are the dimmest bulbs on the tree. My host tells me her group has included an accountant, a state education administrator, and a law student. Leaders of the Sacramento circle included a college English professor, a former corporate personnel executive, and the co-owner of a Montessori school. So why do they do it?

FitzPatrick, who runs a web site called pyramidschemealert.org, wrote his book after a friend recruited him to join the *Airplane Game* in South Florida in the 1980s. He speculates that gifting circles are rebounding in popularity because of real fears Americans face. "We have a deep-seated insecurity about our ability not to fall under the wheels of this economy," he says. "You lose your job, or your husband loses his job, then you lose your health insurance, then you lose your home. Then you project ahead: What about old age? These things are on people's minds, and somebody walks into your house and says, 'I can get you $40,000 in a matter of weeks.' And it's not some seedy con artist—it's your next-door neighbor, your sister-in-law, someone from the church who's just like you."

Even the leader of the circle who invited me on the conference call expresses these fears. "I have no retirement fund, period, no savings account, nothing to my name, and that's kind of scary to me," she says. "When I'm 70 will I be able to pay for groceries? So I want to make it really work for me and that's what the circle is all about—helping women." But inviting women into a process where 90 percent will lose their money doesn't strike me as particularly helpful. My host genuinely believes the circle will have no end, though, so she doesn't see any problem in recruiting others to join. "Circles go through lulls and people get discouraged and want to drop out," she says. "There are no guarantees. People come on thinking that they'll get money-back guarantees. It doesn't work like that, you have to be really committed to the process. It's like the stock market—you never know. That's nothing more than gambling, isn't it?"

Well, no. Investing in the market is about something else entirely. When you choose equity investments using research instead of emotion, it's about an exchange of value: You put your money into a business that has a specific plan to grow, and the business rewards you, the share-holder, with a portion of the profits. True, there are no guarantees. The company may not achieve its plan, and the stock will decline in value. But there are federal laws regulating the sale of securities; a company has a legal obligation to report their results in compliance with certain accounting principles; and U.S. financial markets are the most transparent in the world. The Internet has made more research about companies available today than in the history of investing.

But there is one aspect of the stock market that's exactly like a pyramid scheme. It's called fraud. Enron, Worldcom, Rite Aid, Adelphia, HealthSouth—companies where executives deceived investors and employees, resulting in billions of dollars in devastating losses. As Fitz-Patrick notes, you can do your homework, but "what if the managers of the company are lying, the financial statements aren't true, the auditor is lying, and the analyst who told you the company has great promise is lying? Where is transparency in that?" And who can forget the dot-com boom and bust of the late 1990s? Start-up firms were financed, promoted, and sold by venture capitalists to investors, who bought them in a frenzied mania based on the promise of the Internet and a "New Economy." Investors ignored simple truths like: If you sell dog food online, your shipping costs will probably eat up any profit you make on the sale. But fear and greed have a funny way of twisting reality, and can prompt spectacularly poor investment choices. I learned this valuable lesson when I bought a technology stock at $35 a share and watched it rocket to more than $160 a share five months later. I had faith it would become the next Microsoft, despite the fact that it didn't actually make a product or sell a service. (It was a holding company for firms that did those things.) The investment wasn't tied to a specific value or goal, and I had no strategy regarding when to sell. I just kept greedily wishing it would zoom higher, and when it began to decline, anxiously hoping it would stop falling. I rode it down to about $2 before I finally let go. "People weren't buying stocks based on their ability to deliver value," FitzPatrick remarks. "They were basing the investment on capital gains—and capital gains can be a manipulated by-product of inducing other investors to buy the stock. That's what a pyramid scheme is: Where did my profit come from? It came from the last guys in."

The dot-com spectacle and the scandals on Wall Street were perversions of the stock market that shook the confidence of millions of investors. It's not surprising some women shy away from the market. But fraud isn't the market's operating principle, and there are thousands of managers, auditors, analysts, brokers, and federal regulators who are honest people. Maybe *Dinner Party* participants figure that in a pyramid scheme, you only have to rely on the actions of 32 people to make your money. Plus you have a 10 percent chance of pocketing a gigantic profit if you get in at the right time. But I doubt circle participants analyze things this way. In many cases, they're just desperate for money.

Money Therapy?

"It's very unconventional," admits Oola, a participant in the *Dinner Party.* "People really freak out about it. It makes everybody say, 'What are you doing, are you crazy?'" Oola was more than $30,000 in debt when she joined the circle, hoping to move into the dessert position, pay off her debt, and get a clean start financially. For years, Oola says she was a "gypsy," traveling the world, taking work where she could find it. Her parents divorced when she was a child; she and her mother lived on a shoestring while her father's family enjoyed substantial wealth. "I was always bombarded with the philosophy that money is not there to enjoy or share—it's to save. Subconsciously it made me do the opposite—I blew it whenever I got it," Oola explains. "Money would come my way, I'd use it, and it would come again, and I'd use it—without realizing that way of life isn't very sustainable. It's gotten me places I wanted to go, and I had the time of my life. But in one circumstance on my travels, I was so poor, I lived on the beach and used food stamps."

"The circle has allowed me to open up and talk about money," she says. "I am really taking the position that I created this debt and need to take responsibility for it. I think living within one's means is a healthy way of living. I've learned so many tools, I can really be different about money now." Oola cut up her credit cards, closed her accounts, and worked with a friend who helped her reduce the interest rate on her debt.

Then something remarkable happened. Oola decided to ask some affluent relatives for a low-interest loan to further reduce the cost of her debt. To her shock, they came forth with a $20,000 gift—no strings attached. "A miracle happened," Oola says. "It's a whole new lease on life." Without the support of her circle sisters, Oola says, she would not have had the courage to ask for help, and she believes her relatives wouldn't have recognized her newfound sense of accountability. "The circle brings up so much fear and anxiety; all your issues around finances and abundance come up, but in a safe and supportive environment," she explains. "It's really a break in consciousness. Money can really mess with your self-concept. Is it okay to have money in my life? The concept of the circle, and working with like-minded women, helps to explore and redefine what abundance is in our lives, and to learn that we're all worthy of having it, and it is possible to have it." The leader of Oola's circle insists that Oola's lucky break with her relatives is an example of the kind of "synchronicity" that occurs all the time for circle participants.

So maybe the *Dinner Party* isn't investing at all. Maybe it's $5,000 worth of therapy. Although Oola may never see her money again, it beats playing the slots in Vegas. In this particular circle, at least, women get a sympathetic ear, make friends, and share some groupthink on abundance and overcoming their fears of the unknown. I asked psychotherapist and author Olivia Mellan, who has done money counseling since 1982, about the phenomenon of gifting circles. "It's wishful thinking for magical abundance, for safety and nurturing on all levels," Mellan says. "Who doesn't want the perfect mother? It's a wish for a benevolent parent to a degree, who will make the world safe and make things easy, someone you can trust. And they're getting that emotionally, somewhat, from the group. They just don't get money in most cases." Weigh those benefits against a year's worth of weekly sessions on the couch with a decent New York psychotherapist.

On the other hand, a good New York shrink won't demand you recruit two other patients for him (who may never actually get their therapy). This is where the Dinner Party concept is most troubling: in its ideology. As my host explains, after she wrapped up her $5,000 in a gift box and sent it off to the woman in dessert, she languished on the bottom rung, the appetizer position, for nine months. "A lot of women were so stuck in some of their patterns, it was hard for them to bring on women," she explains. "They would say, 'All the women I'm talking to have seen this on

The Oprah Winfrey Show and they think I'm loony and want nothing to do with this.' Something happened and Oprah gave it a bad name because of one incident. I said to one of the women, 'I think I'm seeing a pattern of being a victim'—and I laid it out the way I saw it. And she said, 'You are absolutely right, this has been a pattern all of my life—relating to me in my relationships with everything—I'm going to shift this.' And the minute she shifted we started drawing in a different type of woman—things happened with a couple different women and suddenly we split." Nine months later, the circle had split two more times, putting my host in dessert.

In other words, the circle offers the opportunity to break free of being a victim—by victimizing other people. Just invite two other women to join and overcome your fear and paradigm of scarcity at their expense. (Easy to do for true believers who ignore the math.) Of course, it sounds so much prettier when it's put in terms of "women's empowerment." Gifting scams always speak the language of the people they are targeting, FitzPatrick says. "In blue-collar communities, it's about paying off debt; in Christian programs it's about giving and receiving," he explains. "In African-American communities it has been about making up for past discrimination and unfair losses." FitzPatrick was attracted to the *Airplane Game* by a New Age philosophy very similar to the circle I encountered. "The ideology said 'anything is possible if you visualize it, you can make it happen, perception is reality, the universe is benevolent and provides for everybody,'" he recalls. "Essentially what seemed like positive values were employed in running a truly predatory scam that broke up communities, broke the law, and stole money."[2]

The Oprah Winfrey Show featured the pyramid scheme *Women Helping Women* in a program about scams in 2003. Viewers flooded the web site's message boards after the show, leaving more than 400 posts. Some of them defended gifting circles, and complained that Oprah failed to feature "legitimate" groups. One post suggested that because there are six billion people on the planet, the circles can go on forever. (This somewhat ignores the fact that more than a billion of these circle members will have to come from China, where the average annual income is less than $400.) Others said they had joined their circles strictly to help other women, with no expectation of return.

It's Just a Matter of Greed

If so many women lose money in gifting circles, why haven't we heard more about it? "It costs a lot of money to prosecute these cases," says Sacramento Deputy Attorney General Mary Simmons. "Jurisdictions don't have the time or attention to look into it, they're hoping it will blow over. But we kept getting more and more complaints from people who were losing. Most jurisdictions don't have the evidence because they don't do the undercover investigation and search warrants. That's why we had successful prosecutions."[3]

Authorities originally identified 100 people to prosecute for promoting the scheme before zeroing in on 12 ringleaders, all women. Prosecutors say the organizers skimmed money off the top and manipulated tables so friends vaulted quickly to the "birthday girl" position. One woman even put her husband on a table under the pseudonym "Paulette." In addition, women were allowed to split an appetizer position eight ways and join for just $625. That meant instead of eight women at the bottom of the pyramid, there were 64. "You got market saturation fairly quickly," says Simmons. "They solicited everybody. It began going up and down the state. A lot of people who got into it would get cash advances on Visa cards, putting in money they couldn't afford to lose." *Women Helping Women* even made its own recruiting video, showing groups of women meeting in someone's home or a hotel conference room, sharing drinks and hors d'oeuvres. Big bills were flashed around, and women who made it to the top of the pyramid offered tearful testimony about how their "gifts" would change their lives. "It showed ordinary women getting $50,000 in cash," Simmons says. "It was pretty compelling." The video became state's evidence against the group's organizers.

When a circle falls apart, women tend not to contact authorities. Few witnesses came forward to testify against the organizers of the Sacramento ring. In fact, crowds of supporters broke in spontaneous cheers when the defendants arrived at an arraignment hearing. "The other people who showed up were friends of the defendants who had made quite a bit of money," says Simmons. "It becomes a cult. It was a fascinating experience for me—in 25 years in law enforcement I had never been involved in anything like it. You could not convince these people they had done anything wrong. They made a lot of money off it, and socially, got a lot of respect from other women."

In March 2004, Christine Suzanne Ney, one of the group's ring-leaders was convicted of a felony—"operating an endless chain scheme." In September she was sentenced to five years probation, 540 hours of community service (or 90 days in jail), and had to make formal restitution. Prosecutors said she received $53,000 and was awaiting another $180,000 when law enforcement closed in on the scam. Eleven other leaders were convicted earlier by either guilty or no-contest pleas. Their sentences included fines and community service. While Ney had claimed the program had a charitable aspect to it, evidence showed of the $53,000 she received, just $50 was donated to charity.

In several states, women have gone to court and the legislature to try to get their gifting groups legalized under the constitutional right to assembly. "When I was in it and people got arrested, those of us that knew them ran like rats," FitzPatrick says. "Total paranoia paralyzed everybody. We were so ashamed that we could be associated with a scam. Now you hear about gifting circles demanding to be allowed to do this, saying if people want to come in and take their chance, government should have no part in it."

Participation in a gifting circle used to be a misdemeanor in California, but it became such a problem the state upgraded it to a felony. "It's all around the country, and the number of losers keeps growing and growing and growing," says Simmons. "We hope that these sentences will be a deterrent. Although these women made $40,000 to $50,000 personally, they have to make restitution and pay $30,000 to $40,000 in attorney's fees, and now they have a felony conviction. They didn't believe anything was going to happen to them, even up to the time of sentencing. They entered their pleas very reluctantly. They still don't admit they have done anything wrong, and you know, I can't make them believe that. It's just a matter of greed. And it's a greed that you justify—it's the spin, the belief this is a private charitable thing and we're all helping each other. Well, you're not helping each other. You're taking other people's money."

The biggest stumbling blocks to women's financial success are fear of failure, and fear of the unknown, according to a study by the National Center for Women and Retirement Research.[4] Gifting circles exploit these fears. If you're looking to overcome your money anxieties, form your own support group—one that has a genuine sense of responsibility for its members. Start a book club that focuses on personal finance books like this one. Talk about the issues—emotional, psychological, informational—that are blocking you from taking control of your financial life and achieving peace around money. Talk about work, relationships, and health issues related to money. Or join an investment club. Meanwhile, if you want to offer financial support to needy women, give to a local food pantry (you can find one at www.secondharvest.org). Ask a local church, synagogue, mosque, or other charitable group how you can help the neediest women in your community. Visit www.guidestar.com and choose among one of the hundreds of worthy nonprofits listed there. Exchange your talents and ideas, energy and friendship. Don't exchange your money.

In Chapter 1, when I suggested you put your money where your heart is, I meant to use your emotions to help identify values and priorities. Don't rely on your feelings to pick an investment. Identify your values, set goals based on them and devise a financial strategy to achieve them, using the principles and tools outlined in Chapter 7. Then just stick with your plan. Otherwise, your heart may urge you to buy a stock based on a hot tip; sell your holdings in a panic when the market declines; buy investments you don't understand from a crooked broker who showers you with personal attention—or join a pyramid scheme.

9

MONEY MILESTONES

Rhonda J., 52, is the director of human resources for a Wall Street investment firm. She earns $350,000 a year. But when she orders take-out from her local Chinese restaurant, she always washes out and saves the plastic containers. "One night my friend said, 'Don't you think you have enough?' And she opened the Tupperware drawer and there were 50 of them in there," she says. "Some habits are hard to kill."

Rhonda grew up with two younger siblings in a blue-collar family in New Jersey. "My mother always saved and planned and lived frugally; she washed aluminum foil and reused it," Rhonda says. "One of my most vivid memories is going shopping for food with a $25 budget and filling up the shopping cart. Money is security. I feel that way because I grew up without it."

Rhonda excelled in school, and one of her teachers urged her to apply to a private East Coast college. But the scholarship offer wasn't adequate, so she went to a state school where she majored in sociology and psychology. A mentor encouraged her to go to graduate school, and she received two master's degrees from an Ivy League university. She worked in career counseling on college campuses before Wall Street's fast-paced environment swept her off her feet. "I went there to be a salesperson, but people are my product," she says.

Rhonda fell in love with her college sweetheart and got married at 24. At first, her husband worked in the district attorney's office as a prosecutor, then moved into private practice. "He was the youngest in a very successful family," she explains. "His brother is a multimillionaire, his cousins are multimillionaires. Money was a way they kept score. The way you presented yourself in life was important—you always had to look good. I was the first non-Italian, non-Catholic for anyone in his family to have married. It's not like he married a doctor's or lawyer's daughter—he married below his station in life. I rose to become his equal professionally and financially. He saw me as more successful than he was."

Over nine years, they had three children. "Early on he'd say, 'I'm getting a big check, let's go to Hawaii for vacation.' And I would say, 'Don't you have to put 50 percent away for taxes?' And he would say, 'Keep out of my business,'" Rhonda recalls. "He was a lawyer, I was a blue-collar kid, but I kind of knew that you had to put some away for taxes. That $10,000 fee is not $10,000; it's $5,000 in real money, but he never got that." When their oldest daughter was in middle school, they purchased a larger home. "We bought the house in February—which doubled the mortgage; but I paid the mortgage and I knew our income was at a point where that would be okay," she recalls. "I said, 'If you can support our other expenses we can do this.'" The following October, on Rhonda's birthday, her husband bought her a Mercedes; for Christmas, a Rolex watch. "When I got all these gifts, I thought that was weird because we had just moved into our house in April," she says.

A few months later, her husband dropped a financial bombshell: He owed the government $36,000 in back taxes. "I found out he borrowed from his brother, the year before from his mother, and before that from his cousin," she says. "Then he was so reckless with his spending on gifts. I had a hysterical meltdown, because I couldn't figure out how this could happen. We were smart, we had great educations, we were dual career. I grew up with these lessons—'you save money to buy a car,' 'you don't get into debt'—and this was humiliating and embarrassing, because we were smarter than this."

Rhonda says her husband suggested the marriage would improve if she quit her job and became a stay-at-home mom. "I said, 'I don't think that's an option right now. We owe the government $36,000; we need my income just to survive,'" she recalls. They started marriage counseling, but he quit. The marriage fell apart.

Money can't make a relationship, but it can surely break it. "Money is symbolically loaded for most people," says Olivia Mellan, a psychotherapist and author who has specialized in money therapy for two decades. "It represents love, power, security, control, happiness, self-worth. Couples tend to polarize around everything. They get in opposition modes and attack each other for their differences." [1]

For Rhonda, money meant security, control. For her husband, money was linked to prestige and self-worth. "By buying me all these things, he was showing other people what a good provider he was," she says. "That wasn't my value set but it was important to him." Their money beliefs created an intense power struggle: Working helped Rhonda feel secure; her financial success caused her husband to feel insecure. Spending made her husband feel worthy; it made Rhonda anxious. When the crisis of back taxes brought the issue to a head, she wanted him to control his spending—a significant part of his self-worth and prestige. He responded by asking her to sacrifice her job—a crucial source of her security and competence. In their earning-spending tug of war, the fight for survival had everything, and nothing, to do with money.

In this chapter, we examine some "money milestones": marriage, changing jobs, buying real estate, and having children. This chapter helps simplify financial decisions by breaking them down by major life transitions. Each milestone comes with key practical and emotional issues to navigate, to ensure money happiness through the transition. Each milestone also requires specific documents that should be put in a safe deposit box or other secure location.

Money and Relationships

Like her mother before her, Rhonda's oldest daughter works on Wall Street. "She knows she always wants to work so she can have her own

money, because she doesn't want to ask her husband for money,"
Rhonda says. "It's the quality of life she wants to lead. She also says, 'I
have to marry someone very successful.' I never thought in those terms
at age 21—I was looking to fall in love. I didn't even think about having an economic stake at that stage. Maybe it's because she's experienced all of this."

What do you expect from your partner, financially speaking? It's a
question we don't often ask. It seems crass. You didn't marry for money,
after all. But honestly confronting that very question can rid us of false
expectations and assumptions that lead to marital trouble. Because
money carries so much symbolic meaning, if we avoid talking about
money, we also fail to address powerful issues that can sink a relationship.

Money also creates marital conflict because opposite money styles attract, says Mellan: "I see a lot of couples where the men are spenders and
the women hoarders. If they don't attract, then they create each other. If
you have two money worriers, one person will become an avoider to get
away from the worry. If you have two hoarders, they'll fight each other
to see who can become the superhoarder—and the other will learn to
spend by comparison."

Mellan advises couples to find a low-stress time to discuss money.
Don't have the conversation while you're paying bills or doing taxes.
"Talk about what money was like in your family of origin, what money
messages you might have gotten from that, and how it might have affected you up to today," she says. "Don't interrupt; really listen to each
other. Then talk about your secret envies and appreciation of your partner's style. A hoarder will admire a spender's generosity and ability to
give, but they don't say that because they are afraid the partner will
spend more. Then share your fears and hopes and dreams—and share
what scares you about the other person's style. Do it in a way that's not
attacking; talk about your own feelings." Separately create lists of your
short-, medium-, and long-term goals, then come together to harmo-
nize both lists, she advises. And try on your partner's money style, at
least once a week, writing down how you feel about playing that role.

Huntley S. met her husband in college. She was raised in an upscale
suburb, riding horses, playing tennis, and vacationing in Nantucket.
He grew up the only child in a blue-collar family, the first to go to college. He is cautious with money; she's a free spender. "We were both

raised with similar morals and values but both had very different lifestyles," she explains. "He wouldn't buy a shirt until it was on sale, and when it would go on sale, it wasn't available in his size anymore. I would say, 'Just buy it!' But he was very uncomfortable with that. I grew up in house where my mom bought whatever she wanted. If she wanted to buy a Gucci bag, she'd figure out how to pay for it later."

When they got married, he was working as a business analyst and she had a job in human resources for a marketing firm. They were both making good salaries when they merged their joint finances. "I said, 'I never want to feel I can't buy something I want because someone is watching over me,'" she recalls. "He said, 'Good, because I don't want to be your dad and watch over you.' We agreed that at the end of the day, the money has to come from somewhere."

They set up a household budget based on their salaries, and Huntley agreed to cut back from five credit cards to two to make tracking expenses easier. They use Microsoft Money, a management software program that links up their checking and credit card statements. They pay bills online, and the program allows Huntley and her husband to examine credit card charges, click on a drop-down menu and allocate each expenditure to a particular category—dining, groceries, household improvements, mortgage payments, clothing, and so on.

Huntley and her husband decided that he would take the primary responsibility for managing their finances, but that they would sit down once a month and review everything together. They recently bought a townhouse and settled on the budget for furnishings. "We had some good pieces of furniture, and we didn't want to spend all of our money in decorating perfectly right away," she says. Huntley made a list of the most essential items and then agreed to save for other purchases down the road. "We gave ourselves a spending budget and committed to $10,000. Sticking to it is a lot harder than I thought it would be. I see something and think, 'oh, I want to have that, too.' I play around with the budget and I'm constantly reallocating from different categories—but I know how much I have, and when it's done, it's done."

An open discussion and a little planning go a long way toward eliminating money-related marital strife. Creating a reasonable budget that focuses on the most important purchases gave Huntley the freedom to spend and reassured her husband that expenses wouldn't spiral out of control. "If we didn't have same philosophy, I think it would put a real strain on our marriage," she says.

Before you merge your money in marriage, do some realistic planning. First, review your mutual spending over the last month, withholding nothing but judgment. Contribute equally to a joint account for household expenses—either a set amount each month, or the same percentage of your incomes. But keep separate checking accounts for those crucial indulgences—football tickets, hot stone massages, or whatever else you love. That's how Georgia medical writer Liza D. and her husband compromised. "We talked about everything before we got married, all the potential sticking points, from 'Would you want to put kids in daycare?' to 'How do you want to handle finances?' When we were both working full time, we put the same percentage of our salaries in a joint account, and whatever was left over after paying the bills went into our own accounts," she explains. "The joint account was for the mortgage, utilities, anything for the house; but then we would each pay for our own activities—dance classes for me or golfing for him. Now that I work part time and make very little, I put 50 percent of every paycheck into the joint account, 25 percent into an emergency savings account, and the other 25 percent is for me to keep. He puts the vast majority of the money into our joint account and keeps a couple hundred for himself every month, which I think is fair. You have to discuss it and figure it out."

Talk it out: How much money is okay to spend without consulting the other person? Also decide which one of you will be the family's chief financial officer. If you both hate dealing with money, trade off paying the bills month to month and talk to a financial planner about the bigger picture (for how to find one, see the next section). No one should be in the dark about how much you have or where the money is going.

Next, come clean about your debts. Once you're wed, you are both legally responsible for them, so decide upfront who will pay them off and on what timetable. If one of you is coming into the marriage with a mountain of credit card debt and it's already a source of tension, be very clear about the plan to pay it down. You may even want to specify your deal in a prenuptial agreement. I'm a big believer in the whole "in good times and in bad" part of the vows; I said them myself once, and still honor them. But bankruptcy is not one of those life memories you cherish putting in the family album. A prenuptial agreement doesn't mean you can't negotiate ways to help the indebted partner; the other partner, for instance, could agree to pay a larger share of the household expenses until the debt is gone. But roughly half of marriages end in divorce; a written agreement that is realistic and specific about who is taking charge of the debt may help to keep your union whole. Next, talk about how you want to handle childcare. Will someone put a career on hold to raise the kids? If so, who? How will you structure your finances, and the division of household labor?

Once you decide how to divvy up the responsibilities, establish and hold on to your own money identity. Aside from maintaining your own checking account, contribute to your own retirement savings account, even if you are not working outside the home, and keep at least one credit card solely in your name. One study found that a quarter of women over age 50 still have credit only in their spouse's name.[2] That makes it tough to get a credit card or make other important financial moves should something happen to him.

Finally, pay cash for your wedding. Don't start your life together in the red by paying for a one-night event with plastic. Consider registering at web sites such as theBigDay.com and The Honeymoon.com, which allow your guests to sponsor a portion of the honeymoon, everything from plane tickets to a snorkeling excursion on a Hawaiian beach. Maybe you would prefer a little help with a home purchase instead of crystal candlesticks? Register at Greenwish.com, which allows gift givers to contribute to the down payment. Or perhaps you already have matching Calphalon cookware and other household essentials, and what you really desire is that $7,000 flat-screen television. Web sites such as Felicite.com allow you to register for that item at any store, and well wishers can contribute a portion of the cost.

Moving in with a Partner

What if your relationship isn't official? Should you combine bank accounts with a live-in partner? The short answer is: No. Keep everything separate—from credit cards to savings accounts. My friendly neighborhood banker shared the tale of a client who opened a joint account with her boyfriend, only to have him drain it when they broke up. When you're married, the government recognizes your assets as legally owned by both of you. If someone absconds with all the cash, the other person has the power to get restoration in a divorce court. But if you're not hitched and your partner walks away with the dough, you have no legal recourse, because when you opened your joint account you signed a customer access agreement that gave your partner the key. Another risk: If your partner is a check bouncer, you're both liable for his bad habits in the event he bounces out of the picture.

If you are a long-term, live-in couple with no plans to marry (Susan Sarandon/Tim Robbins, Goldie Hawn/Kurt Russell), consider a written property agreement that notes who owns what, and how you split up income and expenses. Why bother? Because many states recognize an oral contract, or one implied by a living arrangement. So if you're an investment banker supporting an unpublished poet, theoretically, he could go before a judge and say that you promised to split your take-home pay 50/50 with him. Tough to prove, yes, but who wants a court fight? You can download forms for a written property agreement at the web site Selfhelplaw.com.

✔ Marriage/Live-In Partner Checklist

What Goes in the Safe Deposit Box: Copies of your marriage certificate, will, living will, durable power of attorney, prenuptial agreement; written property agreement (for cohabitating couples).

The Will: If you die without a will, the state gets to divvy up your possessions. Steer clear of those generic forms you find on the Internet or at an office supply store. You want an up-to-date document that conforms to your state's laws, so see an attorney who can guide you through the process. If you are an older couple with significant financial assets, discuss the possibility of setting up a revocable living trust with your attorney. A trust is an arrangement in which someone (the trustee) holds legal title to property for another person, called the beneficiary. Trusts may help reduce estate taxes and avoid probate, the legal process that takes place after someone dies, which can be lengthy and expense. Young couples with few assets do not need a trust. For more information on trusts, see www.nolo.com.

A Living Will or Advance Medical Directive: This gives you the right to die free of the artificial measures a hospital will take to keep you alive in a vegetative state if you're gravely injured. A living will makes your wishes clear and saves your family from having to make agonizing decisions in the event the worst happens. You can download a living will at www.partnershipforcaring.org, or get one free at most hospitals.

A Durable Power of Attorney: This allows your spouse to make important financial, legal, and health decisions on your behalf in the event you become incapacitated. Without one, your family has to go to court and have someone appointed as your guardian—a time-consuming and expensive proposition. It's easy to change your mind later if you want to appoint someone else—simply tear up the document.

Financial Paperwork and Tax Matters: Update the beneficiaries named on retirement accounts, and meet with an accountant or financial planner to review how your combined income affects your taxes, and possibly rethink your investments from a tax perspective. If both of you are coming to the altar with substantial assets or children in tow, consider a prenuptial agreement.

Life Insurance: If you have a mortgage or other fixed expenses that require a dual income, consider buying enough term life insurance (see discussion that follows) to pay it off, so the surviving partner won't have to sell the home.

A final word on relationships: Understand all assets you own in the marriage. Keep a careful record of the names of the institutions, account numbers, tax records, and so on. If you divorce, you will want to know everything that should be discussed in the settlement, and how to locate it. Divorce encompasses complex short-term issues—such as figuring out how to continue health care coverage from a spouse's plan; as well as long-term issues, including an equitable division of retirement savings. The matter is obviously more painful if children are involved. For more tips on what to do in divorce, see the Women's Institute for Financial Education at wife.org. The site offers books and other resources related to ending a marriage.

Job Change

Ursula V. grew up in Manhattan's Soho district in the 1970s, when Soho was a mostly undiscovered industrial neighborhood where artists went to find cheap studio space. Her mother was a sculptor who taught part time; her dad abandoned the family when she was a toddler. "We got by, but it was tough. When I was little, my mom would send me to the grocery store with food stamps and they would look at you crooked," she recalls. "The little coins were plastic. It literally looked like play money."

Ursula says she saved every penny she got, even money from the tooth fairy. "I remember I had a friend when I was 7 or 8, and her mother was an investment banker. I actually asked her how I should invest this money," she recalls. "She told me a mutual fund is a good idea, and she helped me set the whole thing up. I had saved about $500. I still have that fund."

Ursula didn't notice how different her circumstances were from other Manhattan kids until she was a teenager, but it never affected her self-esteem. "By high school, I was gallivanting with the Hamptons crowd and hanging out in these amazing houses in Long Island. I knew there was a big difference between those kids and me. I was eating soup every day and these guys were going to their beach houses. I was aware of being different but it was a cool, funky different, because my mom was an artist and we lived in a loft in Soho. It was 'oh cool, let's go play at Ursula's because she's got a loft and you can skateboard through it.'" When Ursula was 16, her mother met her second husband and their finances greatly improved.

Ursula is still very cautious with her money—she doesn't own a single credit card. But she never lets money dictate her career decisions. She recently quit a prestigious producer job at a cable television network and took a pay cut because a shift in management left her with a toxic boss. "I was totally not happy," she says. "You can't be stupid about stuff—you have to make informed decisions. I didn't just quit from one day to the next. But I was really thinking about things and talking to my supervisors. I also talked to (author) Anna Quindlen. I was interviewing her because we were doing a segment on her. She quit her job at the *New York Times* twice and everybody thought she was nuts. But somehow, someway, I thought, 'It doesn't have to be like this, I don't have to be stuck somewhere and be unhappy.' You spend a lifetime trying to build something up, but I know what it is to have nothing. I didn't think it was horrible. My mother loved me to no end, so that makes all the difference in the world. Sometimes less money means more power to live your life as you choose—if you don't let money control what your career goals are."

✔ Job Change Checklist

What Goes in the Safe Deposit Box: Copies of your employment contract, retirement beneficiary forms.

Money Issues: If you have retirement assets in a 401(k) or other plan from your previous employer, do not withdraw the funds: Roll them over into your new employer's plan or into an Individual Retirement Account (IRA). If you withdraw the money you'll pay a 10 percent penalty and tax on the funds. (If you are being laid off and you are not fully vested in your 401(k), try to negotiate full vesting as part of your severance package, so you can take all the money with you. For more on 401(k) plans see Chapter 7.) Join your new firm's retirement plan as soon as possible and contribute at least enough to get any employer match. If your new job comes with a raise, use the extra cash to pay off credit card debt and build an emergency cushion. Set aside three to six months salary in a conservative place: a money market fund, CD, savings bonds, U.S. Treasuries, or a short-term bond fund. (For details, see Chapter 6.)

Benefits: Sign up for health insurance and disability insurance if your employer offers them. Also consider flexible spending accounts for medical expenses or dependent-care, because you get a double bonus: The money you put in the account is deducted from your gross income; and is set aside in the account on a pretax basis. Let's say you spend $20 a month—$240 a year—to pay for prescriptions not covered by insurance or an over-the-counter drug. If you are in the 28 percent tax bracket, your prescriptions will only cost around $175, because you pay for them with pretax dollars. The benefits can be substantial for parents who use the accounts for qualified daycare expenses (see below). Check with your employer regarding the regulations. If your employer does not offer health benefits, find out if your state offers an affordable policy, or at minimum buy a "catastrophic" policy that will cover major hospital expenses in the event of an accident.

Buying Real Estate

Nina K., her husband, and toddler live with Nina's mother in a three-bedroom apartment in New York. Nina's mother cares for her grand-daughter while the parents are working. The living arrangement, while not ideal, has allowed the couple to super-save for eight months: Half of Nina's paycheck goes to savings; a quarter of her husband's does. They are planning to move to Ireland to buy a home near her husband's family. "We slip now and then, but we have managed to save quite a bit," she says. "I don't want to be a zillionaire, but just have enough to buy a couple of acres and be able to go on a holiday and not feel we can't afford the nuts in the mini-bar."

Before you dive into homeownership, start with the obvious: Can you afford it? A year's worth of monthly mortgage payments should add up to no more than 30 percent of your income. Lenders prefer that your mortgage and other debts (auto and student loans, credit cards) comprise no more than 40 percent of your gross income. (If your income is $60,000, your mortgage and other debts should be no more than $24,000.) In terms of cash upfront, you will need at least 3 to 10 percent of the purchase price of the home to cover a down payment and closing costs. If you can afford it, aim for 20 percent down to avoid paying private mortgage insurance (PMI). PMI is a part of your mortgage payment that protects the lender in case you default. The smaller the down payment, the more PMI you pay, and it can add up to thousands of dollars over time.

Does it make sense to buy in your market? Some real estate markets are so inflated that renting may be a better option. For instance, if your monthly rent is at least 35 percent below the cost of ownership (mortgage payment, property taxes, homeowners insurance, and utilities), it may be worth it to continue renting and investing your savings in stocks and bonds instead. Just be sure to do an *after-tax* comparison— since the interest paid on a mortgage is tax deductible. If you do buy, plan to stay in the home at least five years. In general, the home won't appreciate enough in value to cover your transaction costs if you sell earlier than five years.

✔ Home Buying Checklist

What Goes in the Safe Deposit Box: The deed, title, mortgage closing statement, home warranties, inspection/appraisal documents, copy of your homeowner's insurance policy. Keep a separate folder with receipts from all major home repairs, improvements, or additions. They are considered part of the cost of your home (or *cost basis*). When you sell your home, you subtract your cost basis from the sale price to get the total profit. If your profit is above a certain threshold, capital gains taxes apply. Keeping track of home improvement costs could help you reduce those taxes when you sell. Your homeowner's policy should cover "replacement value", not "actual value" of your home, so you have enough money to rebuild if the worst happens. Create a master list of what you own and take photos, or videotape, the rooms in your home and the expensive belongings. Get separate floater insurance to cover big-ticket items like jewelry.

Boost Your Credit Rating: Request your FICO score at myfico.com, and get a copy of your credit reports from the major credit bureaus, Equifax.com, Experian.com, and Transunion.com. Pay off credit cards, school loans, and other debt before you apply for a mortgage to get the best rate and the flexibility to borrow more money. (See Chapter 5 for more details on how to boost your credit rating.)

Get to Know Your Market: Real estate is an extremely local business. Web sites such as realtor.com allow you to search for homes by price and specific features, but there's no better way to burn calories than walking through a town and chatting up the locals. Contact a real estate broker, and ask to see inventory levels for the past 12 months. Homes will take six to eight months to sell in a weak market, compared to four to eight weeks in a robust one, says Robert Irwin, author of *Irwin's Power Tips for Buying a Home for Less*.[3] Also ask to see comparable sales, or "comps" in a neighborhood you like. These snapshots detail all the features of the nearby homes, as well as asking and selling prices—essential information when figuring out what to bid on your dream home.

Get Preapproved: Be ready to buy by getting preapproved for a mortgage. This will make you more attractive to the seller than someone who does not have financing lined up.

Do Not Tap Your 401(k) for a Home Purchase: If you need cash for the down payment, and you're thinking about borrowing it from your 401(k), think again, says Wisconsin-based financial planner Kevin McKinley: "Other than needing a new kidney, I can't think of a reason to borrow from your 401(k) plan."[4] Many plans allow participants to borrow up to 50 percent of their account balance, and return the money over five years. But the transaction has hidden costs and huge risks. First, Uncle Sam collects *twice* on the money you borrow—because you pay back the loan and interest with after-tax dollars. When you withdraw the money at retirement, you'll owe taxes on it again. Moreover, if you lose your job, you have to pay back the loan immediately—at a time when you can least afford to do so. If you can't, the Internal Revenue Service will consider the loan a withdrawal, and you'll owe income tax on it, along with a 10 percent penalty if you're under age 59½. Then there's the so-called "lost opportunity cost" of 401(k) borrowing. The money you borrow doesn't earn the tax-free interest it otherwise would. Figure in compounding and it can add up to a significant loss,

McKinley says. "Imagine a 25-year-old worker takes a $10,000 loan from the plan—loses his job and can't pay it back. At age 65, that amount would have been worth $452,000, at a 10 percent annual rate of return. He lost not just the gain on the loan amount—the $10,000— but $5,000 in taxes and penalties he had to pay, too."

Do Not Tap Your IRA (unless you really have to): The government has made it possible for consumers to take $10,000 out of an individual retirement account or a Roth IRA one time only without penalty for a first-time home purchase (see Chapter 7). The provision has a funky definition of "first time"—it doesn't have to be the first home you ever buy; you just can't have owned one for the two years preceding the date you acquire this home. If you and your spouse each have IRA accounts, you can each take $10,000 out. Also, the $10,000 can be applied to the purchase of your own home, or that of a child, grandchild, or even a parent. (So if Mom and Dad are retired zillionaires, they can tap their IRAs for your home down payment.) But in general, try to avoid draining funds you will need for your retirement.

Play the Ownership Game: Figure out what it would cost to own (over and above your rent), and set that money aside every month for a year. In 12 months' time you'll know whether ownership is for you— and may have a tidy sum saved for a down payment.

Parenthood

There's nothing like a few kids to rock your world and your financial priorities. Katherine H. has four children, age six and younger. They recently moved to her husband's hometown in Massachusetts, where a developer was building a country club. "They designed it as a kid's club, with a beautiful pool, tennis, day camp," she says. "In my mind, it was a good place for our kids to do all their stuff." The club wouldn't open for two or three years, but Katherine convinced her husband to spend the money in advance for a membership to reserve a spot. To come up with the fee, they decided to cash in a portfolio of technology stocks. It was a lucky move: Had they left the stocks alone, they would have lost most of their value in the 1990s stock market meltdown.

Katherine works full time as a managing director of an energy company. "Money can make you more comfortable and happy, it can give you more freedom, more flexibility," she says. "But you've got to have a healthy family, you have to have a stable marriage, you've got to be able to raise your kids with the right values. Money can give you comfort, freedom, and flexibility but it can also destroy. You see how it is in families when they inherit an estate and fight over it; or the lottery winner, who five or six years later is divorced and penniless. I don't dwell on what it can buy me—I spend more time thinking about how to prepare so it will give us security and give us freedom and flexibility."

Flexibility is the utopia that so many working women strive toward to balance career and children. Katherine, for instance, says she has sometimes considered quitting her job, but has reached a high enough position in her company where she can make her own schedule and call her own shots to a certain extent. Plus she doesn't want the whole breadwinning burden to fall on her husband's shoulders.

Kay S., a communications executive for a Fortune 100 company in the Midwest, worked full time after the birth of her first child. When she was due with her second, she told her boss she wanted to go part time. He asked if she would stay full time if the company put a computer in her home and allowed her to telecommute three days a week. She agreed to try the experiment for a few months—and ended up working that way for several years. "I don't know that my kids even realized I was working. They knew I had a computer and I talked on the phone, and when I said 'Mommy has to get this done' they probably knew. I would work until 2 A.M. and then get up the next morning to play with them. But my work was not a source of stress for them," she explains, adding with a laugh, "At times I had to do a conference call, and the kids were noisy, so I would do the call standing in the bathroom."

Kay says being completely clear about what she valued made the difference: "Had I not stood up for myself and known what my limits were, I could have been a very miserable person," she declares. "My advice would be to establish yourself in your career to some extent before you go asking for flexibility. But know your limits and be bold enough to propose what you think might work. Chances are, if you're good, people will be flexible with you." Kay says the situation put her career in "maintenance mode" for a few years, but she was able to resume her progress when she returned to the office full time.

Heidi B., 37, a New Jersey independent marketing consultant, also sought more flexibility in her last job—and had a less supportive experience. "When I cut my schedule to four days at the consulting firm, I got a lot of flack that I wasn't as billable as other people and got laid off," says Heidi, who has an MBA from a top business school and three kids under age 8. "That was sort of a blessing in disguise, because I tried going out on my own and finding my own clients. As long as I deliver good work in a timely manner, my clients don't care where or when it is done. Now I have all the flexibility I need. I'm well paid for what I do, I love it, and I totally structure it around being with my kids." Heidi now works 20 to 25 hours a week. Her advice for people seeking balance? "Figure out what skill set you already have and find a way to do it as an independent," she suggests. "You can take any skill in business and find a way to do it as a consultant." That kind of risk-taking isn't for everyone, she adds; it requires a self-starter with an entrepreneurial spirit. Moreover, Heidi didn't start her business from scratch; during her tenure with the consulting firm, she made critical contacts that helped her build a client base.

Parenthood not only sparks a quest for flexibility, it also changes the dynamics of career transition. Traditionally, women have been the ones who move in and out of the workforce to take care of kids, shifting to part-time or freelance work, while men supply the steady income and the stable career. Now it's not uncommon to see stay-at-home dads, men who telecommute or work flexible hours to spend more time with their children, or men and women switching roles as the breadwinner so that one can go back to school or start a business. According to the 2000 Census, there were nearly 19 million U.S. families with children where both parents work, and just 7.2 million with one working spouse.

Ellen T., for example, works in the entertainment business. She has two young children and a third on the way. After 16 years working full time, she shifted to part time. "It was a huge decision—I took a sizable cut in salary. I feel better about myself that I did something that was better for my children, by being more present for them," she says. "But I feel overworked for what I'm earning now and it gets me a little frustrated. I've talked to a lot of women who work part time—they're trying so hard to prove they can do it that they end up almost working a full-time job on part-time pay."

Ellen's husband is an entrepreneur pursuing a dream of building his own production company. "I'm insuring the family; I was able to keep my benefits which was a huge thing," she explains. "I feel trapped in my job sometimes. There are times when I envy women who have husbands who are Mr. Stability, who have these great jobs. On the other hand, those men are rarely home. His work is interesting and he's involved in his family and making his own path and I think there's real value to that. I'm on board—I'm not sitting here saying, 'Get a job!' I think when I'm sitting on my rocking chair reflecting on my life someday, what feels like such a hard thing is going to be nothing. That will make all the sacrifices that much sweeter in the end."

Mellan suggests that when couples talk about their money, they also openly discuss the earning part of the equation. "There should be a lot of gratitude expressed for person carrying the burden while the other is free to live out the dream," she says. "They should also reassure the person that they have the right to be anxious. Someone may be anxious and it may have nothing to do with her confidence in her partner; they are just worried about things they can't control. And they should discuss time limits. If someone starts his own business, the other person should know she doesn't have to do this forever. They should talk about what's going to happen next if this doesn't work." [5]

In the mid-1990s, Mary Snyder was a regional marketing manager for a Fortune 500 staffing company earning more than $50,000 a year and contributing half her family's income. She decided to quit to stay home with her children, who were then 3 and 9. But she planned ahead: For several months before she quit, Snyder tracked every penny she spent. To her surprise, much of her outlay was work related—day care, transportation, lunches, cappucinos, fast food (because she had no time to cook), weekly manicures, and a professional wardrobe. "I immediately stopped buying anything that came in a prepackaged box," she says. "I started cooking from scratch, which is very inexpensive. Whatever was in season or on sale was what we would eat that week. But it's also a whole lot healthier." Snyder took the lessons she learned and coauthored a book called *You Can Afford to Stay Home with Your Kids.*[6]

Before taking the leap to a single income, parents should research the cost of benefits like health insurance, since your employer likely foots most of the bill. Also, take last year's tax return and run it through tax software—minus the second income—to figure out what you would save in taxes. Calculate the cost of commuting, and see if you can eliminate a second car. Despite the loss of income, Snyder found quitting work and cutting costs actually left her family in a much sounder financial position. They eliminated credit card debt and auto loans, and fully funded their children's college savings. Snyder eventually started working again, but freelances from home, so there are few work-related expenses. "The stress level of getting home with two kids in tow, starting dinner and getting that going was just unbelievable," she says. "Just not having to rush through the day and parent on the fly—getting rid of that stress—was so worth it." Thinking about cutting back to one income? FinanCenter offers a financial calculator called "Should my spouse work too?" that figures out what the second income is actually worth after taxes and work-related expenses. See www.financenter.com/consumertools/calculators.

Even if living on one salary is out of the question, it's not a bad idea to try it—at least in theory—for your family's financial health. The number of dual-income families declaring bankruptcy or having their homes go into foreclosure has skyrocketed—and it's not because of wasteful spending on vacations or clothing, according to *The Two-Income Trap: Why Middle Class Mothers and Fathers Are Going Broke* by Harvard Law School bankruptcy professor Elizabeth Warren and her daughter, management consultant Amelia Warren Tyagi.[7] According to these authors, the dual-income family of today earns 75 percent more money than a single-income family a generation ago—but has 25 percent less discretionary income to cover living expenses. Both incomes, the authors found, went to fixed costs such as mortgage and car payments, health insurance, and children's education. Bidding wars for housing, especially in high-quality school districts, are largely to blame for the heavier financial burden on families. With both parents already working, there are fewer resources to cushion the blow when misfortune strikes, such as an illness or a job layoff. In a study of bankruptcies from 2001, the authors found that nine out of 10 families cited one of three reasons for their filing: job loss, medical problems, or divorce. They suggest dual-income couples try to live on one income, by cutting fixed costs—staying in a smaller home, looking for a lower-cost preschool—and reserve the other person's salary for savings and discretionary spending.

 Parenthood Checklist

What Goes in the Safe Deposit Box: Birth certificates, social security cards, savings bonds, life insurance policy, an updated copy of your will.

Life Insurance: There are basically two kinds of life insurance: term (you pay premiums, the insurer pays cash if you die) and cash-value policies, which offer a death benefit as well as a tax-deferred investment account. Term insurance is a great, cheap choice when you're in your 20s, 30s, and 40s—a few hundred dollars a year can buy you hundreds of thousands of dollars in coverage. However, the policy gradually gets more expensive as you age. One variety of term insurance is a *level-premium* policy, where the premiums remain steady for 10 or 20 years—ideal if your kids are in their early teens and you want protection until they're out of college. You can get a quote online at quotesmith.com, instantquote.com, or iquote.com. If you've just had your first child at age 45, term insurance may be too pricey, so look into cash-value policies. Premiums are significantly higher, but usually remain the same for life. Watch out for the hefty fees and expenses of the investment account attached to cash-value policies. Talk to a fee-only investment planner (see the discussion that follows) about which insurance is right for you *before* you talk to an insurance agent. How much life insurance do you need? A common rule of thumb is to buy insurance equal to five to seven times your annual gross income. To get a ballpark idea of insurance needs, check out the life insurance needs estimator at insure.com (http://info.insure.com/life/lifeneedsestimator).

Disability Insurance: If your employer offers long-term disability coverage, buy it; it's usually less expensive when purchased with a group. Disability typically pays 60 percent of your salary while you're out of action (but caps monthly income at a certain level). Get a policy that is noncancellable to age 65 (this locks in your cost of premiums as long as you pay on time).

Update Your Will: Would you trust a court to decide who raises your children? Then name a guardian, and a back-up guardian, in your will.

Take Advantage of a Flexible-Spending Account for Day Care: Flex-spending accounts allow you to set aside up to $5,000 in pretax dollars to pay for qualified care, which includes licensed preschools. So if your four-year-old's tuition is $5,000 per year, and you're in the 28 percent tax bracket, your actual tuition cost will be closer to $3,600. Plus you'll have reduced your taxable income by $5,000 by putting the money in the account.

Start Saving for College: My husband went to college on a basketball scholarship, so I hope he'll teach the girls a thing or two about jump shots. But just in case, we save for them in a 529 plan. These are college savings plans sponsored by the states that allow you to put aside money that grows tax-free and is free of federal income tax when its withdrawn, as long as it's used for qualified higher education expenses. (In 2010, Congress must renew the provision exempting the withdrawals from federal taxes. Even if it is not renewed, these plans are still a great way to save for college.) Other 529 plans allow you to prepay state tuition now, locking-in today's rates. Some states also give you a tax deduction when you invest, and allow you to withdraw the money free of state tax. Take a close look at the fees, expenses, and investment performance—some state programs are excellent; others are duds. Check out your home state's program first, and then compare it to other states. Some plans are opened directly through the state program; in other cases, you have to enroll through a financial advisor. It's smart to research and choose your plan yourself. Some plan advisors have been investigated for steering clients to out-of-state plans rather than their home-state plan, even when their home-state plan offered a tax break—presumably because the broker got a higher commission by enrolling the client in the other plan. (See "choosing an advisor" below.) To compare state plans, check out the web site savingforcollege.com. or collegesavings.org. The National Association of Securities Dealers web site also has a tool that allows you to analyze fees and expenses of 529 plans you're considering. See www.nasd.com /Investor/Smart/529/Calc/529_Analyzer.asp. Another good college savings plan is the Coverdell Education Savings Account (previously known as an Educational IRA), where you can put up to $2,000 away for education each year. Coverdell savings can be used for elementary or secondary schools, including tuition, room and board, books, and computers. Contributions are not tax deductible, but the contributions and earnings can be withdrawn tax-free as long as they are used to pay eligible schooling costs.

How to Choose a Financial Advisor

To create a comprehensive plan for all of these life transitions, consider sitting down with a financial advisor. Be extremely choosy. Anyone can call herself a financial advisor. These individuals must be registered and licensed to do certain activities, such as selling investments or insurance—but they do not need specific education or credentials as, say, an attorney or a physician would. Anyone can use the title "financial advisor" or "financial planner"—accountants, attorneys, stock brokers, insurance salespeople, and so on.

"Never place blind trust in an advisor," says attorney John Allen, author of *Investor Beware: How to Protect Your Money from Wall Street's Dirty Tricks.*[8] For instance, your broker may suggest you can profit from the market's ups and downs by jumping in and out of stocks quickly. Then she excessively trades your account to generate more commissions, which explains why her wallet is Prada and yours is faux leather from Target. There is a confusing array of planner credentials such as chartered financial consultant, chartered financial analyst, and certified public accountant/personal financial specialist.

One way to simplify the process is to find a certified financial planner (CFP). CFPs must pass a comprehensive exam that includes financial, investment, tax, retirement and estate planning, insurance, and risk management. They have to practice in the field for at least three years and meet continuing education requirements to maintain their certification. How are financial planners paid? They either charge an hourly fee; get a percentage of the assets under management; or receive a commission from companies whose products they are selling to you. This is where conflicts of interest enter the picture. As mentioned earlier, in 2004, the National Association of Securities Dealers (NASD) began investigating 15 unnamed securities firms and their sales of 529 college savings plans. The NASD noticed the firms steering investors into 529 plans outside their home states—even though in some cases the investors would have received a tax break by choosing their home state's plan. Why would an advisor do this? Because they get better commissions from certain plans.

Certainly there are honest individuals—financial advisors, stock brokers, insurance salespeople—who work on commission. But the investments that meet your objectives may not be the ones that generate the biggest commissions for the broker—and therein lies the temptation to put his or her financial goals above yours. One way to avoid conflict of interest issues is to find a *fee-only* certified financial planner. These advisors will either charge you a one-time fee for a financial plan, an hourly fee, or a percentage fee based on your assets (but they don't get paid by anyone but you). Be prepared to spend at least $100 or more an hour. According to Forrester Research, clients who worked on fee-only retainers spent an average of $500 a year on advice.[9] If you choose to work on an hourly basis, you are paying for a plan—you have to be motivated to implement it.

In sizing up a financial planner, the Securities and Exchange Commission recommends you ask the following:

- What training and experience do you have? How long have you been in business?
- What is your investment philosophy? Do you take a lot of risks or are you more concerned about the safety of my money?
- Describe your typical client. Can you provide me with references, the names of people who have invested with you for a long time? How often do you meet with clients?

- How do you get paid? By commission? Based on a percentage of assets you manage? Another method? Do you get paid more for selling your own firm's products? Will you recommend general kinds of investments or specific funds? (Decide if you want to walk away from the meeting with a specific list of recommended investments.)
- How much will it cost me in total to do business with you?

To save yourself time and money, sort out your financial goals, the time frames in which you would like to achieve them, and your comfort level with risk (see Chapter 7). Lay out the specifics, for example, "I would like to accumulate $20,000 for a down payment on a home in five years; pay off $3,000 in credit card debt and $10,000 in student loans; save enough to cover four years of public college for my child in 14 years; and retire at age 63 at 90 percent of my income." The more prepared you are to talk about your goals, time frame, and appetite for risk, the better a planner can help you achieve your objectives. Look for a planner who engages you about your financial life, who is interested in your whole financial picture.

Other questions you may want to ask include:

- Should I be investing in other retirement vehicles besides my 401(k), like a Roth IRA, and how much?
- How does a recent salary increase affect my taxes, and what can I do to shelter my income?
- Do I need any life insurance? How much? Do I need to consider disability insurance? How much should I have? (It's not a bad idea to bring a copy of any plans offers by your employer.)
- Do I need a will?
- Here are the funds I've chosen in my 401(k)—what do you think of them? Should I consider others? (Bring a list of all the funds your plan offers.) How much should I be investing in my company's 401(k)—versus using the money to pay down debt?
- Consider tracking your expenses for a month before your meeting, so you have a realistic idea of your costs, and can figure out how much extra you have to meet other goals (debt reduction,

retirement savings, house fund). See Chapter 5 for details on how to do this.

- Does your company offer stock options? When should you exercise them and what are the tax implications?

Now if you have a significant amount of money to invest, say $50,000 or more, you might consider a CFP who works on a percentage basis—that is, they get paid a percentage of your portfolio's value every year, ranging from 1 to 2 percent. This is a good option if you have no time or interest in keeping tabs on your investments. But here's the drawback: You pay the advisor a fee, and you also pay expenses on the mutual funds in which she invests your money. (See Chapter 7 for more on mutual fund fees.) If you go with this kind of planner, try to get your overall fee—both advisors' fee and investment-related fees—down to around 1 percent. The more money you bring to the table, the more likely they'll accommodate the request. But talk about the possibility of lowering costs by investing strictly in index funds, individual bonds, and exchange-traded funds (ETFs). Exchange traded funds act like index funds—tracking a specific index—but trade like stocks. That means there are no management fees attached to the investment. If you buy and hold them for long periods of time, they may be less costly than index funds. However, if you are investing a little bit of money month after month, ETFs are not cost efficient, because you'll pay a brokerage fee each time you invest. Those fees can quickly equal or surpass the management and other fees on the index fund.

Advisors who give specific investment advice must register with the Securities and Exchange Commission or their state securities agency. The registration form, known as "Form ADV," has two components, one outlining the planner's services and fees and the other detailing any conflicts with clients or regulators. You can find the form online at www.adviserinfo.sec.gov. If you are working with a broker, call the National Association of Securities Dealers at (800) 289-9999 to verify her license and registration and find out if there's been disciplinary action against her. Also contact your local securities regulator—go to www.nasaa.org on the web and click "find regulator." They'll tell you if she has a history of arbitration claims, or if she's ever been sued.

Read your monthly statements—they will be your first warning that something's amiss. Are there any stock purchases or sales you didn't authorize? Immediately ask your broker for an explanation, and keep a log of your conversations. Compare the previous month to the current one and note changes in overall value, plus the price and value of each investment. Do you know why something declined? If you're still concerned, take your last few statements to an independent professional and get a second opinion.

Start your search for a planner by getting recommendations from relatives, friends, or trusted advisors like an attorney. Every woman I interviewed for this book who worked with a planner found the professional through a personal contact who had a favorable experience. Other places to search include:

- The Financial Planning Association, fpanet.org (includes both fee-only planners and those who work on commission)
- National Association of Personal Financial Advisors, feeonly.org (a group of fee-only planners)
- Personal Financial Specialist Consumer Web site, cpapfs.org (certified public accountants who have received the personal financial specialist designation)
- Garrett Planning Network (garrettplanningnetwork.com), a group of fee-only advisors who charge by the hour.

Remember, investing isn't paint by number; it's truly personal, based on your own Technicolor dreams. So choose a compatriot who asks probing questions about your life goals, your investment style, and your appetite for risk. She should explain (in your native language) both the downside risk and upside potential of specific investments. If she speaks "Brokerese," guarantees profits, suggests she's got insider information, or pressures you to make decisions, run the other way.

Now you have a road map to handling some of life's most important financial milestones. In the next chapter, a final word on money, values, and happiness.

10

THE FINAL WORD ON MONEY, VALUES, AND HAPPINESS

There is something higher than happiness, and that is blessedness.
—Thomas Carlyle

What's the best way to put your money where your values are? In this book, we've looked at ways to merge your values and financial life by shifting your perspective on money, defining wealth on your own terms, and appreciating the affluence you already enjoy. We've discussed methods to identify your values and explore their source—family, community, personality, and worldview. We've focused on tools to control spending, increase savings, and navigate the issues triggered by major financial milestones. This chapter offers some final thoughts on how to put your money where your values are, balance giving and receiving, and keep the faith as you progress toward the good life.

Socially Responsible Investing

The values we talked about in Chapter 1 focused on personal beliefs and priorities—family, friends, independence, kindness. You can express your values in your vocation, spending, saving, and charitable donations. But how can you manifest your values in the larger financial world? Over the past few decades, mutual fund companies have answered that challenge with a new category of funds called socially responsible investing (SRI). SRI funds are mutual funds (explained in Chapter 7) that weigh companies' social, environmental, and ethical practices as well as their financial performance when choosing which stocks to purchase for the fund. The fund managers seek profitability, but they are interested in more than the numbers. For example, some funds won't invest in military contractors, casinos, or companies that make guns, alcohol, or tobacco products. Others analyze how companies treat the environment, their employees, and their communities. Still other funds adhere to the tenets of a specific religion, such as Christianity or Islam. Each fund offers its own unique investment strategy and area of social or environmental concern. More than $2 trillion in assets are now invested in these portfolios. In 2003, an estimated $1 of every $9 invested in mutual funds went to a socially responsible portfolio.[1] And you don't have to sacrifice solid returns on your investment when choosing a socially responsible fund: As a group, these funds perform as well as funds that pay no attention to social issues.[2] Some boast superior long-term track records, and others underperform the market. That simply means you have to apply the same criteria and research to find an SRI fund that you would for any fund (see Chapter 7). Among the leaders in category are Calvert Funds, Domini Social Investments, and Citizens Funds, although industry giants such as Vanguard and TIAA-CREF also offer SRI funds. For a full listing of SRI funds, see socialinvest.org or socialfunds.com. You can also use Morningstar's "Premium Fund Screener" to find the right fund. (You may be able to sign up for a free trial membership or pay a small fee for a one-month membership.)

Curious to know if a mutual fund you currently own lives up to your values? At Calvert.com, you can take a fund you own and run it through a socially responsible investing screen to see if it contains any stocks that violate your values. Click on "Socially Responsible Investing," and then "Know What You Own." Then choose a personal area of interest to screen—such as "Environment." Calvert provides a report listing the stocks owned by your fund that failed the screen. (You can click on "Issue Brief" to see exactly what environmental or other concerns the screen considers.)

"Money should never be separated from values," writes Rosabeth Moss Kanter, a former editor of the *Harvard Business Review* and the author of numerous books on business management. "Detached from values it may indeed be the root of all evil. Linked effectively to social purpose it can be the root of opportunity."[3] Socially responsible investing gives you the opportunity to support businesses aligned with your vision for a better world.

Socially Responsible Spending

American women represent the largest economic force in the world—spending nearly $5 trillion a year.[4] We possess awesome potential for change, if we unite to make value-driven spending decisions. One helpful way to do that is to know exactly how the companies that receive your business are treating the world. Co-op America is a nonprofit group whose mission is to harness consumer strength to create a socially just and environmentally sustainable society. The organization sponsors a web site, www.responsibleshopper.org, that allows you to check up on the brands you buy and the stores you frequent, to see if they are polluting oceans, buying products from sweatshops, violating human rights, and more. The report also looks at a company's positive activities, whether it's humanitarian giving or a commitment to improving the environment. A separate Co-op America site, sweatshops.org, shows you how to avoid buying products made in sweatshops. And GreenPages.org is a directory of companies that have agreed to be screened by Co-op America. They must be value driven as well as profit driven; focused on using business as a tool for positive social change; socially and environmentally responsible in the way they source, manufacture, and market their products and run their offices and factories; and employ extraordinary and innovative practices that benefit workers, communities, customers, and the environment. All of these sites can be accessed through coopamerica.com. Another worthwhile organization, Center for a New American Dream, carries the motto: "More fun, less stuff!" Newdream.org contains hundreds of ideas for regaining life balance and consuming responsibly.

Balancing Giving and Receiving

Looking for a great holiday gift? Consider the gift of compassion. Alternative gift web sites, such as Alternative Gifts International (altgifts.org) and Heifer International (catalog.heifer.org), can help you finding a more meaningful present for the man or woman who has everything. A few brief comparisons for your shopping list:

- A DKNY Pink Leather Strap Watch: $85
- Eye screening, glasses, and surgery to prevent a child in Nepal from going blind: $83
- Waterford Crystal Cross by Marquis: $59
- Shelter for a homeless family in the United States for one week: $60
- Cole Haan leather keychain (in emerald, ocean, or tangerine): $25
- Two shares of seeds or tools to grow a garden to feed orphans in Kenya: $20
- Mini Panasonic Cell Phone encrusted with pink Swarovski crystals: $500
- One dairy cow and livestock training to help a small-scale farmer in the United States or overseas gain economic self-sufficiency; (each farmer who receives livestock donates the offspring to another family to continue the cycle): $500

Now here's a perfect gift: Give someone the soundtrack from the musical *Oklahoma* and a donation of chicks, ducks, and geese to a poor community in their name. (Get it? "Chicks and ducks and geese better scurry. . . .") Never mind. Anyway, I'm not sitting up here on my high horse-drawn-surrey-with-the-fringe-on-top trying to take you on a guilt trip. Just offering a couple suggestions for a different kind of holiday. Or birthday, or anniversary. I brought the Alternative Gifts catalog to a Brownie meeting and those seven-year-olds went wild! They were looking for something to do with the proceeds from the annual cookie sale. We booked the slumber party at the local museum for them, sent seeds and supplies to help a family in South America grow a vegetable garden, and provided basic medicine for a community clinic in Africa. Earn some, spend some, give some away (and promise to live by the Girl Scout Law).

Online alternative gift catalogs are a great avenue to share the wealth. But before you give to any charity, make sure it's legitimate, and the money is going where it is truly needed. Look at the financials of a charity you're considering: No more than 10 percent of the budget should go to fund-raising and publicity, and no more than 35 percent to administrative costs. Guidestar.com and give.org are online databases that profile hundreds of charities, link to their IRS filings, and offer some guidelines for choosing an organization. For "gift basket" charitable ideas, check out Justgive.org or Networkforgood.org.

Keeping the Faith

Consuela D., 45, used to work in medical administration, earning about $30,000 year. Last year her company outsourced all of the jobs in her division to India, where wages run 80 percent lower. She went back to school to train for a career that can't be sent overseas: massage therapy. "I have a natural knack for healing," she remarks, adding she always gets positive feedback from massage clients. "I like the satisfaction of making people feel better." When she heard rumors about layoffs in her previous company, she started watching for sales on soap, toilet paper, and other household necessities, and stocked up.

"I would love to have more money—but you can have all the money in the world and still be miserable," she says. "You look at celebrities— they have basically everything money can buy—but look at all the problems they have: alcoholism and drugs and relationships that don't last. They're human and, at the end of the day, after they look at all of their things, they still have problems like the rest of us. Freedom is a mental thing. Those demons that run around your head—loneliness or anxiety—you have to solve that yourself."

Consuela says the best way to alleviate money worries is to consider other people's needs. When she's not in school, she checks in on an elderly neighbor. She buys homeless people in her neighborhood something to eat. She has an army of nieces and nephews, who she treats before she treats herself. "My money is limited, but I don't walk around saying, 'I don't have any money,'" she explains. "If someone really needs something, I try to help them. But the universe will reward you accordingly—you'll get it back. You might not get it from the same person you helped. You don't do something for someone and expect that person to return the favor. It might be someone who says, 'Do you need a ride somewhere?' Or someone will say, 'Let me take you to dinner.' When I give, I don't look for anything in return, but trust I'll be taken care of when the time comes."

Much of this book has been about control. Control what you spend, control what you save, control how you invest, control your emotions about investing, control how you communicate about money, control your investment advisor so she doesn't end up controlling you. Control, control, control. Now I want to talk a little bit about trust. Here are the seven laws I try to follow to bring my money, values, and happiness in line:

1. Be grateful: A grateful heart is never envious.
2. Be giving, of your talent, time, and money.
3. Be diligent and responsible: Don't expect managing your money to be easy; keep learning and be accountable for your own financial life.
4. Be flexible: In the fires of failure are the seeds of new opportunity.
5. Be positive: Anything is possible, even a better route than the one you had in mind.
6. Be trusting, in your good common sense, in the people you love, in your hard work.
7. Keep it light: It's only money.

A friend of mine recently sat down with a financial planner and asked how much she and her husband would need to start saving to pay, in full, for their two children to go to a good private college. Her children are three and five. The planner said $2,000 a month. "There's just no way I could do that," she told me.

Don't forget, a planner's job is to be cautious. Planners base their numbers on the worst-case scenario: College costs continue to escalate; your children can't work a part-time job; there won't be loans or scholarships available. A financial advisor wouldn't keep her job for very long if she said, "Don't worry about it! It's all works out in the end!" Since I'm not your advisor, I can go ahead and say it: Don't worry about it. It all works out in the end. Focus on your values, clarify your intentions and be totally committed to giving it your best shot. My parents had 11 children. Ten of us graduated from college. My one brother who chose not to finish college owns a thriving business. Five of us have master's degrees (the overachievers have more than one) and one has a PhD. Ten of us own our homes. But much more importantly, we're friends. We make each other laugh. We have healthy marriages and healthy children. In my book, that makes us rich. What I learned from my parents' experience is that anything is possible with focus, commitment, and patience. There are dozens of ways to pay for college—scholarships, financial aid, work programs. There are dozens of ways to buy a home. There are dozens of ways to save for retirement. Declare your values first, set goals that reflect them, be open-minded about the ways to achieve them, then work your way there. Never let money stand between you and something you deeply value. As Norman Vincent Peale once remarked, "Empty pockets never held anyone back. Only empty heads and empty hearts can do that."

If you're reading this book, it may be because you want the power to secure your financial life. (Or perhaps you're related to me and I told you there would be a quiz later on the contents.) Hopefully, the previous chapters will help you get organized so you'll feel more in control of your life. But the truth is, we can't see what's coming down the road. We can't control every aspect of our existence. We can only prepare as thoroughly as possible, and then, as Consuela advised, take care of others and trust you'll be taken care of when the time comes. When I was a child, my mother used to say, "Work as if it all depends on you, and pray as if it all depends on God." Years later, that still works. You don't have to be a spiritual person to see the value in releasing your anxiety about the things you can't control. You're the photographer. You choose the subject, set the lighting, frame and focus the shot. But if you yank the film out of the camera before it has a chance to develop, you may destroy your work. When we let go of anxiety, let go of the need to know and control the ultimate outcome, we make space for something new to enter our lives. As Abraham Lincoln once said, "God is the silent partner in all great enterprises."

And this is the end of this enterprise. Be wealthy, be happy, live the good life.

NOTES

Chapter 1

1. Sallie McFague, *Speaking in Parables: A Study in Metaphor and Theology* (Minneapolis, MN: Fortess Press, 1975), p. 1.
2. The World Bank, *World Development Report 2004,* http://web
   .worldbank.org/WBSITE/EXTERNAL/NEWS/0,,contentMDK
   :20194973~menuPK:34463~pagePK:64003015~piPK:6400301
   2~theSitePK:4607,00.html.
3. U.S. Agriculture Department, www.usda.gov/news/releases/1999
   /10/0415.
4. *World Development Report 2004.*
5. U.S. Census Bureau, Current Population Reports, *Supplemental Measures of Material Well-Being: Expenditures, Consumption and Poverty, 1998 and 2001* (September 2003), www.census.gov/prod
   /2003pubs/p23-201.pdf.
6. The Office of the United Nations High Commissioner for Refugees, www.unhcr.ch/cgi-bin/texis/vtx/home.
7. *World Development Report 2004.*
8. U.S. Department of Labor, Bureau of Labor Statistics.
9. Centers for Disease Control and Prevention, *Surgeon General's report on Physical Activity and Health,* www.cdc.gov/nccdphp/sgr/intro
   .htm.
10. The National Sleep Foundation, www.sleepfoundation.org
    /PressArchives/lessfun_lesssleep.cfm.

11. U.S. Census Bureau, August 2004, www.census.gov/hhes/www /income.html.

12. World Health Organization, *The World Health Report 2003: Shaping the Future,* www.who.int/whr/2003/en/overview_en.pdf.

13. *World Development Report, 2004.*

14. *World Development Report, 2004.*

15. Statistics on percentage of Americans attaining various levels of education, average salaries, and lifetime earnings from U.S. Census Bureau, Census 2000, www.census.gov/prod/2002pubs/p23-210.pdf.

16. Figures on household income and poverty from U.S. Census Bureau, www.census.gov/Press-Release/www/2003/cb03-153.html.

17. Centers for Disease Control and Prevention's National Center for Chronic Disease Prevention and Health Promotion, *Health and Quality of Life Outcomes* (July 28, 2004), p. 40, www.hqlo.com /content/2/1/40.

18. Statistics on checking accounts, debt, and vehicle ownership. U.S. Department of Labor, Bureau of Labor Statistics, *Consumer Expenditures in 2002* (February 2004), www.bls.gov/cex/csxann02.pdf.

19. Federal Reserve, *Survey of Consumer Finances 2001,* www .federalreserve.gov/pubs/oss/oss2/2001/scf2001home.html.

20. From an analysis of 2001 Federal Reserve data by economist Ed Wolff of New York University for the Economic Policy Institute. Wolff is the editor of the academic journal *Review of Income and Wealth.*

21. Federal Reserve's *Survey of Consumer Finances 2001.*

22. Fair Isaac Corporation, *Average Credit Card Statistics,* www.myfico .com/myfico/CreditCentral/AverageUse.asp.

23. Employee Benefit Research Institute, www.ebri.org/findings /ret_findings.htm.

24. U.S. Department of Labor, Bureau of Labor Statistics, *Consumer Expenditures in 2002.*

25. National Association of Realtors, www.realtor.org/publicaffairsweb .nsf/Pages/DecEHS04?OpenDocument.

26. Sandy Baum and Marie O'Malley, *College on Credit: How Borrowers Perceive Their Education Debt: Results of the 2002 National Student Loan Survey* (February 6, 2003), a study sponsored by the Nellie Mae Corporation, www.nelliemae.com/library/nasls_2002.pdf.

27. Bob Condor, "In Pursuit of Happiness: Social Connections," *Chicago Tribune* (December 9, 1998).

28. Barry Schwartz, *The Paradox of Choice: Why More Is Less* (Ecco, 2004).

Chapter 2

1. Mihaly Csikszentmihalyi, *Finding Flow: The Psychology of Engagement with Everyday Life* (New York: Basic Books, 1998), p. 49.

2. Russell Connors Jr. and Patrick McCormick, *Character, Choices and Community: The Three Faces of Christian Ethics* (Mahwah, NJ: Paulist Press, 1998), p. 45.

3. Thomas Kostigen, *What Money Really Means* (New York: Watson-Guptill Publications, 2003).

Chapter 3

1. For a more thorough discussion of moral worldview, see Charles L. Kammer, *Ethics and Liberation* (Maryknoll, NY: Orbis Books, 1988).

2. *World's Richest People, 2004,* www.forbes.com/finance/lists/10/2004/LIR.jhtml?passListId=10&passYear=2004&passListType=Person&uniqueId=CRTT&datatype=Person.

3. www.madamecjwalker.com.

4. See note 2.

5. *Special Report on CEO Compensation,* www.forbes.com/static/execpay2004/LIRQDES.html?passListId=12&passYear=2004&passListType=Person&uniqueId=QDES&datatype=Person. Speech at Massachusetts Institute of Technology commencement ceremony, http://web.mit.edu/newsoffice/2000/fiorinaspeech.html.

6. Lucille Ball profile, library.thinkquest.org/CR0215629/lucilleinfo_.htm?tqskip1=1.

7. Rosa Parks profile, www.rosaparks.org.

8. *100 Top Celebrities, 2004,* www.forbes.com/maserati/celebrities2004/LIRO0ZT.html?passListId=53&passYear=2004&passListType=Person&uniqueId=O0ZT&datatype=Person.

9. David Montgomery, "Billions Served; McDonald's Heiress Joan Kroc Took Her Philanthropy and Super-Sized It," *Washington Post* (March 14, 2004), p. D01.

10. Ian Irvine, "The Real Philadelphia Story," *Sunday Telegraph* (April 16, 1995), p. 1.

11. Sister Maria José Hobday, *Parabola* (essay) vol. 4, no. 4 (November 1979), p. 5.

Chapter 4

1. Richard Easterlin, "Does Economic Growth Improve the Human Lot? Some Empirical Evidence," in *Nations and Households in Economic Growth: Essays in Honour of Moses Abramowitz,* P. A. David and M. W. Reder (Eds.) (New York and London: Academic Press, 1974).

2. Ed Diener with J. Horwitz and Robert A. Emmons, "Happiness of the Very Wealthy," *Social Indicators,* vol. 16 (1985), pp. 263–274.

3. Robert Biswas-Diener and Ed Diener, "Making the Best of a Bad Situation: Satisfaction in the Slums of Calcutta," *Social Indicators Research,* vol. 55 (2001), pp. 329–352.

4. Philip Brickman, Dan Coates, and Ronnie J. Janoff-Bulman, "Lottery Winners and Accident Victims: Is Happiness Relative?" *Journal of Personality and Social Psychology,* vol. 36 (1978), pp. 917–927.

5. For more comprehensive essays on the hedonic treadmill and studies of subjective well-being see Daniel Kahneman, Ed Diener, and Norbert Schwarz (Eds.), *Well-Being: The Foundations of Hedonic Psychology* (New York: Russell Sage Foundation, 1999).

6. Roper-Starch Organization, 1979, *Roper Reports 79-1* and Roper-Starch Organization, 1995, *Roper Reports 95-1* (Storrs, CT: University of Connecticut, the Roper Center), referenced in Richard Easterlin, "Building a Better Theory of Well-Being," presentation at the conference *Paradoxes of Happiness in Economics,* University of Milano-Bicocca, March 21–23, 2003, Institute for the Study of Labor (IZA), Bonn, Germany, www.economics.ucr.edu/seminars/10-03-03easterlin.pdf.

7. *Foundations of Hedonic Psychology,* Preface, p. x.

8. Daniel Kahneman, "Toward a Science of Well-Being" lecture given at the University of New South Wales, Sydney Australia and rebroadcast on "All in the Mind with Natasha Mitchell" (August 17, 2003), ww.abc.net.au/rn/science/mind/s923773.htm. See also Daniel Kahneman and A. Tversky (Eds.), *Choices, Values and Frames* (Cambridge: Cambridge University Press and New York: The Russell Sage Foundation, 2000), pp. 673–692, www.iies.su.se/nobel/papers/utility3.pdf.

9. George Loewenstein and David Schkade, "Wouldn't It Be Nice? Predicting Future Feelings," in *Well Being: The Foundations of Hedonic Psychology,* p. 96.

10. Daniel Kahneman, "Toward a Science of Well-Being" lecture (June 12, 2004), wy2x05.psychologie.uni-wuerzburg.de/PSY2-PHP/werbung/kahneman_ppt.pdf.

11. Daniel Kahneman, "Objective Happiness," in *Well Being: The Foundations of Hedonic Psychology,* Daniel Kahneman, Ed Diener, and Norbert Schwarz (Eds.) (New York: Russell Sage Foundation, 1999), p. 20.

12. See note 8.

13. See note 9, p. 98.

14. L. M. Ausubel, "The Failure of Competition in the Credit Card Market," *American Economic Review,* vol. 81 (1991), cited in "Wouldn't It Be Nice? Predicting Future Feelings," p. 98.

15. Sonja Lyubomirsky, "Increased Happiness," presentation at the *2003 International Positive Psychology Summit,* Washington, DC, sponsored by the Gallup Positive Psychology Center, www.gallup.hu/pps/2003/Lyubomirsky.pdf. For all archived papers, including presentations by Kahneman, Diener, and Seligman, see www.gallup.hu/pps/2003_ipps_archives.htm.

16. Bob Condor, "In Pursuit of Happiness: Social Connections," *Chicago Tribune* (December 9, 1998).

17. David Myers, *The Pursuit of Happiness* (New York: William Morrow, 1992), p. 45.

18. Martin Seligman, *Learned Optimism: How to Change Your Mind and Your Life* (New York: Simon & Schuster, 1990), pp. 40–53.

19. Richard Easterlin, "The Economics of Happiness," *Daedalus: Journal of the American Academy of Arts & Sciences,* vol. 133 (2004), pp. 26–33.

20. Andrew Oswald and David Blanchflower, "Well-Being over Time in Britain and the USA," *Journal of Public Economics,* vol. 88 (2004), pp. 1359–1386, www2.warwick.ac.uk/fac/soc/economics/staff /faculty/oswald/finaljpubecwellbeingjune2002.pdf.

21. Thich Nhat Hanh, *Heart of the Buddha's Teaching* (New York: Broadway Books, 1999), p. 67.

22. See note 9.

23. Mike Collett-White, "Materialism Link to Depression and Anger: Study," Reuters, London (July 2001). Shaun Saunders and Don Munro, "A Psychological Profile of Materialism in Australia," presented at the Seventh European Congress of Psychology, London, July 2001. See also Shaun Saunders and Don Munro, "The Construction and Validation of Aconsumer Orientation Questionnaire (SCOI) designed to measure Fromm's (1955) 'Marketing Character' in Australia," *Social Behavior and Personality,* vol. 28, no. 3 (2000), pp. 219–240. See also Shaun Saunders, Don Munro, and Miles Bore, "Maslow's Hierarchy of Needs and Its Relationship with Psychological Health and Materialism," *South Pacific Journal of Psychology,* vol. 10 (1998), pp. 15–25.

24. Virginia Postrel, *The Substance of Style* (New York: HarperCollins, 2003), pp. 102–103.

25. Tim Kasser and Richard M. Ryan, "A Dark Side of the American Dream: Correlates of Financial Success as a Central Life Aspiration," *Journal of Personality and Social Psychology,* vol. 65 (1993), pp. 410–422.

26. Tim Kasser, *The High Price of Materialism* (Cambridge: MIT Press, 2002).

27. Kennon Sheldon et al., "What Is Satisfying about Satisfying Events? Testing 10 Candidate Psychological Needs," *Journal of Personality and Social Psychology,* vol. 80 (2001), pp. 325–339, www.apa.org/journals/psp/psp802325.html.

28. J. C. Brunstein, "Personal Goals and Subjective Well-Being: A Longitudinal Study," *Journal of Personality and Social Psychology,* vol. 65 (1993), pp. 1061–1070.

Chapter 5

1. Joe Dominguez and Vicki Robin, *Your Money or Your Life* (New York: Penguin Books, 1999), pp. 109–145.
2. "Myvesta Survey Finds Debt Equals Depression for Many" (November 29, 2001), press release, Myvesta.org.
3. Judy Lawrence, *The Budget Kit,* 3rd ed. (Chicago: Dearborn Trade, 2001).
4. Cohen, Lizabeth. *A Consumers' Republic: The Politics of Mass Consumption in Postwar America* (New York: Alfred A. Knopf, 2003), pp. 263, 293.
5. Lawrence Mishel, Jared Bernstein, and Sylvia Allegretto, *The State of Working America, 2004–05* (Ithaca, NY: ILR Press, 2003), p. 1, www.epinet.org/books/swa2004/swa2004web.pdf.
6. Federal Reserve.
7. See note 2.
8. Massachusetts Public Interest Research Group.
9. See note 8.
10. See note 8.
11. Martin Seligman, *Authentic Happiness* (New York: Free Press, 2002).
12. See note 8.
13. Bob Hammond, *Repair Your Own Credit,* 3rd ed. (Franklin Lakes, NJ: Career Press, 2001).

Chapter 6

1. *The Disposable Worker: Living in a Job-Loss Economy,* Survey 14 in the *Work Trends* series (July 28, 2003). A Joint Project of the John J. Heldrich Center for Workforce Development and Edward J. Bloustein School of Planning and Public Policy at Rutgers, State University of New Jersey, www.heldrich.rutgers.edu.

2. For more information on savings bonds see www.savingsbonds
   .gov or treasurydirect.gov.

3. Deborah Taylor-Hough, *Frozen Assets: How to Cook for a Day and
   Eat for a Month* (Fredonia, WI: Champion Press, 1998).

4. "66 Ways to Save Money," government publication, www.pueblo
   .gsa.gov/cic_text/money/66ways.

5. "50 Ways to Save Money," *Consumer Reports* (May 2002).

Chapter 7

1. Information on all of the tax-advantaged vehicles in this chapter
   can be found at www.irs.gov.

2. Employee Benefit Research Institute, www.ebri.org/findings
   /ret_findings.htm.

3. "Understanding Long-Term Investment Performance," by Ibbotson
   Associates, www.ibbotson.com.

4. "Fidelity Investments Reports Higher 401(k) Balances," press
   release (September 29, 2004) personal.fidelity.com/myfidelity
   /InsideFidelity/index_NewsCenter.shtml?refhp=cp.

5. For more information on stocks, visit the "Path to Investing" web
   site by the Securities Industries Association, www.siainvestor.com
   /categories/choosinginvestments/stocks/stocks_011.htm.

6. For more on bonds, see "An Investor's Guide to Bond Basics"
   published by The Bond Market Association,
   www.investinginbonds.com.

7. Investment Company Institute, *2004 Mutual Fund Fact Book: A
   Guide to Trends and Statistics in the Mutual Fund Industry,*
   www.ici.org/funds/abt/2004_factbook.pdf.

8. For more information on mutual funds, see the Securities and
   Exchange Commission's "Introduction to Mutual Funds,"
   www.sec.gov/investor/pubs/inwsmf.htm.

9. See note 3.

10. The National Endowment for Financial Education, www.nefe.org
    /pages/multimedia.html. This site offers a variety of personal
    finance information.

11. Jeremy Siegel, *Stocks for the Long Run: The Definitive Guide to Financial Market Returns and Long-Term Investment Strategies* (New York: McGraw-Hill, 1998).

12. Harry M. Markowitz autobiography, nobelprize.org /economics/laureates/1990/markowitz-autobio.html.

13. For an excellent primer on investing for other goals, see the Securities and Exchange Commission's "Road Map to Saving and Investing," www.sec.gov/investor/pubs/roadmap.htm.

Chapter 8

1. Interview, October 14, 2004.

2. Robert FitzPatrick, and Joyce K. Reynolds, *False Profits: Seeking Financial and Spiritual Deliverance in Multi-Level Marketing and Pyramid Schemes* (Charlotte, NC: Herald Press, 1997). Interview with FitzPatrick, August 31, 2004.

3. Interview, October 21, 2004.

4. The National Center for Women and Retirement Research (NCWRR), "Women Cents Study" (1995).

Chapter 9

1. Interview on October 21, 2004.

2. Women's Financial Network at Siebert, www.wfn.com.

3. Robert Irwin, *Irwin's Power Tips for Buying a Home for Less* (New York: McGraw-Hill, 2000).

4. Interview on November 17, 2004.

5. Interview on October 21, 2004.

6. Mary Snyder and Malia McCawley Wyckoff, *You Can Afford to Stay Home with Your Kids* (Franklin Lakes, NJ: Career Press, 1999).

7. Amelia Warren Tyagi and Elizabeth Warren, *The Two-Income Trap: Why Middle-Class Mothers and Fathers Are Going Broke* (Philadelphia: Basic Books, 2003).

8. John Allen, *Investor Beware: How to Protect Your Money from Wall Street's Dirty Tricks* (New York: John Wiley & Sons, 1993).

9. Benajmin Ensor, *How Consumers Pay for Financial Advice* (September 2, 2004), www.forrester.com.

Chapter 10

1. Statistics on socially responsible investing. Social Investing Forum, *2003 Report on Socially Responsible Investing Trends in the United States,* www.socialinvest.org/areas/research/trends /sri_trends_report_2003.pdf.
2. Emily Hall, "Evaluating Socially Responsible Funds: Is it a Good Idea to Invest with Your Heart?" Morningstar.com (July 7, 2004), news.morningstar.com/doc/article/0,1,110270,00.html.
3. Quoted in Ben Cohen and Jerry Greenfield, *Ben & Jerry's Double Dip: How to Run a Values-Based Business and Make Money Too* (New York: Simon & Schuster, May 1998), p. 88.
4. Economist Intelligence Unit, *The Economist,* 2002, quoted in a presentation by Women & Co., a subsidiary of Citigroup.

RESOURCES

American Association of Individual Investors
Nonprofit educational group founded in 1978.
www.aaii.com

American Savings Education Council
Nonprofit national coalition of public- and private-sector institutions trying to raise public awareness about saving for retirement. Offers on-line tools.
www.asec.org/tools/index.htm

Consumer Action
Nonprofit consumer education and advocacy group founded in 1971. Offers free publications on all aspects of personal finance.
www.consumer-action.org/English/library/money_mgt/index.php

Consumer Federation of America (CFA)
Advocacy, research, education, and service organization founded in 1968. Offers a number of publications on personal finance issues.
www.consumerfed.org

Department of Education
Offers a "financial aid" portal with information on financing higher education.
http://studentaid.ed.gov

The Dollar Stretcher
Online web site focused on saving money and time since 1996.
www.stretcher.com/index.cfm

Fannie Mae Homepath
Information on buying a home.
www.fanniemae.com/homebuyers/homepath/index.jhtml?p=Homepath

Federal Trade Commission
Information on consumer topics including credit, investments, working at home, and evaluating franchise and business opportunities.
www.ftc.gov/ftc/consumer.htm

The Federal Reserve
"There's a Lot to Learn About Money" contains a variety of personal finance articles.
www.federalreserveeducation.org/fined

The Federal Reserve Bank of Chicago
Financial education research center offers information on budgeting, saving, and other topics.
http://chicagofed.org/cedric/financial_education_research_center.cfm

The Federal Reserve Bank of Dallas
"Building Wealth: A Beginner's Guide to Securing Your Financial Future" contains money basics.
www.dallasfed.org/ca/wealth/index.html

The Federal Reserve Bank of Boston
Economic educational publications offered free; generally designed for schools, from elementary to college level, although also helpful for the individual consumer.
www.bos.frb.org/education/html/edpub.htm

Federal Citizen Information Center
Click on the "Money" tab for free and low-cost publications on personal finance.
www.pueblo.gsa.gov

Finaid.org

Free comprehensive guide to financial aid for college established by college planning author Mark Kantrowitz.

www.finaid.org

FinanCenter

Offers a comprehensive package of personal finance tools and calculators.

www.financenter.com/consumertools/calculators

Financial Literacy and Education Commission

Comprehensive educational web site created as a result of Title V of the Fair and Accurate Credit Transaction Act. (Title V established the Commission with the purpose of improving financial literacy and education.)

www.mymoney.gov

Garrett Planning Network

Group of financial planners who will meet with clients for a one-time or periodic consultation, charging by the hour—good option for professional advice if you have a handle on your finances.

www.garrettplanningnetwork.com

GE Center for Financial Learning

Educational web site sponsored by General Electric.

www.financiallearning.com/ge/home.jsp

GreenMoneyJournal.com

Encourages and promotes the awareness of socially and environmentally responsible business, investing, and consumer resources in publications and online.

www.greenmoneyjournal.com

IHateFinancialPlanning.com

Good source for basic personal finance articles, but keep in mind the site is not independent. It is owned by financial services giant ING; and many of the products and services described on the site are offered by

ING companies. For example, a section that helps you find a financial planning professional refers you to individuals affiliated with ING. www.IHateFinancialPlanning.com

Ivillage.com
The money portal on Ivilllage.com offers basic personal finance advice and message boards, including debt support groups and budgeting tips and ideas.
www.ivillage.com/money

Moneyandhappiness.com
Web site affiliated with this book; contains personal finance tips and more.
www.moneyandhappiness.com

Morningstar
Indispensable source for all information related to mutual funds.
www.morningstar.com

MyFico.com
Run by the company that creates the Fico credit score; the "Credit Education" section of the site explains how credit scores work and offers tips on boosting your credit rating.
www.myfico.com

National Association of Investors Corporation
Nonprofit group of individual investors and investing clubs focused on education and support; 66 percent of members are women. Founded in 1951.
www.better-investing.org

National Association of Personal Financial Advisors
Organization of planners who do not accept commission for the products they sell. They get paid either a flat fee or a percentage of assets under management.
www.napfa.org

National Association of Securities Dealers (NASD)

A private regulatory group that licenses brokers. Its web site includes an "Investor Information" tab that allows you to check if your broker or advisor has been disciplined for their sales practices. Look for the "investor brochure" series on all aspects of personal finance and "investor alerts" to help avoid scams and problems.

www.nasd.org

National Foundation for Credit Counseling

Nonprofit debt counseling group founded in 1951.

www.nfcc.org

Sallie Mae

A leading provider of education funding, providing federally guaranteed student loans originated under the Federal Family Education Loan Program.

www.salliemae.com

Savingforcollege.com

Comprehensive guide to 529 savings plans.

www.savingforcollege.com

Securities & Exchange Commission (SEC)

Regulates the sale of securities; its primary mission is to protect investors and maintain the integrity of the securities markets; see the Office of Investor Education & Assistance for investing information. Also, all companies, U.S. and foreign, are required to file registration statements, periodic reports, and other forms electronically through the SEC. These filings are all available free to the public through the SEC's EDGAR database. The SEC's web site offers a tutorial on how to search the EDGAR database.

www.sec.gov/investor.shtml

TaxSites.com

Offers a database of various tax information sites on the web.

www.taxsites.com

Tomorrow's Money

Basic personal finance information, sponsored by the Bond Market Foundation, a nonprofit charitable and educational group organized by members of the bond market industry.

www.tomorrowsmoney.org

Women's Institute for a Secure Retirement

Nonprofit organization devoted to providing women with skills and information to improve their economic circumstances and plan for a financially sound retirement. Founded in 1996 with a grant from the Heinz Foundation.

www.wiser.heinz.org

Women's Institute for Financial Education

Nonprofit group founded by financial advisors Candace Bahr and Ginita Wall in the 1980s. Offers general information and special focus on issues related to divorce and widowhood.

www.wife.org

401k Help Center

Click on the "Plan Participant Channel" for information on how 401k plans work and how to manage money in a 401k.

www.401khelpcenter.com

Financial News Web Sites

Bankrate.com	Kiplinger.com
Bloomberg.com	Moneycentral.msn.com
Businessweek.com	Money.cnn.com
CNBC.com	Quicken.com
CBSmarketwatch.com	SmartMoney.com
Finance.yahoo.com	Taxsites.com
Fool.com	Thestreet.com
Forbes.com	WSJ.com
Fortune.com	Yahoo Finance
Ft.com	

INDEX